Susan Dabney Smedes

A Southern Planter

Fourth Edition

Susan Dabney Smedes

A Southern Planter
Fourth Edition

ISBN/EAN: 9783337005320

Printed in Europe, USA, Canada, Australia, Japan

Cover: Foto ©ninafisch / pixelio.de

More available books at **www.hansebooks.com**

A SOUTHERN PLANTER.

BY

SUSAN DABNEY SMEDES.

"The memory of so honest and noble a life deserves a suitable record."
—Wm. M. Green, *Bishop of Mississippi.*

"A priceless heritage for his posterity; the record of a life crowned with honorable deeds."
—*Extract from a letter of* Hon. E. Barksdale, *of Mississippi.*

FOURTH EDITION.

NEW YORK:
JAMES POTT & CO., Publishers,
Astor Place.
1890.

Press of J. J. Little & Co.,
Astor Place, New York.

PREFACE.

The materials for these memorials were collected a few weeks after the death of my father. There was no thought then of having them made public. They were gotten together that the memory and example of his life should not pass away from his grandchildren, many of whom are yet too young to appreciate his character. They will come to mature years in a time when slavery will be a thing of the past.

They will hear much of the wickedness of slavery and of slave-owners. I wish them to learn of a good master: of one who cared for his servants affectionately and yet with a firm hand, when there was need, and with a full sense of his responsibility. There were many like him. Self-interest—one might, with truth, say self-protection—was with most masters a sufficient incentive to kindness to slaves, when there was no higher motive. My father was so well assured of the contentment and well-being of his slaves, while he owned them, and saw so much of their suffering, which he was not able to relieve after they were freed, that he did not, for many years, believe that it was better for them to be free than held as slaves. But during the last winter of his life he expressed the opinion that it was well for them to have their freedom.

It has been suggested by friends, in whose judgment I trust, that these memorials may throw a kindly light on Southern masters for others, as well as for my father's descendants. Should this be so, I shall not regret laying bare much that is private and sacred.

He was like his Jaqueline ancestors in appearance. The "grand look" of the first Jaquelines and what we knew as the "Jaqueline black eyes" were his. Several times in his life he was asked as a favor by painters to sit for his portrait; on two occasions by distinguished artists whom he met casually. "I want a patrician head for an historical picture that I am painting," one said.

He never suspected any one of wishing to be otherwise than strictly upright, and, consequently, was frequently defrauded in his dealings with dishonest people. Once, during the latter years of his life, when in extremest poverty, he made a rather worse bargain than usual.

"I do not think that you ever made a good bargain in your life," some one said.

"No, I never tried," was the emphatic answer. "A good bargain always means that somebody makes a bad one."

"Uncle Tom," one of his brother's children said to him, "why do you deny yourself everything? Your credit is good. You could get thousands of dollars if you chose."

"Yes, my dear, my credit is good; and I mean to keep it so," he replied, in a manner that precluded further argument on that subject.

S. D. S.

BALTIMORE, 1303 JOHN STREET, June 1, 1886.

CONTENTS.

CHAPTER	PAGE
I.—Birth and Early Years	17
II.—Marriage and Life at Elmington	31
III.—Leaving the Old Home	47
IV.—Mammy Harriet's Recollections	52
V.—Early Days in Mississippi	65
VI.—Plantation Management	76
VII.—Still Waters and Green Pastures	87
VIII.—Management of Servants	101
IX.—A Southern Planter's Wife	108
X.—A Southern Planter	115
XI.—Home Life	130
XII.—Holiday Times on the Plantation	160
XIII.—The Valley of the Shadow	166
XIV.—Summer Travel	171
XV.—Summer-Time—Falling Asleep	179
XVI.—Slaves and War-Times	190
XVII.—A Week within the Lines	202
XVIII.—Refugees	214
XIX.—Old Master	223
XX.—The Crown of Poverty	231
XXI.—The Crowning Blessing	244
XXII.—Life at Burleigh	259
XXIII.—Quiet Days	292
XXIV.—Rest	322

Hawarden Castle,
Chester.
Oct 12. 89.

Dear Madam

When you did me the honour to send me the Memorials of a Southern Planter, I in acknowledging your courtesy said (I think) that I should peruse it with lively interest. I have finished it this morning and my interest in the work is not only lively but profound.

What I expected that the world might reap from it — may I roughly described as justice to the South: to which as matter of course something less than justice has latterly been done in the common estimation.

My expectation was thoroughly fulfilled. But what I also found was the exhibition of one of the very noblest of human characters: affording to every one (and least may I say to one who is himself a happy father in old age) food for admiration, for love, and for woe so distant and woe so humble imitation.

I am constrained to go on & add that the family picture is one of rare beauty, and that the Memoir is such as he would have wished it to be: I cannot give it higher praise.

get men. I am very desirous that the old world should have the benefit of this work. I write to my bookseller in London to order me three copies which I may give to friends. I shall ask Mr. Knowles the Editor of the Nineteenth Century (our most widely known periodical of the highest class) to allow me to draw attention to it there by a brief notice. But I now ask your permission, I hope your _immediate_ permission (if you like to send it by telegram "Gladstone Hawarden England Proceed" will suffice) to publish it in England. Pray do this through any channel which may be agreeable to you. Should you desire to do it through me, I shall on receiving your answer communicate with one or the other of my own publishers in London (Mr Murray and Mr Macmillan) and you will probably hear from one of them as to the terms on which he would propose to proceed. Either of them may be entirely trusted.

In any case allow me to thank you, dear Madam, for the good this book must do; and may the blessing of the Almighty rest richly on the heads of all the descendants of one noble born among Nature's nobles.

I remain dear Madam
Faithfully yours
H Lyellwoom

Mrs Smedes

INTRODUCTION.

GENEALOGICAL.

In the fair land of France the old Huguenot name and family of d'Aubigné still live. They form but a small colony in their native land, never having increased much. From the earliest times they seem to have had a strong religious vein.* All the branches of this family in America claim a common ancestry. They have the same armorial bearings,—an elephant's head, three footless martins, and the fleurs-de-lis of France,—the same traditions, and the same motto, which they hold in three languages. In France they have the motto in the Latin, *Fidelis et Grata*. One of the American branches has it in French, *Fidèle et Reconnaissant;* while most of the name in the United States have it in English, *Faithful and Grateful*.

The name has undergone many changes since the American branch left France, two centuries ago. It is variously written, as Daubeny, Daubney, Bigny, D'aubenay, Dabnée, and Dabney.

The traditions among all say that they are descended from that fearless Huguenot leader, Agrippa d'Aubigné, who flourished from 1550 to 1630.

But Agrippa was not the first of his name known at the French court. According to tradition in the family, a d'Aubigné commanded a company of Swiss guards at the court of Louis XII.

Agrippa d'Aubigné wrote a minute history of the

---

* The following is an extract from "Don Miff," a romance written by my brother, V. Dabney: "This Huguenot cross gave the old Whacker stock a twist towards theology. Two of the sons of Thomas and Elizabeth took orders, much to the surprise of their father."

fearful times in which he lived,—one of the best that has come down to us. Agrippa was the father of Constant d'Aubigné, who was the father of Mme. de Maintenon, and her brother, Chevalier d'Aubigné. Constant d'Aubigné was twice married. The first wife, Ann Marchant, left a son Theodore. The second wife, Jeanne Cardillac, was the mother of Mme. de Maintenon and Chevalier d'Aubigné; the latter was never married. The d'Aubigné line was continued through Ann Marchant's son, Theodore.

We find the name on the rolls of Battle Abbey among the list of knights who fell at Hastings. Others survived the conquest, and are mentioned in Hume's History as champions of Magna Charta.

After the revocation of the Edict of Nantes (1685), a branch of the d'Aubigné family left forever the land of their ancestors, because they could no longer there worship God with freedom of conscience. They took refuge in Wales. Somewhere between 1715 to 1717 two brothers, Cornelius and John d'Aubigné, left this land of their adoption, and sailed for America. Perhaps about the same time their brother Robert came over, and fixed his home in Boston. Cornelius and John came to Virginia and settled on the two banks of the Pamunkey River,—Cornelius on the northern and John on the southern side.

In the hand-book in the land office of Richmond, Virginia, is recorded: "Cornelius de Bany, or de Bonés or de Bony—a grant of land (200 acres) in New Kent, dated 27th September, 1664. Again, another grant to same of 640 acres, dated June 7th, 1666. Again, this last grant was on Tolomoy Creek, York River. Again, Sarah Dabney, a grant of land (179 acres) on Pamunkey River, in King and Queen Co., April 25th, 1701." Then follow other grants to other Dabneys in these early days of our country.

From Robert d'Aubigné, of Boston, sprang the men who for three generations, and almost from the beginning of our republic, have held the United States consulate in the Azores, or Western Islands. During this period the government has seen many changes, but only

INTRODUCTION. 9

one attempt has been made during eighty years to take the consulship out of the hands of the descendants of Robert d'Aubigné. They have borne themselves so well in their office as to win the confidence of Whig and Democrat and Republican. Under General Grant's administration it was thought advisable, for political reasons, to bestow this consulship on Mr. Cover. Accordingly, in 1869, it was taken from Charles William Dabney and given to Mr. Cover. Charles William Dabney, who had succeeded his father in the consulate, who had held it since 1806, received the new consul in his own house, as he could not be suitably accommodated elsewhere. But Mr. Cover lived only two years, and on his death the consulate passed again into the hands of the Dabney family. Charles W. Dabney had held it for forty-three years. He did not desire it again, feeling too old to serve. His son, Samuel W. Dabney, was appointed consul in 1872, and still holds the office. Honorable mention was made by President Cleveland, in reappointing him to the consulate, of the services of Samuel W. Dabney. A younger brother of Charles W. Dabney, William H. Dabney, held for twenty years the consulship of the Canary Islands, having resigned in 1882.

In the court record at Hanover Court-House, unfortunately destroyed in the Richmond conflagration of 1865, occurred this entry in the first minute-book of that county, at the beginning of the entries, which were begun when the county was cut off from New Kent County, in 1726 :

"Ordered, that it be recorded that on — day of April, 1721, Cornelius Dabney, late of England,* intermarried with Sarah Jennings." All accounts agree that his first wife died soon after coming to Virginia, leaving an only son, George. From this English George came the William Dabney who gave two sons to the Revolutionary army,—Charles, who commanded the Dabney Legion, and George, who was a captain in that legion. The brothers were present at the siege of

---

* He seems to have gone to England before coming to America.

Yorktown and the surrender of Lord Cornwallis. They received the thanks of Congress for services rendered. George Dabney's powder-horn, that he carried into battle, is still in existence, and in the possession of one of his descendants. Patrick Henry, who was a kinsman and companion of these brothers, was on very intimate terms with them.

From the marriage of Cornelius Dabney and Sarah Jennings sprang three sons and four daughters. The descendants of their half-brother George and of this band of brothers and sisters have their homes in Louisa and Hanover Counties. Of late years they have spread over nearly every State in the South and Southwest, and some have found their way to the Middle States.

The distinguished Presbyterian minister, Rev. Robert L. Dabney, well known as the author of the "Life of Stonewall Jackson," and now professor in the State University of Texas, is descended from Cornelius Dabney's son George.

John Dabney established himself on the lower Pamunkey River, at what has been known ever since as Dabney's Ferry, and this became the original nest of the Dabneys of King William and Gloucester Counties.

"Most of the families of Lower Virginia are descended from John d'Aubigné; also the Carrs, Walters, Taylors, Pendletons, Nelsons, Robinsons, and Carters and Fontaines, Beverleys and Maurys, the Lees, of Loudoun, the Seldens and Alexanders, of Alexandria. There is hardly a Huguenot or Cavalier family in Virginia that has not in its veins an infusion of the blood of that sturdy confessor, Agrippa d'Aubigné. From the original pair of French Huguenots, married in 1685, no less than six thousand descendants have their names inscribed on a gigantic family-tree. Several thousand more could be added, if the twigs and boughs were filled out with the names of the lineal descendants known to exist."

John d'Aubigné was married twice. George was the offspring of his first marriage. James, his son by his second wife, was famous for his great strength.

George was twice married, and died, leaving two sons, George and Benjamin, by his first wife, and two, James and Thomas, by his second wife. His second son, Benjamin, refused to receive his share of his father's property, leaving it to be used in educating his younger half-brothers. His brother George lived at the old homestead, Dabney's Ferry, and became the father of sixteen children, eleven of whom lived to be grown. Of these, four were sons and seven daughters. These sisters were noted for their beauty. One of them, Mary Eleanor, attracted the admiration of General Lafayette.

A daughter of this lady, now sixty-seven years of age, writes thus:

"General Lafayette, you know, visited this country in 1825. He was the guest of the city in Richmond. No private house could do for his entertainment, but a suite of rooms in the great Eagle Hotel was secured for him. I have seen the rooms many a time, as my mother boarded there with my brother and myself. Cousin H. R. was the most gifted person with her pen, and she would, with indelible ink, make lovely leaves, flowers, doves, or scrolls, with the name in them. Well, Lafayette's pillow-cases were of the finest linen, marked by her with *her own hair*, which was a lovely auburn, very long and smooth and even, and a motto was also on them with the name. I saw them often. I believe he was in Richmond some time. All his pillow-cases were marked in that way. My dear mother had then been a widow four years, and was only twenty-four years old, and in the very height of her beauty. Everybody who could get to Richmond was there to see the great welcome of the city to Lafayette. Many people were not even able to find shelter. Of course, my mother and young aunts were among those who went there. There was a ball, spoken of to this day as the Lafayette Hall. My mother danced with him and became well acquainted. People used to come over with such tales to grandpa's, and he made me cry many a time, teasing me by saying that mother was going to marry Lafayette and go to France to eat *frogs*. You know Lafayette was a married man, well advanced in years; but, of course, I did not know that. He really told several persons, Mrs. H. among them, that my mother was the most beautiful woman he had ever seen, either in France or America. When he left Richmond many ladies kissed him, and he requested a kiss from my mother."

Benjamin Dabney married first Miss Patsy Armstead. She lived only a few years, leaving three children, George, Benjamin, and Ann. A year or two later he married his second wife, Miss Sarah Smith, the daughter of the Rev. Thomas Smith. My father was one of the children of this marriage. The sons, George and Benjamin, grew up to be of so great physical strength as to become famous at their college of William and Mary. In physical development they resembled their grandfather's half-brother, James Dabney, who bears the surname of "the Powerful" on the family-tree. George went into the navy, and was engaged in the battle of Tripoli, and was so fortunate as to save Decatur's life in that fight. He grew tired of the navy and left it for a planter's life. Benjamin also became a planter, and married his cousin, Ann West Dabney, the daughter of his uncle George.

The Smiths from whom my father was descended on the maternal side were known in Virginia as the Shooter's Hill Smiths,—Shooter's Hill, in Middlesex County, Virginia, being the home which they founded in this country. His mother was Sarah Smith, the daughter of the Rev. Thomas Smith, of Westmoreland County, a clergyman of the Established Church, and Mary Smith of Shooter's Hill. The earliest record in the old Shooter's Hill Bible is of the marriage of John Smith of Perton and Mary Warner of Warner Hall, Gloucester County, in the year 1680. One of Mary Warner's sisters, Mildred, married the son of George Washington's uncle, Lawrence Washington. A descendant of John Smith of Perton, General John Bull Davidson Smith of Hackwood, was a thorough Democrat, sharing with other Americans of that day in a revulsion and animosity against everything English.

Seeing that some of his family took more interest in genealogy and family records than he thought becoming in a citizen of the young republic, he made a bonfire of all the papers relating to his ancestors and family history. It is necessarily, therefore, rather a tradition than a fact recorded in family history, that John Smith of Perton was the son of Thomas Smith, the brother of the Captain John Smith so famous in colonial history. The Smiths of this line adopted Captain John Smith's coat of arms, the three Turks' heads, and now hold it.

The grandson of John Smith of Perton, John Smith of Shooter's Hill, married in 1737 Mary Jaqueline, one of the three beautiful daughters of the French emigrant, Edward Jaqueline. The ceremony was performed at Jamestown by the Rev. William Dawson. They were the parents of Mary Smith of Shooter's Hill, who was married in 1765 to the Rev. Thomas Smith. In Bishop Meade's book on the old churches and families of Virginia are some interesting accounts of Mary Smith's Jaqueline ancestors and Ambler relations. The following extracts are from his pages:

"The old church at Jamestown is no longer to be seen, except the base of its ruined tower. A few tombstones, with the names of Amblers and Jaquelines, the chief owners of the island for a long time, and the Lees of Green Spring (the residence and property, at one time, of Sir William Berkeley), a few miles from Jamestown, still mark the spot where so many were interred during the earlier years of the colony. Some of the sacred vessels are yet to be seen, either in private hands or in public temples of religion. . . . The third and last of the pieces of church furniture—which is now in use in one of our congregations—is a silver vase, a font for baptism, which was presented to the Jamestown church in 1733 by Martha Jaqueline, widow of Edward Jaqueline, and their son Edward. In the year 1785, when the act of Assembly ordered the sale of church property, it reserved that which was passed by right of private donation. Under this clause it was given into the hands of the late Mr. John Ambler, his grandson. . .

INTRODUCTION.

"Edward Jaqueline, of Jamestown, was the son of John Jaqueline and Elizabeth Craddock, of the county of Kent, in England. He was descended from the same stock which gave rise to the noble family of La Roche Jaquelines in France. They were Protestants, and fled from La Vendée, in France, to England during the reign of that bloodthirsty tyrant Charles IX., of France, and a short time previous to the massacre of St. Bartholomew. They were eminently wealthy, and were fortunate enough to convert a large portion of their wealth into gold and silver, which they transported in safety to England."

"Whilst I was in Paris (says one of the travellers from America), in 1826, the Duke of Sylverack, who was the intimate friend of Mme. de La Roche Jaqueline (the celebrated authoress of 'Wars of La Vendée'), informed me that the above account—which is the tradition among the descendants of the family in America—corresponds exactly with what the family in France believe to have been the fate of those Jaquelines who fled to England in the reign of Charles IX. I found the family to be still numerous in France. It has produced many distinguished individuals, but none more so than the celebrated Vendean chief, Henri de La Roche Jaqueline, who, during the revolution of 1790, was called to command the troops of La Vendée after his father had been killed, and when he was only nineteen years of age. Thinking that he was inadequate to the task, on account of his extreme youth and total want of experience in military affairs, he sought seriously to decline the dangerous honor; but the troops, who had been devotedly attached to the father and family, would not allow him to do so, and absolutely forced him to place himself at their head in spite of himself. As soon as he found that resistance was useless, he assumed the bearing of a hero and gave orders for a general review of his army: to which (being formed in a hollow square), in an animated and enthusiastic manner, he delivered this ever-memorable speech: 'My friends, if my father were here you would have confidence in him; but as for me, I am nothing more than a mere child. But as to my courage, I shall now show myself worthy to command you.'

"This young man started forth a military Roscius, and maintained to the end of his career the high ground he first seized. After displaying all the skill of a veteran commander and all the courage of a most dauntless hero, he nobly died upon the field of battle, at the early age of twenty-one, thus closing his short but brilliant career."

The Jaquelines have English as well as French ancestors. A branch of the family in America still cherishes a lock of Queen Elizabeth's red hair. This was acquired through Cary, Lord Hunsden, whom they claim as their English ancestor. His mother was Mary, daughter to Thomas Bullen and sister to the unfortunate Anne Bullen.

Through the Smiths and Jaquelines my father was related to the Washingtons, Marshalls, Amblers, Joneses, Pages, Carys, and many other Virginia families. My father's grandfather, the Rev. Thomas Smith, was not related to his wife, Mary Smith, although she bore the same name. The result of this union was a family of three sons and four daughters. Among the list of their names in the family Bible we find a Mary Jaqueline. Their fifth child, Sarah, was born on the 27th of February, 1775, and her brother, John Augustine, seven years later. A thirteen-year-old sister, Ann, was struck by lightning and burned to death in her closet.

Thomas Smith was rector of Nomini Church, Cople Parish, Westmoreland County, from 1765 to 1789. At one time during the residence of his family at the rectory attached to this old church, there came an alarm that the British ships were coming up the Potomac River. The rector ordered everything that could be hastily collected to be put into a wagon to be driven off to a place of security. As the servants were engaged in loading up the wagon, the oxen moved one of the wheels against a plank on which a line of beehives were standing. The plank was upset and the hives thrown to the ground. The bees flew in every direction, stinging every living thing within reach.

The family and servants fled into the house. They were obliged to stuff even the keyholes to keep out the infuriated bees. The oxen ran entirely away, and the fowls which were in coops in the wagon were stung to death.

The Rev. Thomas Smith died in May, 1789. Two years later, in December, 1791, his wife died. In October, 1791, their daughter Sarah, in her seventeenth year, was married to Benjamin Dabney. He was a widower with three children, though but twenty-seven years old. Sarah's step-daughter, Ann, afterwards married her brother, Major Thomas Smith.

Benjamin Dabney had given up the family mansion at Dabney's Ferry, together with his patrimony, on his father's death, to his brother and his half-brothers, and he made his home on the York River at Bellevue, in King and Queen County. He had also, to some extent, used his own means in the education of his half-brother, James Dabney, and his wife's favorite brother, John Augustine Smith. Both young men received medical educations abroad,—James Dabney in Edinburgh, and John Augustine Smith in London and Paris. His kindness and trust were not misplaced. When his own early death deprived his children of a father's care, Dr. James Dabney and Dr. John Augustine Smith were the best friends whom his children had.

MEMORIALS

OF

A SOUTHERN PLANTER.

CHAPTER I.

BIRTH AND EARLY YEARS.

My father, Thomas Smith Gregory Dabney, was born at Bellevue, his father's country-seat on the York River, in the county of King and Queen, Virginia, on the 4th day of January, 1798, and he used to tell us that he was two years in the world before General Washington left it.

Two brothers had died in infancy before his birth, and the vigorous boy was hailed with much rejoicing. The christening was a great event. It was celebrated at Bellevue on so large a scale that the cake for the feast was made in a churn. Often as children we heard the old servants refer with pride to this occasion, and to the large company invited to witness it. In the old Smith Bible, for the rebinding of which one hundred dollars of Continental money is said to have been paid, is found this entry, in his mother's small, old-fashioned handwriting: "Thomas Smith Gregory Dabney, our third child, was born on the 4th day of January, 1798; was baptized the 11th May, 1798. His godfathers were Messrs. Robert Wirt, Harvey Gaines, Thomas G. Smith, James Dabney, Thomas Fox, and Edward Jones. His godmothers were Mrs. Lee, Mlles. Milly Williams, Elizabeth Robinson, Mary S. Whiting, Mary Camp, and Ann S. Dabney, and Ann Baytop." The first incident recorded of the baby was his great terror at the sight of a very ugly lady, a visitor of his mother's. "Missis, he didn't know if she was folks," was his nurse's explanation when his screams had drawn attention to her charge. When only one year of age he was inoculated, having been sent with his nurse to a public hospital, as the custom then was in Virginia. In due time he passed safely and without disfiguring marks through the dangers of varioloid. He used to relate to us that his mother had said that one of the happiest moments of her life was when her spool of cotton fell from her lap, her little Thomas, then eighteen months old, picked it up and handed it to her. When he was two years old his brother, Philip Augustine Lee, was born, and, two years later, his sister, Martha Burwell. This little flock were taught their letters and to read by a favorite servant, the daughter of their mother's maid. Thomas had great difficulty in remembering one of the letters. Finally, a cake was promised, all for himself, if he would try still harder. So, all day he went about the house repeating "G, G," and the next day, when lesson hour came, his mother put his cake before him as fairly earned.

My father's recollections of his father were very distinct, considering that he died in the forty-third year of his age, when his son Thomas had only attained the tender age of eight years. The memory of this father was ever a most cherished one, and his children remember the almost pathetic manner in which in his own old age he lamented the untimely cutting off of that young life and brilliant career.

Benjamin Dabney was at the head of the bar in King and Queen County, and was engaged by the British government to settle British claims. In nearly every case that came to trial in his county he was engaged as counsel on one side. He was considered by his brethren in his profession to be the most learned man in the law in his section. The judge who at that time sat on the bench appealed to him when doubtful on any legal point, saying that Mr. Dabney knew the law, and there was no need to look into the books when he was at hand. My father used to tell us of his vivid recollections of seeing him drive home every evening when the court was in session. He was accompanied by his body-servant, who followed the gig on horseback, and who, after my grandfather got out, carried into the house the shot-bags of gold doubloons that had been stowed away under the seat in the gig-box. He sometimes brought home several of these. One of his fees amounted to four thousand dollars, which, considering that he died when barely in his prime, and the value of money at that time, was exceptionally large.

His eight-year-old son was already learning from him some of the fond, fatherly ways, which were destined years after to endear him to his own children and grandchildren, and which he practised in imitation of this tender father eighty years after that father was laid in his grave. One of our earliest recollections of our father was his having some treat for us always on his return home from a visit. This dainty was invariably put in the very bottom of his great-coat pocket, and the delightful mystery of feeling for that package and bringing it up to light, and then, with eager, expectant fingers untying the string before the treasure could be seen, was a pleasure not to be forgotten. My father's face at such times was one of the great charms of the scene, so merry and loving, and almost as full of the pleasant little excitement as the group of bright young ones gathered around him. In explanation to a visitor who might be looking on, he would say, "This is the way that my father treated me. I shall never forget how I enjoyed running my hand down in his great-coat pocket when he came back in the evening from court. I was always sure of finding there a great piece of what we called in Virginia 'court-house cake.'"

He was like his father in his thorough business methods and his punctuality. On the days when Benjamin Dabney did not attend court he retired to his study after breakfast, and his wife used to say that her orders were not to have him disturbed unless the house was afire. Promptly at three o'clock he left his books and his business cares behind him in his study, and, after dressing for dinner, joined his family in the drawing-room. He was invariable in his rule of being there ten minutes before dinner was announced, and he expected all in the house to conform to this. Many guests came and went at Bellevue, but this was never allowed to interfere with his business. After breakfast he would say to the gentlemen, "Here are guns and horses and dogs and books; pray amuse yourself as you like best. I shall have the pleasure of meeting you at dinner." After dinner he was like a boy on a holiday, ready to join in anything that was proposed, and the life of every party. He was so elegantly formed that after his death it was said that the handsomest legs in America were gone. His death was caused by a violent cold, contracted in the discharge of his law business. At this time a young and rising lawyer, Mr. Charles Hill, was already beginning to share many of the important cases and large fees with Benjamin Dabney. This gentleman was destined to become the father of a child who, years after, married the son of his rival, Benjamin Dabney, and whom we knew as our dearest mother.

Our faithful old nurse, Mammy Harriet, who grew up from childhood with my father, being only two years younger than himself, and who was scarcely ever separated from him, sits by me as I write, and she gives me an incident connected with the death of my grandfather too touching to be passed by.

"Yes, honey," she says in her affectionate way, that seems to claim us still as her babies, "'course I 'member when ole marster die. I 'member well de ole 'oman, Grannie Annie, who sot wid him night an' day—sot wid de coffin up-stairs—all by herself; lay by de corpse all night long, put her arms roun' de coffin, an' hold on to it, cryin' all night long. She foller de coffin twenty miles to Bellevue, whar dey bury him; foller behin' it cryin' an' hollerin' an' hollerin' an' cryin' to marster to say how d'ye to Toby—dat was her son—an' to Mars Gregory Smith,—dat was marster's uncle, what was dead. De ole 'oman use to wear gre't big pockets, wallet-like, an' she used to fill 'em full o' peanuts an' hickory-nuts an' apples an' dem kind o' things, an' carry 'em to Mars Jeemes Dabney, de brother o' her own marster, what was dead. He was Doctor Dabney, you know, your cousin Jeemes's father. He thought a heap on her. Yes, to be sho, he was a married man den, wid two chillun. She mighty good ole 'oman. When she die her hyar was white as my cap."

When Thomas was nine years old his mother, feeling that her brother, Dr. John Augustine Smith, would be a better judge than herself of the necessary requirements for the education of her sons, sent them to him, and Thomas was under his care for nine years. Augustine had never been a strong child, and it was soon decided that he was not able to stand the rigorous climate of Elizabeth, New Jersey, where the boys had been placed at boarding-school. At this early age the devotion of a lifetime had begun between the two children. The tender care and admiration of Thomas for his gentle, studious brother knew no bounds. He used sometimes to tease him himself, but never allowed any one else to do so. He was the self-constituted champion of this younger brother, whose thoughtful, retiring habits might otherwise have drawn on him many petty annoyances from his heedless school-fellows. At this time Augustine possessed the gift, which he lost later in life, of handling bees and other insects without danger of being stung. When he was missed from the playground, he might often be found in some secluded spot, with various stinging insects tied to strings, flying and buzzing around his head. He was quite fearless, and so gentle that they seemed to understand that no hurt would be done them. Thomas was occasionally deluded into trying the same experiments on seeing how easily it seemed to be managed, but in an instant he was off roaring with pain, and bitterly rueing his misplaced confidence. He always believed that Augustine was by nature fitted for a naturalist, and he deplored that his education was not turned in that direction. The harsh climate that froze the blood of the delicate boy and made his return to his mother's care in the Virginia home necessary, built up for the elder and stronger lad the iron constitution that was during his whole life the wonder and admiration of all who knew him.

In talking of these school-days, he used to amaze his Southern-born children by his stories of the moonlight races that he and his schoolmates took over the New Jersey snows. This they did without an article of clothing on. They sometimes ran a mile, diversifying things on the way by turning somersaults in the snow-drifts that were waist-deep. When they got back, they would creep softly up-stairs and jump into their beds and sleep like tops. At last old Parson Rudd, the head of the school, got wind of all this, and strictly forbade it. Nothing daunted, the boys were out again like rabbits when the snows and the moonlights were propitious. They were captured once, as they entered the door, after one of these escapades, and Parson Rudd did not fail to flog them soundly all around. In those days flogging was considered as necessary for a boy as his food, and as good for him.

The habits formed at this time clung to Thomas through life. He used frequently in winter to stand in the cold night-wind in his shirt and get thoroughly chilled, in order, he said, to enjoy returning to bed and getting warm. His family feared that revulsions so sudden would endanger his life, or his health, and tried to persuade him to give up what they could not but look on as a dangerous habit, but his laughing assurance that he liked it, and it agreed with his constitution, was the only satisfaction they received in answer to their solicitations.

On one occasion during his school-days in Elizabeth his mother came to pay him a visit, and Mrs. Winfield Scott called on her there. As Mrs. Scott was taking leave her coachman, an ignorant Irishman, got the fiery horses into so unmanageable a state that they stood on their hind legs and pawed the air. In vain did he try to make them move off. Thomas, seeing the difficulty, asked Mrs. Scott to allow him to drive her home.

She had not seen him before, and asked, "My little man, where do you come from, that you know how to manage horses?"

"I am from Virginia," he answered.

"If you are a Virginia boy you may drive me home," she said.

In a moment he was on the box by the coachman, and had shown to the unruly horses that a fearless hand had taken the reins. They yielded at once to him, and in a short time Mrs. Scott was at her own door.

General Scott came out to meet her as he heard the carriage roll up, and as he handed his wife out, asked, "What young gentleman am I indebted to, my dear, for bringing you home?"

"He did not tell me his name," she replied; "he only said that he was a Virginia boy. I do not know who he is."

General Scott turned to thank him, but he was already speeding away across the fields. When he had gotten too far away to be thanked, he could not resist looking around to see how the horses were behaving. They were standing on their hind legs pawing the air.

Thomas was taken from this school into the household of his uncle, Dr. Smith. This gentleman was admirably fitted by nature and education for the trust committed to him by his sister in the care of her sons. His character was so strong, and of such uncompromising integrity, as to impress itself on all who came under his influence. He received his medical education in London and Paris, and was a practising physician in the city of New York when Thomas was put under his charge. When only thirty-two years of age his native State of Virginia called him to the presidency of William and Mary College. From this post he was recalled to New York by the offer of a professorship in the College of Physicians and Surgeons. Ultimately he rose to be president of the college.

In order to stimulate Thomas's ambition in the city school which he now attended, Dr. Smith urged him to try to take the Latin prize. He did succeed in winning this prize, a handsome set of Plutarch's Lives, and when he carried the volumes home, his uncle took a five-dollar gold piece from his pocket and put it into the boy's hand. His first thought was to spend the whole of this in candy and raisins, and he went as fast as his feet could take him to his favorite resort, a little candy-booth kept by R. L. Stuart. Unfortunately, sulphur had just been weighed out in the scales, and the raisins had a strong taste of sulphur when they were handed to the lad. He was made so ill by this that he could not eat a raisin for years. R. L. Stuart was, fifty years after this time, one of the millionaires of New York.

Mrs. Smith heard Thomas say one day that he had never had as much pound-cake as he could eat. She made one for him, about the size of a grindstone, he used to say, and had it set before him when the dessert came on the table. "Now, Thomas," she said, "that cake is all for you." Thomas was cured of his fondness for pound-cake for the rest of his life by the very sight of this huge one, for he ate only a very small slice of it.

But the lively, gay boy was more fond of going to the theatre than of his Latin books. He spent nearly all his pocket-money in this way; and during the nine years that he was with his uncle he saw almost everything that was brought out on the New York stage. He went nearly every night, and the inexhaustible fund of amusing songs that were the delight of his children and grandchildren, and that are indelibly associated with him by his friends, who cannot recall them without a smile, were learned in this way.

After the horror of the burning of the Richmond Theatre the play-houses were not entered in New York by the public for some weeks. Every night the managers had their plays performed to houses absolutely empty. One night Thomas went to a theatre, and finding a man sitting there, stayed during the half of the play. But the situation of having all the actors and actresses looking at them, and going through their parts for them alone, became more and more embarrassing, and both Thomas and the man slipped quietly out. Curiosity to see the end prevailed, however, and finding a little crack in the lobby, the two stationed themselves so as to be able to peep through that, and held their posts till the curtain went down on the last act.

His memory was very strong, and so clear in the minutest detail as to be the admiration of all who came in contact with him. Everything that he heard or read seemed graven on steel. Hence, by this constant attendance at the theatre, he became familiar with Shakespeare's plays, and with all the standard works of the English drama. He was especially fond of Shakespeare's plays, and of "The Rivals" and "She Stoops to Conquer," and he quoted from them with ease. This, however, he rarely did, having an unconquerable shyness in making anything like a premeditated speech. At dinners he often made speeches and proposed toasts when the occasion called for them, but those who knew him cannot fail to recall the mounting color and slightly husky voice which accompanied even the shortest address.

When he was nine years old he saw Robert Fulton make the trial trip with his steamboat on the Hudson River. He never forgot the appearance of Fulton as he stood on the deck with folded arms, looking as if he were chiselled out of stone. All along the river-banks were the crowds who had gathered to witness what most of them had predicted would be ignominious failure, and they would have shouted in derision if their evil predictions had been verified. Instead, involuntary shouts of wild applause and admiration burst forth as the wheel made its first revolution and the steamer moved off from her wharf like a thing of life. The river-bank all the way was lined with people who came to see the wondrous thing. In the city of New York it was known that the steamer was on her way down the river while she was yet several miles off by the loud shouts of the crowds on the river-banks. Thomas, like most boys born on tide-water, was exceedingly fond of boats and of all sorts of water sports, and used to amuse himself by climbing the masts of the vessels in New York harbor. From the roundtop-mast of an English ship, just brought in as a prize, he one day witnessed the steaming in of Robert Fulton's steamboat. When he went back to his uncle's house, his mother, who had arrived on the boat, told him that she had seen a little fellow no bigger than himself up in the rigging of a big ship, and was amazed to hear that he was no other than her own boy.

His admiration of naval courage and prowess was boundless, fostered in childhood by the recitals of his half-brother George, the midshipman, and later by the stirring scenes of the war of 1812. He was one in the funeral procession that bore our heroic "Don't-give-up-the-ship" Lawrence to his last resting-place in Trinity church-yard.

At one time during his residence under his uncle's roof Dr. Smith became dissatisfied with his want of application to his studies, and advised his mother to set him to work at some handicraft. Accordingly, he was set to work in a printer's shop, and he printed a Bible before he concluded to apply himself to the cultivation of his mind. At the same time Augustine was sentenced to learn the business of a coachmaker for the same offence of idleness. He was actually in his mother's carriage, on his way to be apprenticed to a coachmaker, when, at Dr. Smith's suggestion, he was given one more opportunity of showing that he was not hopelessly indolent. The result with both boys was quite satisfactory; they returned to their books with new interest, and there was never again occasion to find fault with them on this subject.

One night when Thomas was about fourteen years old he had run to a fire. This he always did when near enough to reach the scene. Above the uproar of the flames could be heard the screams of a poor woman entreating some one to save her baby, which she said was in the burning house. No one moved to attempt to rescue it. The smoke was already puffing out of the windows, and it was considered as much as a man's life was worth to enter the building. The boy seized a piece of rough scantling, which he adjusted to the second-story window that she indicated, and on this he climbed until he reached the window. He got into the room and felt his way to the bed, where the woman had said that her child lay. The bed was empty. Unknown to the mother, the child had been taken out and was in a place of safety. The boy now groped his way to the window. The fire had made such progress that the window-panes were falling in great drops of molten glass. Not a moment was to be lost, and he seized the scantling with both hands and slid to the ground. The liquid glass fell on his hands, and the splinters and nails, of which the scantling was full, lacerated them. The scars left by these wounds were so deep as to be plainly visible during his whole life. The crowd had watched with breathless suspense his climbing into the house, and it was believed that he had gone to certain death. His reappearance at the window was hailed with tumultuous cheers and applause. The police crowded around him, asking his name, and the woman fell on her knees before him to bless him for his efforts in her behalf and to beg to know his name. He refused to give it, being quite embarrassed at finding himself the centre of so much attention, when he had been doing what seemed to him so plain and simple a duty. He got away as fast as he could, and did not even tell his uncle of his adventure. The New York morning papers contained an account of the "heroic action of a young boy who had refused to give his name." It was many years before he mentioned the circumstance to any one.

One cold day, when he was about nineteen years old, he noticed on the ferry-boat, as he was coming from New York to Jersey City, a poor woman, who was shivering in her calico dress. He took off his great-coat and put it around her.

In after-life he amused his friends very much by his stories of a certain Mr. ——, who, as some sort of expiation for having killed a negro, built a church, and undertook to gather a congregation and to preach to them. His efforts brought together a number of the

wild spirits of the city. Thomas, who was afraid of
Dr. Smith's displeasure if it were known that such a
place was his Sunday evening resort, introduced himself to this man under the name of Gregory. "Brother
Gregory," as Mr. —— always called him, was promoted
in this motley assembly to be the raiser of the hymns,
and he was besides the senior warden. One of his
duties was to snuff the candles; he also handed around
the plate for the contributions of the congregation.
He received nothing but wads of paper and cigar-ends,
but the man persisted in having the plate handed
around regularly. There were no end of practical jokes
played on him by his unruly congregation. They shied
rotten apples at his head and blew out the candles, and
tried in every way to interrupt him, especially when
his eyes were tightly closed in prayer. It was observed
that no amount of disorder or noise could make him
unclose his eyes at these times, and so the merry fellows invariably played the wildest pranks on him as
soon as he began the prayer. Thomas was often the
leader of these, but the man never suspected him, as
he always seemed so ready to help to catch the offenders. It must have been remarked even by Mr. ——
that he was singularly unsuccessful in these efforts at
assisting him. One night he threw the snuff of a can-
dle-wick on a fuse that he had arranged so that it
would go off in the midst of the prayer. At the same
moment the candles were put out all over the house.
This time the unfortunate man was really so alarmed
that he shrieked for Brother Gregory to come to him,
that they meant to kill him. With a most officious
show of zeal Thomas rushed forward. The two pursued the supposed offenders through the church, and
up the stairs and through the gallery, Thomas taking
good care not to overtake the fugitives. In the gallery
they fled through a door, which they held against the
united efforts of the preacher and his ally. At a pre-
concerted signal they suddenly sprang from the door,
which now gave way, and the poor man and his
trusted friend were precipitated headlong on the floor.
It is almost needless to say that the police frequently

appeared on the scene when this horse-play became very uproarious. Mr. —— became so fond of his young friend that he took him to tea at his house one evening, and introduced him to his daughters, two very pretty girls. After tea he asked his guest to lead in prayer. But this was a length to which the boy could not be induced to go. Indeed, that he was asked to do it made such an impression on him that he made up his mind never again to attend the Sunday evening meetings. Years after this Mr. —— had occasion to go to Richmond, Virginia, and he made many inquiries about a much valued friend, young Mr. Gregory, who had come, he said, from that part of the world, and whom he had lost sight of, much to his regret. Of course he found no trace of him. His mother, who heard of these inquiries, was greatly diverted. She had had many a hearty laugh over the stories of his escapades under the assumed name, for it was all too good to be kept from her. His mother went very often from her Virginia home to visit her brother in New York. The devotion of Thomas to her was one of the strongest feelings of his nature. After her death, which did not occur till he was nearly sixty years of age, he said that he had never said a disrespectful word to his mother in his life. During her lifetime he never failed to go to visit her every other year, after he moved out to Mississippi. Until railroads were built this journey was performed in stages and by steamboats, and it could not be made in less than two weeks. Each time he took one or two of his children with him, that he might show them to her in turn. The last child that was taken to her of the nine that she lived to see was the first-born girl, her own little namesake, Sarah. He had greatly desired to have a daughter, that she might bear his mother's name.

While he lived with Dr. Smith he did all the family marketing. He also frequently went with him when surgical operations were to be performed. He learned so much from him in surgery as to be of lasting service to him in the care of his servants on his plantation. It was often said of him that he should have been a physician. His steady hand and strong nerve fitted him especially for the practice of surgery. When he was fourteen years old the war of 1812 broke out. A report came to the Gloucester home that the British were making a demonstration of landing at Old Point Comfort. The State of Virginia called for men to go to the defence of the Point, and among the drafted men was Mrs. Benjamin Dabney's overseer. I shall give the account of this in Mammy Harriet's words. She was a child twelve years of age at the time, and never forgot the scenes then witnessed.

"'Course I 'member when Mars Thomas went off to de wars. What's to hender me from 'memberin'? He warn't grown, you know. He was just like Mars Ben, he own son Ben, when he went off to fight. You all know how you fix him up to go off to fight? Jest so he ma fix him up, and put him on de horse to ride to Old Point Comfort. De horse was Juno colt. Don't I know Juno? She was one of missis carriage-horses, an' she used to stan' straight up on her hin' legs when she was put to de carriage. You see dey come an' call for de overseer, Maja, an' he was mighty skeered, an' he cum hollerin' to de house, 'Mrs. Dabney! Mrs. Dabney! Whar is she?' Den she cum out an' tell her son Thomas to go in de overseer place, 'cause de overseer was of use on de place. Mars Thomas was delighted to go."

Mrs. Dabney sent him on a lame horse, telling him that a lame horse was good enough to advance on, but would not do for a retreat. Her brother, Colonel Thomas Smith, was already in camp at Old Point Comfort, and Thomas was sent to join him. At the end of three weeks it was seen that this place would not be attacked, and Thomas returned home. He was through life a soldier at heart. Perhaps this early taste of the military life made the indelible impression. His step and bearing were those of a soldier, and this appearance was heightened by the old style of dress,— the swallow-tailed, blue cloth coat and gold-plated buttons. This was his dress till he was over sixty years of age, when he no longer had the means to pay for the costly clothes.

On the breaking up of the camp at Old Point Comfort, Thomas and Augustine were sent to the college of William and Mary. Here they were once more under the eye of Dr. John Augustine Smith, who had just been called to the presidency of the college. A house was rented for the two boys, and, with the assistance of a cook and a body-servant apiece, they kept house during their collegiate course. Thomas was there for a comparatively short time, being called to take charge of Elmington. At this time his mother contracted a second marriage, with Colonel William H. Macon, of New Kent County, and she moved to his home, Mount Prospect, in that county.

CHAPTER II.

MARRIAGE AND LIFE AT ELMINGTON.

On the 6th of June, 1820, Thomas was married to Miss Mary Adelaide Tyler, daughter of Chancellor Samuel Tyler, of Williamsburg. He was at this time twenty-two years old. This lady lived only three years. Of this marriage were born two children, Benjamin Augustine and Samuel Tyler. Samuel died in infancy. Augustine lived to be nine years old, a gentle, quiet boy, who early showed signs of the disease of which he died, water on the brain.

When Thomas Dabney had been a widower about three years, he met at the county ball at King and Queen Court-House Miss Sophia Hill, the daughter of Mr. Charles Hill of that county. She was but sixteen years of age, and this was her first ball. All who saw her at that time say that she was one of the most beautiful creatures that the eye ever rested on. Her hair and eyes were of that rare tint called the poet's auburn, and her complexion was the fair, fine skin that is found only with such hair. Teeth of snow, a shapely head on lovely shoulders, hands and arms that might have served as models for a sculptor, and a charming smile, and one of the sweetest voices in the world, made up a combination that is rarely met with. To this matchless beauty was joined a sunny, happy disposition and bright manner that made her irresistible in her youthful grace.

Thomas Dabney always said that he fell violently in love with her as soon as his eyes fell on her across the ball-room. He lost no time in securing an introduction, and before the evening was over he was resolved on winning this lovely girl for his wife. He found several formidable rivals in the way, but he was so fortunate as to win her young heart. He drove from his home in Gloucester to her father's home, Mantua, on the Mattapony River, in King and Queen County, every two weeks during the two months' engagement. He went in his gig, with his body-servant following on horseback. Each time he took a gift,—sometimes handsome jewelry, and at other times volumes of standard English authors.

On each alternate week he wrote a letter to her. None of these letters were answered. He looked for no acknowledgment,—his thought was that he was honored sufficiently by her receiving them. This he expressed many years after, in speaking of a nephew who had complained that his betrothed did not write as often as he did.

The marriage took place at the Mantua house, on the 26th of June, 1826. The ceremony was performed in the midst of a large company of relatives and friends. One who saw the bride the next day said that as she sat in her soft white gown, with her fair hands crossed in her lap and a smile on the beautiful face, she was like the vision of an angel.

On that day Thomas took her home to Elmington. Her beauty and gentleness and modesty won the hearts of his friends. Mrs. Mann Page, of Gloucester, was celebrated for her beautiful hands, but after Sophia came, it was acknowledged that hers surpassed Mrs. Page's in beauty. She found Elmington full of her husband's servants, who had been accustomed to take care of him during his life as a widower. She felt shy about taking things into her own hands, fearing to excite their jealousy, and she took no voice in the housekeeping for two years.

The butler, George Orris, was quite equal to the trust committed to him. It was only necessary to say to him that a certain number of guests were looked for to dinner, and everything would be done in a style to suit the occasion. George himself was said to know by heart every recipe in Mrs. Randolph's cookery-book, having been trained by that lady herself. Virginia tradition says that Mrs. Randolph had spent three fortunes in cooking. At the appointed hour, in knee-breeches and silk stockings and silver buckles, George came to announce that dinner was served.

George was so formidable in his dignity of office that the timid young wife stood quite in awe of him, and before she learned to know the good, kind heart that beat under that imposing appearance, was actually afraid to ask for the keys to get a slice of bread and butter in her husband's house. Some one asked George how he liked his new mistress. "I like her very much," was the reply, "only she wears her under petticoat longer than the top one." She was much amused on this being repeated to her, and explained that the white satin wedding-gown which George had seen her wear to her own dinner-parties was longer than the lace overdress that covered it. George was sincerely mourned at his death, which occurred a few years later.

The lady's-maid, Abby, whom Sophia found at Elmington, was in her department as accomplished and as faithful as George Orris was in his. She took the new mistress at once all over the house, giving her an inventory of everything that had been left in her care. In speaking of this afterwards, when both mistress and maid were grown old together, Sophia said that not even the smallest thing had been misappropriated by those honest hands.

On the 27th of March of the following year the first child was born. The happy parents gave him the name of Charles. But the child lived only nine months. On Christmas-day, 1828, a second son was given to them, whom they named Thomas. Then followed James, another Charles, and Virginius.

The life at Elmington was the ideal life of a Virginia gentleman. Elmington was situated on an arm of the Chesapeake Bay, the North River, in the county of Gloucester, that has so often been called the garden-spot of Virginia.

The house was of red brick, quaint and old-fashioned in design. It was built very near the water's edge. The lapping of the waves of the incoming tide was a sweet lullaby to the quiet scene, as the eye rested on the greensward of the lawn, or took in the bend of the river that made a broad sweep just below the Elmington garden. The North River is half a mile wide. On the other shore could be seen the groves and fields and gardens of the neighboring country-seats. The low grounds on the river-shore extend back a distance of a mile and three-quarters, and lie like a green carpet, dotted here and there with grand old forest-trees, and corn, wheat, rye, and tobacco fields. Far as the eye can reach stretches this fair view around Elmington. And far over, beyond field and grove and creek, rises the line of soft, round hills that mark the highlands of Gloucester.

On the land side, the Elmington house was approached through the fields by a lane a mile and three quarters long. It was broad enough to admit of three carriage-drives. Many of the lanes in Gloucester lie between avenues of cedar-trees, and the fields in most of the estates are divided by cedar-hedges. It was so on the Elmington lands.

About four miles inland from the North River, in a quiet spot, surrounded by venerable oak and pine and walnut and other native trees, stands old Ware Church. It was built in colonial times, and its age is unknown. It is nearly square in form, and altogether unlike the present style of church architecture in this country. But its ancient walls are churchly, and the look of unchangeableness is soothing to the spirit in this world of unrest. This was the parish church attended by the North River people. The old pew-backs at that day were so high that the occupants were invisible to each other. Many of them might read the names of their deceased ancestors on the tombstones that served as a floor for the chancel. The floor of Ware Church was made of flagstones. Stoves were not then in use in churches, nor was any attempt made to heat them. Delicate people stayed at home in the winter, or had warming-pans of coals carried in by their servants to put to their feet.

Gloucester County had been settled by the best class of English people who came to this country, the younger sons of noble houses, and other men of standing, who were induced to make their homes over here by an inherent love of change, or because they had not the means to live in the mother-country in the extravagant style required by their station. These brought to their homes in the New World the customs and manners of the Old. The tone of society has always been truly English in Lower Virginia, the "tide-water country," as the people love to call it. Everybody kept open house; entertaining was a matter of course, anything and everything was made the occasion of a dinner-party. The country-seats were strung along the banks of the North River in a way to favor this. A signal raised on one could be seen for several miles up and down the river. If one of the colored fishermen, whose sole occupation was to catch fish for the table at the Great House, as they called their master's residence, succeeded in catching a sheep's-head, his orders were to run up a signal-flag. This was an invitation to dinner to every gentleman in the neighborhood. If a rabbit was caught the same rule was observed. Rabbits were not common, which seemed to be the pretext for this, for they were not really esteemed as a dainty dish. A rabbit was served up rather as a trophy of the hunt than as a part of the feast intended to be eaten. But the sheep's-head in those waters were not uncommon, and one was taken by the fisherman of one house or another nearly every day. At five minutes before the time for dinner the gentlemen would ride up, or come by boat to the door of the house that had the signal flying. If any one was unable to attend, his servant rode up promptly with a note of regrets. Punctuality in the observance of all the rules of courtesy and good breeding seemed inherent in the men and women in Gloucester society. In his Mississippi life Mr. Dabney was often annoyed by the different manners of his neighbors out there, very few of whom thought it necessary to send regrets or apologies when his invitations could not be accepted.

Bishop Moore would go two or three miles out of his way in order to spend a day or two at Elmington. One night at about ten o'clock, in the midst of a snow-storm, he drove up. A game of whist was going on in the dining-room. Mr. Dabney, hearing the sound of his carriage-wheels, went out to welcome the guest, and found the bishop and his daughter there. While he was helping the old gentleman to get out of his great-coat before taking him in to the dining-room, the company there were busy hiding away the cards. Meanwhile, Bishop Moore was telling him, with hands upraised, of the cause that had brought his daughter and himself out in such weather and at such an hour —the people at whose house they had intended to sleep they had found engaged in a game of whist! Mr. Dabney roared with merriment in telling this story. "The bishop saw the devil behind every card," he always added.

At this time John Tyler, afterwards President of the United States, was among his intimate friends, and he wrote to ask if he could come to Elmington for a week of absolute rest and quiet. Upon the invitation being sent, he came, and his wishes were respected in the true Virginia manner of letting the guests of the house be happy and comfortable in their own way. He sat all day over his papers, no one being allowed to intrude on his privacy. Every evening, when he came down to dinner, he found a company invited to dine with him.

Augustine Dabney had married Miss Elizabeth Smith,

of Fredericksburg, and lived in Gloucester, back in the country some miles from the North River. Thomas's nearest neighbor and most valued friend was his father's half-brother, Dr. James Dabney. Living on adjoining estates, their homes were barely a stone's throw apart, and not many hours of the day passed without intercourse between the two houses. The uncle and nephew were congenial in many ways, and Sophia revered and loved Dr. Dabney like a father. Thomas's aptitude for medicine and surgery was at times so helpful to Dr. Dabney, that he fell into a way of calling on him frequently to assist him. He used to say that Thomas's soft hand and acute sense of touch enabled him at times to diagnose a case that would baffle a practitioner of considerable experience who was not possessed of these natural advantages. He always had him at hand in his surgical cases if possible, and thus, under this uncle, were renewed the lessons given by Dr. Smith. Dr. Dabney was a man made of no common clay. His hospitality was on so princely a scale that he made no charge for medical services to any stranger visiting his county, thus making the whole county of Gloucester his home. Although for many years a widower, with only two children, both sons, the arrangements of his home were set with a view to a large household. Everything was on a scale liberal even for Gloucester.

A lady now sixty-eight years of age writes thus of Dr. James Dabney: " He stood *very high* in his profession. He was a widower from my earliest recollection. He had a housekeeper and fine servants, and entertained people by the score for months at a time. Even ladies used to stay there from cities."

His home, the Exchange, was seldom without its guests of a day, or a week, or many months. The ample fortune of the host justified the elegant hospitality of the house.

He had expended the whole of his patrimony during his five years at the medical school in Edinburgh. On his arrival in America, after graduating in medicine, he was obliged to borrow five hundred dollars in order to open his office as a practitioner of medicine at Gloucester

Court-House. It was not long before his ability brought him into a large practice, not only in Gloucester County, but he was called to Richmond, Norfolk, and other places as consulting physician.

In the midst of Dr. Dabney's busy professional life his friends and neighbors called on him to represent his county in the Virginia Legislature. This he refused to do, alleging that he had no time for political work. But they were so persistent that he finally yielded. He stipulated, however, that he would not make one electioneering visit or ask for a single vote. In this he remained firm, and even went so far as to absent himself from the polls on the day of election. He was elected by a large majority, and he served the term out. His county people tried hard to induce him to allow his name to appear a second time as a candidate for the Legislature. But he was not to be moved from his resolution of devoting himself henceforth to his profession.

The strong character of Dr. James Dabney made its impress on Thomas. Doubtless he had inherited some of the traits with the blood of this large-souled uncle.

Dr. Dabney's views about his own interment were very simple. He required from his son James a promise to carry them out on his death, and his last wishes were respected. He was placed in a plain pine coffin, and no stone was set up to mark his grave. A brick wall saves it from desecration. Like his uncle, Thomas had a repugnance for costly and showy funeral trappings. He carried out these views in his own household. He always expressed a desire to be buried himself as he buried his loved ones, in a plain pine coffin. "That I may return as quickly as possible to the original elements in the bosom of the earth."

This taste was in accordance with the simplicity of character of the two men. They did nothing for show during their lifetime, and did not desire anything done for show over their ashes.

In colonial days a robe of silk was spun and woven for the Merrie Monarch in Gloucester County, and in the garret of the Exchange the silk-worms spun the silk for two complete suits for General Washington. In color they were gray. Thomas Dabney remembered seeing the silk-worms up there when a child, and his aunt Anderson, who presented these suits to General Washington, used occasionally to give him a cocoon for a plaything.

Thomas Dabney was interested in all that was going on in Virginia. He rode to Richmond frequently. When it was known that Watkins Leigh, or R. G. Scott, or the Stannards, or any other of the distinguished men of that day, were to engage in a debate, he was pretty sure to be there to hear them. Thomas was present at the famous dinner at Yorktown given in honor of the nation's guest, the Marquis de Lafayette. At the table he was placed next to George Washington Lafayette, who occupied the seat next to his father. It was in the month of October, and there was a small dish of red Antwerp raspberries sent by Mrs. Tayloe of Mount Airy. They came from her hot-houses, and were set before General Lafayette. The courteous gentleman leaned across his son and offered the berries to Thomas. He took two.

The story is still told in Gloucester of Thomas's capture of a man by the name of Crusoe, living in the lower part of the county. This man had acted for some years in open defiance of the oyster law. No sheriff had arrested him. He openly boasted that none should. Thomas had lately been elected to this office, and he determined to make an attempt to capture Crusoe. Summoning a posse of three of his neighbors, he proceeded in a boat down the river to Crusoe's schooner, that was lying out in York River. The schooner was well built and in stanch condition, while the boat which held Thomas and his friends was a wretched water-logged craft. As they drew near Crusoe's schooner, the sheriff called out to him to surrender. The only reply made to the summons was to cover the little boat of the sheriff and his party with an enormous old swivel-gun, and to warn them with an oath not to advance any nearer. Thomas held a consultation with his friends, telling them that they must decide whether they were willing to approach the schooner under such circumstances. It was decided that it would be foolhardy to attempt to board a well-equipped boat when they were in a crazy thing that could not be managed in an emergency. So they went back home, leaving Crusoe master of the field for the time.

Ascertaining that Crusoe was in his house on a certain night, it was resolved to capture him there. Accordingly another posse was summoned, and Thomas and his four men rode to the man's house, a distance of about twelve miles. They surrounded the house, and the sheriff knocked at the door and demanded instant surrender. Crusoe's wife put her head out of the window up-stairs and said that her husband was in bed; that if Mr. Dabney would come up-stairs alone and unarmed, he would give himself up. The posse objected to these conditions, and said that Mr. Dabney should at least be accompanied by one of them, or should wear his arms. But he called to the woman that he was ready and willing to come up on Crusoe's terms.

She came down then and unbarred the door, and he followed her up to the man's room. He gave himself up at once, and, at the sheriff's bidding, prepared to mount a horse and go with him as his prisoner. He was greatly dejected at the prospect of being thrown into prison to await his trial, and was very sulky as they rode along. The party did not stop till they had reached Elmington.

When dinner-time came, Thomas ordered dinner to be served to him, but he refused to eat. He had not tasted food the whole day. Thomas said to him, "Mr. Crusoe, would you like to go back to your wife to-night?" The man looked up quickly, his whole countenance changing. "I mean to put you on your honor," the sheriff continued. "You know that it is against the law for me to release you without bail. I will be your surety that you will be at Gloucester Court-House to pay the hundred dollars' fine in two weeks."

The man was much moved, and shed tears. The sheriff lent him his own horse to ride home. On the appointed day he was at the court-house with the hundred dollars in his hand. His gratitude to the man who had trusted him, one who had been an outlaw for years, made a changed man of him. He was ever after a law-abiding citizen, and was Thomas's stanch friend as long as he lived.

Crusoe passed away years ago, but his son, himself an aged man now, loves to tell the story of Mr. Dabney's trust of his father. This son asked Mr. James Dabney of the Exchange if he was a relative of the former sheriff, and on hearing that they were cousins, expressed his own gratitude and his father's for the confidence placed in him in the time of trouble. The fifty odd years that have passed since that time seem not to have obliterated it from the memory of the Crusoe family.

At the time when the negro rising known as the Southhampton insurrection was threatened, Thomas received from Governor Floyd a commission of colonel of militia. He and his men kept their horses saddled and bridled in the stable every night for three weeks, ready for any alarm or emergency. He was an accomplished horseman, and sat his mettlesome, blooded stallion like a part of himself. A boy in the neighborhood, whom his father asked if he would like to go to the court-house to see Colonel Dabney's soldiers drill, said in reply that he would rather see Colonel Dabney on his horse at the head of his regiment than all the soldiers. This boy, now a gray-headed man in Baltimore, delights yet in talking of those days. "When the drum and the fife struck up," he says, "that was the time that we boys had the fun. Colonel Dabney's horse sprang into the air and seemed hardly to touch the ground, and we wondered how he kept his seat."

On the night when it was understood that the negro rising was to take place he called his own negroes up, and put his wife under their charge, as his duty called him away from her. His charge to them was that not only was she to be protected by them, but she was not even to be alarmed; and if harm befell a hair of her head, they should be held accountable for it. The negroes were faithful, and guarded the house all night long, and with so much tact and genuine affection that when Thomas Dabney returned to his home the next day, his wife was amazed to hear from his lips the story of the peril that she, along with every white woman in Gloucester, had passed through during the night.

It is a singular circumstance that, with the exception of the negroes on the Elmington place, not a negro man was to be found in Gloucester County on that night by the patrol. It was supposed that the daring spirits had gone to join in the uprising, while the timid ones had hidden themselves in the woods.

About the year 1835 a great many Virginians were induced to remove with their families to the far South. For several reasons Thomas began to consider the expediency of moving out to the then new country. He was considered one of the most successful wheat and tobacco farmers in his part of the State. But the expensive style of living in Gloucester began to be a source of serious anxiety. He knew that with a young and growing family to educate and provide for the difficulty would be greater each year. He felt also the increasing difficulty of giving to his negroes the amount of nourishing food that he considered necessary for laboring people. In view of these facts, he made up his mind that he must leave his home in Virginia for a new one in the cotton-planting States.

Many and great were the regrets when it became known that Thomas Dabney had determined to leave Gloucester.

The farewell dinner given to him at the court-house was perhaps the most notable ever given within the limits of the county. A copy of the *Richmond Enquirer*, bearing date of September 22, 1835, contains the published account of the proceedings of the day, which is here inserted.

EXTRACT FROM "THE RICHMOND ENQUIRER," SEPTEMBER 22, 1835.

" *To the Editors of the Enquirer:*

"GENTLEMEN,—Under cover you have the proceedings which occurred at a public dinner recently given by many citizens of this county to Colonel Thomas S. Dabney, the insertion of which in your paper of an early day is desired. I have the honor to be your ob't serv't, "JOHN TYLER.

"DINNER TO COLONEL THOMAS S. DABNEY.

"Colonel Dabney being about to move to the State of Mississippi with a view to a permanent settlement in that State, many of his countymen united in giving him a public dinner at Gloucester Court-House on the 12th inst. The following letters passed on the occasion:

"GLOUCESTER COUNTY, Sept. 5th, 1835.

"DEAR SIR,—On behalf of many of the citizens of this county, who have learned, with the deepest regret, your determination shortly to leave Virginia for a residence in another State, we tender you an invitation to a public dinner to be given at Gloucester Court-House, on such day, prior to your departure, as may best suit your convenience. Those whom we represent are desirous of thus publicly manifesting their respect towards you because of their high estimate of your character as a man and your conduct as a citizen. We trust that no consideration will induce you to hesitate in yielding to their wishes, thereby affording them an opportunity, which may never occur again, of shaking you cordially by the hand and bidding you a warm and affectionate adieu.

"We feel ourselves honored in having been made the channel of this communication, and subscribe ourselves, in all sincerity, your faithful and sincere friends,

"WILLIAM ROBBINS,
"THOMAS SMITH,
"JOHN TYLER,
"MANN PAGE,
"ROBERT CURTIS.

"COL. THOMAS S. DABNEY, Elmington.

" *Answer of Colonel Dabney.*

"ELMINGTON, Sept. 8th, 1835.

"GENTLEMEN,—Your greatly esteemed note of the 5th inst. on behalf of many citizens of this county, tendering me a public dinner, has been received. Deeply sensible as I am that the honor proposed to be conferred upon me is immeasurably beyond my merits, yet the footing upon which you have been pleased to place my acceptance or refusal leaves me no alternative, for it is impossible I can refuse my long-tried and best friends an opportunity of bidding me adieu prior to my leaving the State; and it might not become me to prescribe the mode. I therefore accept the invitation of my Gloucester friends with profound sensibility, not only for the distinguished and unexpected mark of their affection and confidence which it bespeaks, but also for the numberless obligations with which they have been loading me for years past. If it should be agreeable to yourselves, gentlemen, and those whom you represent, I will meet my friends on Saturday, the 12th inst.

"I have the honor to be, gentlemen, with perfect respect and esteem, your grateful friend, THOMAS S. DABNEY.

"To CAPT. ROBBINS, COL. SMITH, GOV. TYLER, CAPT. PAGE, and COL. CURTIS.

"The Rev. R. R. Corbin, Benj. F. Dabney, Esq., and Robert Nicholson, Esq., who are also about to leave the land of their nativity, were invited guests, the last of whom alone attended. The absence of the other two gentlemen was much regretted by all who were present. Notwithstanding the inclemency of the day, the seats at the table were filled. The tribute of respect thus paid to one of our most valued and most valuable citizens furnishes an admirable moral to the rising generation. It was the voluntary outpouring of the heart, in testimony of a well-spent life, offered by his neighbors, countymen, and friends, to a private citizen, mingled with the loss which our society is destined to experience in his emigration. Governor Tyler was called on to preside, and Captain Mann Page acted as Vice-President. After partaking of an excellent dinner, the cloth was removed, and the President addressed the meeting in a few brief remarks. He said that he had risen to propose a sentiment which he was sure to find the most cordial unanimity at that table, and he had as little doubt on the part of this whole community, if every citizen of the county was there assembled. Those present had met to render a tribute of respect to a native-born citizen of the county, who, after having passed the spring, and in some degree the summer, of his life among them, was about to migrate to a distant State, where he trusted he might reap the richest harvest of reputation and wealth. Heaven grant that his days may be long in the land which he proposes to inhabit! He will not fail to think of the land of his forefathers and the friends he has left behind. We, on our part, can never forget that Elmington, while his dwelling-place, was the seat of unbounded hospitality and of all the social virtues. He would say no more, but would propose:

"'Our guest, friend, and countyman, Colonel Thos. S. Dabney. His departure from among us leaves a vacuum in our society not easily to be filled. He will be to Mississippi what he has been to Virginia, one of her most useful and valuable citizens.'

"After the applause which this sentiment elicited had subsided, Colonel Dabney returned his thanks in a feeling and appropriate address, of which we regret we are unable to furnish more than the briefest outline. He expressed himself to be most deeply affected by the kindness manifested towards him. The motive which had led to this assemblage, the sentiment just uttered, and the warm response with which it had met, the organ through whom it had been announced,—all—everything was calculated to overpower him with sensibility. He stood in the midst of long-tried friends, to whom he was about to bid an affectionate and perhaps last farewell. He was in the act of leaving his native home, and the land so dear to his affections. Those considerations left him no voice to utter one-half of what he felt. The prospect of bettering, in a worldly point of view, the ultimate condition of his children had induced him to seek a place of abode in another clime; and he would say that if his humble bark, pushed out in what was to him an untried ocean of adventure, could be used as a breakwater by those who were here, or their children's children, when engaged in a similar voyage, he would regard himself as most truly happy. He added many other remarks, and concluded by offering the following sentiment:

"By Colonel Thos. S. Dabney: 'The citizens of Gloucester County, in the Old Dominion:

"'Where'er I roam, whatever realms I see,
My heart, untravelled, fondly turns to thee;
Still *to my brothers turns* with ceaseless pain,
And drags, *at each remove,* a lengthened chain.'"

"By the Vice-President: 'Our friends emigrating from the County of Gloucester: Health, prosperity, and happiness attend them.'

"By Captain P. E. Tabb: 'Our Guest: May the people destined to be his future associates know his virtues and appreciate his merits, as do the warm hearts met this day to testify their love and respect for him.'

"By the Vice-President: 'Our Guest, Robert Nicholson: A worthy son of the ancient dominion.'

"Mr. Nicholson expressed his grateful thanks for the notice that had been thus taken of him.

"By Mr. Nicholson: 'The State of Virginia—the land of my forefathers. My greatest boast shall ever be that I was born a Virginian.'

"By Colonel Thomas Smith: 'Our friends Thomas Dabney, Richard R. Corbin, and Benj. F. Dabney: They possess our love and respect, and when they move from among us we shall not forget them.'

"By Wade Mosby, Esq.: 'The memory of the late Philip Tabb, one of Gloucester's best benefactors.'

"Mr. Mosby preceded this by remarks expressing his great

veneration for the character of Mr. Tabb, which called for an acknowledgment from Mr. Philip E. Tabb, as the representative of the family, which was rendered after the most feeling manner.

"By C. S. Jones, Esq.: 'Colonel Thomas S. Dabney: May the star which guides his destiny lead him and his to prosperity, to everlasting peace and happiness.'

"By John P. Scott, Esq.: '*Mrs. Thomas Dabney*, to whom may be applied the words of the noble Cornelia, when inquired for her jewels, pointing to her sons, "These are they."' Mrs. Dabney's name was received with long-continued applause.

"By John R. Cary, Esq.: 'The State of Mississippi: She will ere long contain some of Virginia's most noble sons; she will not fail to cherish and honor them.'

"By Richard Morriss, Esq.: 'Hinds County of Mississippi: A State within itself,—Jackson, the seat of government; Clinton, the seat of science; Raymond, the seat of justice; and Amsterdam, the port of entry.'

"By Andrew Van Bibber, Esq.: 'Augustine L. Dabney: Though not with us, not forgotten; one worthy of all remembrance.'

"By A. L. Byrd, Esq.: 'Colonel Thos. S. Dabney: I have known him for seventeen years; if he has any superior in those qualities that adorn a man, I should like to see him.'

"By John T. Seawell, Esq.: 'Wyndham Kemp, and those of our fellow-countrymen who will soon join him: May God remember me as I remember them.'

"By Dr. P. R. Nelson: 'Virginia: I can never leave thee or forsake thee,—

'"The bridegroom may forget his bride
  Was made his wedded wife yestereen,
The monarch may forget the crown
  That on his head an hour has been;
The mother may forget her child
  That hangs so sweetly on her knee,
But I'll remember thee, my State,
  And all that thou hast been to me."'

"By Robert Tyler, Esq.: 'The Emigrants: With sorrow and regret we part with our fellow-countrymen; but if they will go, we pray God speed them.'

"By C. S. Jones: 'We lose in our friend Colonel Dabney one of Virginia's most valued sons; but no matter where his destiny may be cast, his motto will still be "States rights forever."'

"By Wade Mosby, Esq.: 'The memory of Thomas T. Tabb, late of Todsbury: Hospitable, generous Virginian,—who that knew thee does not mourn over thy grave, and shed tears for thy too early death?'

"By J. S. Cary, Esq.: 'Wyndham Kemp, Esq., of Raymond, Mississippi: Though far away, thou art not forgot.'

"By A. L. Byrd, Esq.: 'Richard R. Corbin and Dr. Benjamin

F. Dabney: They are about to leave us, with our friend Colonel Dabney,—may Heaven crown their efforts with success.'

"By John Tyler, Esq.: 'The good old County of Gloucester: Her name is identified in history with the names of Nathaniel Bacon and John Page, of Rosewell. The one resisted the arbitrary acts of a king's *governor*, the other of a king. Let us cherish their names and emulate their virtues.'

"By John T. Seawell, Esq.: 'Mrs. Thomas Dabney: "Take her for all in all, these eyes shall never look upon her like again."'

"Numerous other sentiments were given, which unfortunately did not reach the chair, and the day concluding, terminated a feast as full of reason and the flow of soul as ever it has been our good fortune to witness."

Mr. Dabney gave a farewell dinner to his friends at Elmington. As the concluding toast was drunk,—it had been proposed by the host to their meeting again,—he struck off the stem of the delicate wine-glass that he held in his hand, that no future toast should be drunk in it, he said. He requested that each guest present should break his wine-glass and keep it as a memento. One or more of these broken glasses are still preserved in Gloucester.

CHAPTER III.

LEAVING THE OLD HOME.

THOMAS went through a large part of Alabama, Louisiana, and Mississippi looking at the country before deciding on a body of land in Hinds County, Mississippi. He succeeded in purchasing four thousand acres from half a dozen small farmers.

The ancestors of both Thomas and Sophia Dabney had been slave-owners. The family servants, inherited for generations, had come to be regarded with great affection, and this feeling was warmly returned by the negroes. The bond between master and servant was, in many cases, felt to be as sacred and close as the tie of blood.

During the course of years many of the Elmington

negroes had intermarried with the negroes on neighboring estates.

When the southern move was decided on, Thomas called his servants together and announced to them his intention to remove, with his family, to Mississippi. He further went on to say that he did not mean to take one unwilling servant with him. His plan was to offer to buy all husbands and wives, who were connected with his negroes, at the owners' prices, or he should, if his people preferred, sell those whom he owned to any master or mistress whom they might choose. No money difficulty should stand in the way. Everything should be made to yield to the important consideration of keeping families together.

Without an exception, the negroes determined to follow their beloved master and mistress. They chose rather to give up the kinspeople and friends of their own race than to leave them.

Mammy Harriet says of this time, "Marster was good all de time. He do all he could to comfort he people. When he was gittin' ready to move to Mississippi, he call 'em all up, an' tell 'em dat he did not want anybody to foller him who was not willin'. He say, all could stay in Figinny, an' dey could choose dey own marsters to stay wid. Ebery one o' he own, and all who b'long to de odder members o' de fambly who was wid him, say dey want to foller him, 'ceptin' 'twas two ole people, ole gray-headed people, who was too ole to trabble. An' dey was de onliest ones leff behind on dat plantation, an' dey did cry so much I did feel so sorry for dem. I couldn't help cryin', I feel so sorry. Our people say, 'Ef you got a husband or a wife who won't go to Mississippi, leff dat one behind. Ef you got a good marster, foller him.' My husband b'long to Cappen Edward Tabb, an' marster went dyar twice to try to buy him. But Cappen Tabb say dat no money couldn't buy him from him. Den Mrs. Tabb say dat she would buy me, an' two odder people dyar wanted to buy me too. But I say 'No, indeed! Go 'long! I shall foller my marster.' My sister want to go wid marster, too. She had five chillen dat was goin' wid him. I was standin' by marster when he talk to dey father, my brer Billy. He say, 'Billy, your children shall not lack for father and mother. I will be both father an' mother to them.' I heerd him say dat myself, an' he did it too."

The five brothers and sisters were ever favorite and trusted servants. I did not know till I heard this account from Mammy Harriet the special reason of their being favored above others. I often heard my father speak of them very affectionately. One day he said that he had never had occasion to punish one of them but once, when the girl had frightened the baby Virginius by telling him that a lion would catch him. "I hated to punish one of that truthful, honest family," he said; "but my orders had always been that no child of mine should be frightened by any one, and I could not pass it over."

When it was resolved to leave Virginia, the baby boy was named Virginius, after the beloved State that had given birth to his ancestors. This child, the youngest of four brothers, was but six months old when, in September, 1835, the long journey southward was begun.

Sophia's father and mother and her two sisters, one married to Mr. Lewis Smith, with her husband and two children, Augustine Dabney, with his wife and family, and other kinsfolk and friends had become quite infatuated with the desire to go with Thomas to Mississippi, and a number of these arranged to undertake the move along with him. Mr. Charles Hill took charge of the carriages that held the white families, while Thomas had the care of the negroes and wagons. The journey was made with so much care and forethought that not a case of serious illness occurred on the route. The white families were quartered at night, if practicable, in the houses that they found along the way. Tents were provided for the negroes. The master himself, during the entire journey, did not sleep under a roof. The weather was perfect: no heavy rains fell during the two months. He wrapped himself in his great-coat, with sometimes the addition of a blanket, and slept all night in their midst, under one of the travelling wagons.

One of the first nights on the road was spent at the house of Thomas's cousin, Mr. Thornton, of King William County. The cousins had never met, but Mr. Thornton, hearing that the moving families were to pass by his gate, sent to beg that his kinspeople would stop in their journey for a day or two and refresh themselves under his roof. Thomas sent Mr. and Mrs. Hill and Sophia and the children to accept this hospitality, feeling unwilling himself to leave the large number of negroes under his care for even one night. Those who were entertained by Mr. Thornton greatly enjoyed it. It was a regret to Thomas not to meet this kinsman of his father's. This regret was greatly increased when, during the Confederate war, he learned of the death in his country's cause of a noble scion of this house, the lamented Colonel Thornton, known and beloved as "Jack Thornton."

My dear father was very fond of recounting anecdotes and incidents, especially in his table-talk, of brave and generous and honorable deeds. At such times his eye kindled, and his whole face glowed with the intensity of his feeling. It was quite impossible for a young person to look at him, and to hear his words and tones, without an aspiration to be worthy of such commendation.

The stern incorruptibility of his wife's father was a theme on which he had talked with earnest enthusiasm to his children. He was very fond of relating an occurrence that took place on the journey from Virginia to Mississippi. Somewhere in the mountains of Tennessee one of my grandfather Hill's carriage-horses had fallen ill, and was quite incapable of proceeding farther. Thomas set about to look for a substitute; meanwhile trying such remedies as he could think of for the ailing horse. While he was standing by the beast, a countryman rode up on a fine, powerful horse. At once Thomas inquired if he would sell him. To his surprise, the man answered immediately that he would exchange his horse for the sick one, if ten dollars were added. The bargain was made in a few minutes. Then Thomas said to the man, "Now you have the money, there can be no objection to your telling me the fault in this vigorous young creature, that looks to me like a very valuable horse."

"I will tell you what is his fault," the countryman answered. "He is very good for some things,—for drawing in double or single harness, and for a saddle too, and he ain't got no tricks. He is as gentle as a cat. But he won't tote double. Me and my old 'oman wants to go to meetin', that's the main thing that we wants a horse for, and he won't tote us both. That's the reason that I want your horse. I ken cure him very soon. Thar ain't much the matter with him." But the man was mistaken. In a few hours the sick carriage-horse was dead, never having moved from the spot where he had been sold and bought.

The next day Mr. Hill, who had fallen somewhat behind, came along over the same road. He saw the great, hulking mountaineer weeping bitterly by the side of a dead horse, which he at once recognized as his own. He stopped and inquired into the case, and the man related the transaction, attaching no blame to any one. He had made his own terms, and had been quite elated with his bargain until he found that none of his nostrums, in which he had so confidently trusted, availed anything.

Mr. Hill rode forward to Thomas and desired him to return at once, and to see that the man was quite satisfied before leaving him. This Thomas did. The man said that five dollars more "in United States money" would compensate him for the loss that he had sustained, and his tears were dried in a moment when this was handed to him. Tennessee was in those days but sparsely settled, and the simple country people were delighted to receive travellers, and to give them the best that the land produced, almost considering themselves repaid by the pleasure of their company. At one house, after a bountiful supper on chickens, eggs, butter, cream, honey, and other country delicacies, for which the price charged was so insignificant as to seem quite absurd, our travellers asked what the charge would be if they spent a week there. Mine host replied that he could hardly say, that he had had but one boarder. This boarder had come to spend a week, but had stayed on and on till two months were passed, and he had thought that one dollar a week was about the right thing to charge him. His horse, he added, had cost him nothing, and so there had been no charge made for him, and he had kept fat on the mountain pastures.

CHAPTER IV.

MAMMY HARRIET'S RECOLLECTIONS.

I give here Mammy Harriet's account of the journey, taken down by me as she sat by my side a few weeks ago:

"We leff in September, when dey was pullin' fodder, an' we git to Mississippi three weeks to Christmas. Missis had so much patience wid her chillun. Sometimes she gib 'em one pat wid her low slipper. One pat was 'nuff. I say, ef I had all dem chillun I should knock some on 'em in de head wid de odders. On dat road I come to somethin' what I nebber see before; it 'twas a log town. All de houses was made out o' logs; all ' ceptin' de court-house. Dat was weather-boarded. I dunno whar 'twas. I nebber 'quire 'bout dat. 'Twas somewhar 'tween Mississippi an' de old country. We got to de Injun chief's. And de young Injuns come from de muster. Dey had on dey muster-close, and dey had on de appleëttes on dey shoulders and de silver ban's on de hats. Dey was de grummest people what I ebber see. Dey look mad as de ole scratch. I thought cert'nly dey would speak to your pa, but dey didn't dat! Dey was de savagest-lookin' people. But dey was sosherble wid your pa, an' gib him de liberty o' lettin' us hab some lumber to fix a place to sleep. Dey was de headest people what I ebber see. We women buss out larffin' when we hear 'em talk. Dey was mighty savage people. We butt up wid a whole parcel on 'em ebery day. Dyar was mos' as many o' dem trabellin' as dyar was o' us. I was 'feared on 'em. I nebber see a yaller Injun before. In Figinny dey was dark. De wife o' de chief ask marster to let her hab de ferry-boat to go to see her sick daughter. He had 'gaged it to tik us over. He say 'certainly.'

"One day a beggar come 'long, an' marster gib her five dollars. Your pa was always good; good to everybody.

"Marster was so good to us. He do eberything on dat journey dat was for our good.

"Marster do all he could to comfort he people.

"He buy fresh meat, salt fish, eberything. Ef he see a turnip-patch or cabbages or apples or 'taters, he say, 'Go on, see if you can get these things.' Sometimes dey gib 'em to us, sometimes we buy. One ole man say, 'I want a 'oman to live wid me. Don't you think your marster would let me have a 'oman or a chile? I would like to buy you. You seem to be a very likely 'oman.'

"'Buy who! buy me!'" And as my dear old black mammy recalls this insult to herself and to her honored master, her dim eyes kindle, her voice is full of suppressed feeling, her frame at its height, her manner such as might become an enraged pythoness. "'No, not one! Don't you know marster don't want to sell none o' his people? We are follerin' our marster. We ain't no nigger-traders. No, when marster sell any o' his people 'tis 'cause he is made to do it. 'Tis 'cause he cyarn't do nothin' wid 'em himself.'*

"We did live like princes, I can tell you. Sich a cookin'! sich a cookin'! We bile greens an' eberything. We live good; we did that. We didn't want for nothin'. All had umberillas, ebery one, an' when it rain you see all dem umberillas go up.

---

* Mammy's testimony here is pathetic. One of the four negroes whom her master sold was her son.

"Marster did eberything to comfort he people on comin' to Mississippi, eberything to comfort 'em.

"Marster gib we all new fryin'-pans an' buckets for de journey. De big famblys he gib two buckets to. You see we sell all our things. We git good prices for 'em, too, 'fore we leff Figinny. He gib me one bucket. Dey make me very mad, 'cause dey tik my bucket to water de horses and de muels an' eberything. I say, 'Who got my bucket?' Eberybody say, 'I dunno.' So I say, 'Lem my bucket alone; marster done gib it to me. Nobody sharn't hab it.' Den one day I was settin' down, an' my bucket was by me, an' de oberseer or some o' de white folks sen' for my bucket. I say, 'Lem my bucket 'lone. I don't keer who wants it. Marster gib it to me. Ef he want it he ken hab it, but nobody else.' Den de oberseer come an' say, 'Harriet, give me that bucket.' 'I won't. It is mine. Marster gib it to me.' Den he went to marster an' tole him dat I say dat. Den marster say, 'You let Harriet alone; let her bucket alone, every one of you. Do not touch it.'

"When we come to Raymond marster say, 'This is the last town. If you want to buy anything, go in an' buy.'

"So we all 'cluded dat, seein' 'twas de las' town, we would go in an' buy. I went in an' buy cups an' saucers an' plates an' coffee-pot an' things. Den when we got to de Burleigh land we was all right. I was jes' as well satisfied as eber I was in ole Figinny jes' as soon as I got settled."

Mammy Harriet's testimony of the life and character of her master, taken down in the freshness of her grief for his loss, is not arranged with any system. It seems best to set it down just as she said it. She grew up with him. They were never separated until the last few years of his life, when he had not the means of supporting his faithful old servants about his person. He did not fail to provide her with such comforts as he was able to pay for as long as he lived. "Law, I tells eberybody dat mammy is jes' as well off as she was in slave'y times," her daughter has said, in seeing clothing and provisions sent to her mother at stated intervals. "Law, mammy don't hab no trouble like we all, 'cuz de white folks don't forgit her."

"I hates to talk 'bout him," she says, with a groan. "When I hear 'bout it I thought 'twould hab kilt me. I nebber had such feelin's before. I cyarn't 'spress what I did feel 'bout it. Oh, my good marster is in glory, but we cyarn't help missin' him; we cyarn't help it. I nebber was so surprised in my life as when I hear 'bout it. It make me sick an' nervous to talk about him an' about dem times; but for de satisfaction ob you all I talk 'bout him.

"Ain't you ebber see your grandma, honey? She always was pretty, honey, a mighty pretty 'oman. She had black hyar an' eyes. Your pa was like her in dat. An' she had a noble 'pearance. Marster was like her in dat. He move to what dey call de Shipyard from Bellevue. We didn't live dyar no time, 'cordin' to my understandin'. Dat's what de ole people tell me. I don't 'member 'nuthin' 'bout it. Dat was 'fore we move to Elmin'ton.

"I had a weddin'—a big weddin'—for Marlow's kitchen. Your pa gib me a head weddin,—kilt a mutton—a round o' beef—tukkeys—cakes, one on t'other—trifle. I had all de chany off de sideboard, cups an' saucers, de table, de white table-cloth. I had on your pa's wife's weddin' gloves and slippers an' veil. De slippers was too small, but I put my toes in. Miss Mary had a mighty neat foot. Marster brought out a milk-pail o' toddy an' more in bottles. De gentlemans an' marster stand up on de tables. He didn't rush 'mongst de black folks, you know. I had a tearin'-down weddin', to be sho'. Nobody else didn't hab sich a weddin'. Yes, Sis Abby hab a mighty nice weddin', too,—cakes an' things,—a handed roun' supper, you see. Marster promised de fust one what git married arter he did a tearin'-down weddin', an' I was de fust. De whole day 'fore I was to be married Miss Mary— dat was your pa fust wife—kep' me shut up in a room. 'A bride must not be seen,' she said. An' she wouldn't lemme come out to dinner, but she sent my dinner in to me on a plate. De nex' mornin' I went to marster's an' Miss Mary's room 'fore dey was up. 'Who is that?' she say. I say, 'Harriet.' 'Good-morning, Mrs. Bride. I wish you joy.'

"Oh, yes, I'se been see good times!

"In dem days I always dress my hyar very fine an' wear a high top comb in it.

"I don't nebber 'spect to see no sich times again.

"Miss Mary was a lady to de tips o' her toes. She hab de most beautifullest walk dat ebber I see. I used to love to see her walk off. I nebber see nobody walk like her.

"I want to tell you how good marster was to his people in Figinny. De people would ketch a few oysters ebery day, an' by Sadday dey would hab a heap o' oysters piled up on de bank. Den dey would go to marster an' say, 'Marster, I'se got a heap o' oysters dat I would like to sell.' 'Very well,' he would say; 'go along and take the cart and mule and take your oysters around and sell them.' In de harves'-time he had two waitmans to wait on de people who was cuttin' de wheat and de barley. An' dese two waitmans dey had two gre't harmper-baskets full o' bottles o' whiskey,—a pint for ebery man an' half a pint for ebery 'oman. An' dey used to larf an' say to de young gals, 'You young gals ought not to drink whiskey so; you ought to put water in it.' But de young gals always tik de whiskey.

"Me an' Sis Patsy was de milkers, and Miss Mary used to say, 'You young girls* must not drink whiskey in that way.' So she always put mine an' Sis Patsy's in a pail, an' put water an' sugar in it, an' gib it to us so. You see, we was house-servants. She was a good lady, mighty good,—sich a good missis.

"When de harves' was gathered, de dinner for de black people was cooked in de kitchen,—same as for de gre't folks,—all sorts o' nice things. She would go out den an' cut off de house-servants' dinners. Ef there

---

* In quoting her master and mistress, Mammy generally used correct language.

was a piece o' sp'iled meat she would say, 'Throw that out to the dogs. That is not fit for people to eat.' She had a big chany bowl, an' if a roach fell in it, she had ebery drop o' de molasses throwed out. She say, 'That is not fit for the servants to eat. They shall not eat it.' She nebber let her people eat what she would not eat.

"Dey had big doin's, I know, when your ma was married, 'cause Mrs. Hill was a stawmped down fine lady,—a lady from de crown o' her head to de bottom o' her foot.

"In your pa house de servants eat dinner after de marster an' de missus eat,—de same things as dey eat. Uncle George sot de table for de servants to eat. Dyar was plenty on 'em. Dey come wid dey marsters an' missises. Mr. Root come in carriage an' four an' three servants. He nebber trabble wid less. De maid sot by he side in de big carriage, an' de man ride postillion, an' de biggest gre't dinners, gent'mans! George Orris was de cook for dese big dinners. He tik apples or oranges either an' he cut handles an' figgers an' preserve 'em. He feed de tuttles out in de ribber whar he tie 'em. He mik four dishes out o' one tuttle,—forcemeat balls an' things. Mammy can't 'member all de names o' de dishes. De day dat tuttle was cooked de people come fo' what was out! He mik a fine dish out o' chicken-foots an' heads,—fricassee 'em.

"When we fust come out to dis country, Mississippi, marster made de ploughers tik out de muels at eleven o'clock. An' he didn't 'low 'em to put 'em back 'fore three o'clock, an' nobody worked in dem hours. I s'pose dat was to get us used to de new country. Oh, no, we was nebber hurried. Marster nebber once said, 'Get up an' go to work,' an' no oberseer ebber said it, neither. Ef some on 'em did not git up when de odders went out to work, marster nebber said a word. Oh, no, we was nebber hurried.

"In later times our ploughers and de odders worked till twelve o'clock, an' den dey tik out de muels an' eberybody sot down to eat an' res' till three o'clock. Sometimes when we was all settin' roun' one would say to de odder, 'Come, le's we git up an' go to work.

We hab been settin' here long 'nuff.' But marster nebber said sich a thing. In dem days some o' de people used to obersleep deyselves. We used to larf so much at 'em; 'speshully at Sarah, my brer Billy's daughter. Marster would nebber hab no horn to wake us up. When one overseer come dyar wid he horn, marster soon put a stop to dat. He said, 'I do not keep hounds to be called up with horns.' Sarah was a gre't hand to obersleep herself, an' marster didn't nebber let nobody call her, nor any o' de odders what obersleep dyselfs. He say, 'Don't trouble them. They cannot help that.' An' to dem he would say, 'Ef you don't wake up till twelve o'clock, get up and come out to work then. Don't stay at home and say that you are sick, because I don't blame you.' Sometimes I would not get through givin' out de buttermilk to all de little black chillun, an' dat was 'bout eleven o'clock or twelve o'clock, an' I would see marster an' Sarah goin' out to de fiel' together. An' we would all larf at Sarah, and she would say, 'What you all larffin' 'bout? Go 'long. You do like you ain't got no sense. You fools, go 'long.' Sometimes we larf 'bout dat to dis day wid Sarah, an' we set an' talk 'bout it. You ken ask her, an' she will tell you jes' what I tell you 'bout it.

"Yes, honey, dat he did gib us Fourth o' July,—a plenty o' holiday,—a beef kilt, a mutton, hogs, salt and pepper, an' eberything. He hab a gre't trench dug, an' a whole load o' wood put in it, an' burned down to coals. Den dey put wooden spits across, an' dey had spoons an' basted de meat, an' he did not miss givin' us whiskey to drink,—a plenty of it, too. An' we 'vite all de culled people aroun', an' dey come, an' we had fine times. Our people was so good, and dey had so much. Dyar warn't no sich people no whyar. Marster mus'n't be named de same day as udder people. Our people want to help de poor critters what didn't hab nuthin'; dey saved it up for dem. Marster 'lowed us to hab meetin', just as much meetin' as we choose. A heap o' people didn't let dey people hab meetin'; didn't like for dem to visit an' see udder people. Marster warn't dat way. We went 'bout.

" 'Fore we got 'quainted at de Pass,* marster used to tell brer Harrison to tik de carriage-horses an' put 'em to de wagon Sunday evenin's, an' drive we all out down de street, down town. Oh, we was big bugs in dem days, an' we sot up dyar in de wagon; who but we? An' we did hab nice times. And you chillun would say, 'I want to go with mammy, I want to go with mammy,' an' we would tik you little ones an' dress you up an' tik you 'long, too. An' afterwards, when we got 'quainted, de culled gent'mans would 'vite we all to de ice-cream an' things. An' marster made brer Harrison carry us dyar in de wagon. 'Twas 'bout a mile. An' we had cake,—currant cake, plain cake, dis here iced cake,—all kind o' nice things. An' how we did 'joy ourselves! An' do you 'member de green oranges, jes' turnin', dat Mrs. Henderson let her people gib to us? Law, I did drink so much o' dat orangeade. Mrs. Henderson was so good to her people. An' we used to go down dyar to de Pint, all dressed up an' set back on dem pleasurin' benches. Mrs. Henderson had a big watermillion patch ebery year, an' she let her people hab all dey want. An' dey cut a heap ov 'em for we all, an' we sot back on dem benches an' we eat jes' as long as we could. Oh, I'se been see good times!

"An' de fish. Don't you 'member all de fish dat marster gib us? On de first day always when we got to de Pass, marster stop at de fish-house, when we was passin' thro' de town, an' buy a gre't long string o' gre't big fish,—all sorts, croakers an' mullets an' all sorts,— so he hab to gib to 'em all. He say, 'Here, take these home an' cook them for your dinners, but don't make yourselves sick.' An' we did eat fish three times a day, an' sometimes four times. Your pa always buys de best ob eberything for us. Ebery mornin' he go out fishin' at de Pass in he canoe, an' he ketch 'bout half a bushel o' fish. Marster used to buy fine sweet potatoes for all his people in trabellin' to de Pass, an' at night he put he head out o' de tent an' say, 'Beverly, don't make yourself sick on potatoes, so that you

---

* Pass Christian, on the Gulf of Mexico.

will not be able to travel in the morning.' An' Bebly say, 'Yes, sir.' An' all dat time he had a spiderful o' potatoes settin' by him, an' jes' as soon as he got thro' wid one spiderful he put anudder in de fire."

This Beverly, who was one of the wagon-drivers, was a great favorite with my father. I have heard him say, as Beverly's merry laughter sounded over field and wood,—for I never heard any laugh quite so careless or so astoundingly loud as this gay fellow's,—"Well, I do enjoy hearing that." The trip to the Pass was a gala time to Beverly, as to all the other servants who were taken, about nine or ten. The white family still recall with amusement the contest as to who could eat the greater number of fish on the day of the arrival at the Pass. Mammy Maria, one of our dear nurses, of whom much is said in these memorials, and her brother Beverly usually carried off the palm, he having been known to eat at the first meal fourteen silver trout and she thirteen.

"Oh, de Sundays, when all de people dress up in dey finery, an' come thro' de gate, an' walk thro' de yard, an' pass by de porch whyar all de family was settin'! How dey switch by! Don't you 'member Phœbe? She twis', she twis', an' she twis'. You see brer Aaron come down from Raymond ebery Sadday, an' de nex' mornin' he say, 'Gals, lemme show you de steps de town ladies tik.' Den he put he hand 'hin' he back, an' he twis' heself, and we larf 'twell we cry. Dyar's whar Phœbe ketch de step. Brer Aaron was mighty funny.

"We buy things at Christmas ef we choose, but ef we didn't choose to do dat, we had things. We was given flour an' sugar an' coffee an' butter an' whiskey an' things. De sick people call for anything dey want, any time, an' missis sont it to de quarters.

"Joe Nelson was at de Pass, wukkin' on de house down dyar, an' my aunt, Grannie Harriet, ask marster to send for him, 'cause she want to see him. She 'peared to know dat she was gwyne to die.* Marster

---

* Joe was her adopted son. The Pass was two hundred miles from Burleigh.

send for him right off, an' he hadn't been at home more dan three days 'fore grannie was struck wid paralysis. I was settin' wid her, and she was on de bed, an' she look mighty strange all on a sudden. I thought she was dyin'. I run to de house to missis. Marster was out in de fiel'. I tell missis dat I thought Grannie Harriet was dyin'. Missis put on her bonnet an' went to her jes' as fast as she could. When grannie see her she could not speak, but she hold out both arms to her. Missis run into her arms an' bust out cryin'. She put her arms roun' grannie's neck, an' grannie could not speak, but de big tears roll down her cheeks. An' so she die.

"I often begged marster to let a funeral sermon be preached over grannie, but he always say, 'No, Harriet, I do not know anybody good enough to preach a sermon over her.'"

I remember well the death of this aged servant. The master himself led the funeral procession, and all his children followed the coffin as mourners. He ordered out the whole plantation, every one who could walk, and every man, woman, and child carried a torch. The sound of the mournful funeral hymn, and the blazing of the many torches, as we wound down the road to the dark shades of the burying-ground, made a painful impression on me as a child, and caused many a secret tear. I wished much to be excused from going to the funeral; but the master seemed unapproachable in his grief, and I was afraid of incurring his displeasure if he should discover that I was unwilling to pay what he considered fitting respect to the memory of this trusted friend.

His mother had given her to him with the words, "You can trust her in everything. She has never told me an untruth or even prevaricated in her life."

It is recorded of Grannie Harriet that when the wagons drew up at the new home place on the Burleigh plantation, and she looked around at the rude accommodations, she asked, "And is dis what my marster left Gloucester for?"

The master ever treated her as a member of the

family. His daily habit on his return from the fields at mid-day was to dismount at her gate and to sit laughing and talking with her for a half-hour. He consulted her about his plantation affairs as he did no one else, and her judgment was so sound that he relied on it. He missed her much after her death. No one ever filled her place with him either as adviser or friend. Our childish associations with Grannie Harriet were delightful. She petted and spoiled us to our hearts' content, and could not bear to have any fault found with us.

Especially at Christmas did we delight in going to her to beg for cake and other dainties. Mamma took care that she should have a good store on hand; and we, who knew nothing of this, praised grannie's things, and found them ever so much nicer than anything to be gotten at the "great house."

Sometimes we were allowed, as a very great treat, to wrap up in sheets and go to grannie's house to frighten her. Her feigned terror at the sight of the band of little ghosts filled us with rapture, only equalled by that we felt when, on suddenly dropping the sheets, we heard grannie's exclamation of astonishment that the master's children were playing such pranks on her.

She lived alone. We were not allowed to visit any of the other servants with such freedom. Her master said that he would be proud to hang her portrait in his drawing-room, in such esteem and affection did he hold her.

Owing to the delay with the sick horse, which was at the time looked on as an unmixed evil, the travellers did not reach the Mississippi plantation till two weeks later than had been calculated on. When they got there they found that the log houses in which they had expected to find shelter till better could be provided had been completely demolished by a cyclone. They were but a heap of timbers lying on the ground. Had they reached this place at the time set for their arrival they would have been in these houses, and could scarcely have escaped with their lives, for the cyclone had passed over in the night.

Thomas looked at the wreck and remembered his annoyance at the delay to which, under Providence, he owed their safety. The scene made an impression that was life-long. It influenced his character. It gave him a belief in a special Providence that was ever afterwards unshaken. His trust in the wisdom and goodness of God was from that hour so strong that he never for a moment doubted it. Under no circumstances was a murmur or anything approaching to it ever heard to escape his lips. Not even by a wish would he imply that he could desire the decrees of Providence altered.

One of the farmers whose lands he had bought, and who had not yet moved out of his house, was able to spare a few rooms for the white families, and the marquees were pitched for the negroes. All hands were set to work to build houses.

In selecting his plantation, Thomas showed his usual sound judgment in practical matters. It comprised four thousand acres in a compact body, not all bought at one time, but as he saw opportunity to secure the property of small farmers whose land adjoined his. In this way he shaped his place to suit himself; and it was characteristic of his exact methods that after making his final purchase the section lines fell so as to form an almost exact square, with Tallahala Creek crossing it diagonally from northeast to southwest. The lowland bordering the creek, called "The Bottom," was inexhaustibly fertile, and ensured heavy crops in the dryest season. From the creek-bottom the land gradually rises and runs back in a series of hills and plateaus. Those not already cleared for cultivation were covered with a magnificent growth of timber,—oaks of many species, yellow pine, hickory, elm, sweet- and black-gum, besides countless other trees and shrubs of less value. Walnut-trees of magnificent size, magnolia, beech, and laurel grew on the banks of the creek.

Crops raised on the hills flourished best in wet weather; so with the admirable diversity of soil on the plantation there was never a failure of a whole crop in the most unfavorable season.

The land was well watered throughout by Tallahala Creek, with its tributary branches, Indian Jumper and Snake Creek, and a number of smaller bayous. In the hills springs bubbled out, giving rise to spring "branches," which did not go dry in the most prolonged drought. There was always pasturage for cattle along these water-courses, and in the bitterest cold of winter they found abundant green food in the canebrakes of the creek. In this mild climate many wild flowers adorn the fields and woods till late in the fall. Tiny blue innocents dot the grass as early as January. Later come wild violets, roses, the wild lily, rhododendron, clematis, woodbine, snap-dragon, and a host of flowering trees, shrubs, and vines. Among these we find the red-bud, maple, dogwood, crab-apple, hawthorn, and wild peach; but supreme in beauty and in fragrance we have the yellow jasmine. It is the crown and glory of Southern woods, throwing its drapery of golden bells over trees and shrubs for whole acres.

It was Thomas's plan in the management of this large estate to bring under cultivation a certain portion of new land every year. His rule was to clear one hundred acres each season. The cotton-plant delights in a virgin soil, and he counted on making a bale and a half of cotton to the acre on all new ground. This was, of course, above the average. In the hill country a planter thinks himself rewarded for his labor by an average yield of half a bale to the acre. Thomas one year made six hundred bales on six hundred acres, but that was an exceptional season. The fact that this place would be as productive now as ever with the same cultivation goes to show how well the land lies, and how wise Thomas was in the choice of his plantation.

CHAPTER V.

EARLY DAYS IN MISSISSIPPI.

In entering on this pioneer life many difficulties had to be met that were a new experience to people coming from lower Virginia. One of the first was the unavoidable delay in getting supplies of meat for the servants. For two weeks after their arrival they had none. Sophia's sister Emmeline, Mrs. Lewis Smith, was so conscientious that she refused during this period to touch a morsel of meat, although the supply on hand was ample to last the white families till more could be procured.

The roof of the house in which Thomas had to put his wife and children was so leaky, that he had sometimes at night when it rained to sit up in bed and hold an umbrella over her and the baby.

There were then no railroads, and the cotton crop had to be hauled in wagons forty miles, to Grand Gulf. The roads were so bad that to trust the teams to negro-drivers alone was not to be thought of, and the master went with every wagon.

Not more than a quarter of a mile from Thomas's home, in those early days in Mississippi, lived a man named Jack Cotton. He was one of a band of highwaymen who infested the road from Vicksburg to Memphis. Their practice was to waylay planters and rob them on their return from selling their cotton. Jack Cotton's house was a half-way station and a rendezvous for the band. Jack was civil to the new neighbors, and they were ignorant of his reputation as a desperado till he ran away to Texas to escape the law.

There was no doctor or church nearer than Raymond, which was ten miles from Burleigh. The country people around the plantation, seeing that Thomas knew how to take care of his servants, began to send for him when they were sick. He was so successful that his reputation grew more than was convenient. They had a way of sending for him at night that was specially disagreeable, and he had finally to refuse to make night calls. One day he was summoned to attend a woman who was about to die, the messenger said. When Thomas reached the house, he saw tied to the fence and to trees horses with men's saddles and horses with side-saddles, and on the little porch were men, women, and children, evidently a gathering of the sick woman's clan. One woman, sitting in the sick-chamber, was rocking her baby crosswise on the plank floor. Altogether the hubbub was something distracting. The patient herself was in a highly nervous state. The husband explained that she had not been able to sleep for one or two days and nights. Thomas's advice was that every man, woman, and child should be sent away. It was acted on at once. "Folks, the doctor says you must all go home," the man called out from the door.

In a few minutes they were unhitching their horses and getting away as fast as they could. As soon as all was quiet, a soothing potion was given to the sufferer. The next morning the news came to "the doctor" that she had slept all night and was a great deal better, and not at all in danger of dying.

A disease called black tongue appeared among the negroes at Burleigh at one time; very soon forty of them had their tongues protruding from their mouths, swollen and cracked open. The doctors were losing so many cases, for the disease was epidemic in the country, that Thomas resolved not to send for a physician. He made a careful study of the symptoms, and observed that the vital powers were strongly taxed and the system run down very low. Not knowing what medicine would check the disease, he resolved to give none, but to build up the system with stimulants and nourishing food, leaving to the recuperative power of nature to pull his patients through. A liberal use of port wine and mutton-chops (such chops! I never saw their like elsewhere) justified his hopes and expectations. He did not lose a case.

Thomas was misunderstood and misjudged by the people in Mississippi by whom he found himself surrounded. The plainer classes in Virginia, like those in England, from whom they were descended, recognized the difference between themselves and the higher classes, and did not aspire to social equality. But in Mississippi the tone was different. They resented anything like superiority in breeding.

Thomas Dabney was considered cold and haughty. It took them long years to find out that he was a true friend to the poor. As years passed on they learned to look on him as one to be relied on, not only for substantial help but for sympathy. Under the look of stern dignity the heart was tender and compassionate as a woman's.

It was the custom among the small farmers in his neighborhood to call on each other to assist when one of them built his house, usually a log structure. Accordingly, one day an invitation came to the new-comer to help a neighbor to "raise" his house. At the appointed time he went over with twenty of his men, and he did not leave till the last log was in place and the last board nailed on the roof, handing over the simple cabin quite completed to the owner. This action, which seemed so natural to him, was a serious offence to the recipient, and, to his regret, he was sent for to no more "house-raisings." On another occasion, a small farmer living a few miles from him got "in the grass," as the country people express it when the grass has gotten ahead of the young cotton-plants and there is danger of their being choked by it. Again Thomas went over with twenty men, and in a few hours the field was brought to perfect order. The man said that if Colonel Dabney had taken hold of a plough and worked by his side he would have been glad to have his help, but to see him sitting up on his horse with his gloves on directing his negroes how to work was not to his taste. He heard a long time after these occurrences that he could have soothed their wounded pride if he had asked them to come over to help him to raise his cabins. But he could not bring himself to call on two or three poor white men to work among his servants when he had no need of help.

Another neighbor he found more grateful. This man was very sick during the season when his field should have been ploughed. His wife and only servant were quite taken up with nursing him. One day they heard the voices of workers in their field, and, on looking out, recognized Colonel Dabney and his servants. He had heard of the trouble, and had ordered his men to go to this place with their mules and ploughs, and to put everything in order for the crop, not failing to take their dinners along. The man got well, and he and his wife and children were life-long friends to the family at Burleigh.

A young doctor moving to the neighborhood said in his hearing that he found it difficult to buy corn. Thomas made no comment, but the next morning the doctor saw a six-mule wagon at his gate. The driver, whom he recognized as a Burleigh negro, asked where the corn should be stowed away. He showed him his corn-crib, and a day or two after, meeting Thomas, asked what he owed for the corn. "Oh, nothing," was the answer; "I do not charge a neighbor for a wagon-load of corn." This incident is hardly worth mentioning were it not that little things make up a man's life and show the spirit.

His plantation was considered a model one, and was visited by planters anxious to learn his methods. He was asked how he made his negroes do good work. His answer was that a laboring man could do more work and better work in five and a half days than in six. He used to give the half of Saturdays to his negroes, unless there was a great press of work; but a system of rewards was more efficacious than any other method. He distributed prizes of money among his cotton-pickers every week during the season, which lasted four or five months. One dollar was the first prize, a Mexican coin valued at eighty-seven and a half cents the second, seventy-five cents the third, and so on, down to the smallest prize, a small Mexican coin called picayune, which was valued at six and a quarter cents.

The decimal nomenclature was not in use there. The coins were spoken of as "bits." Eighty-seven and a half cents were seven bits, fifty cents four bits, twenty-five cents two bits. The master gave money to all who worked well for the prizes, whether they won them or not. When one person picked six hundred pounds in a day, a five-dollar gold-piece was the reward. On most other plantations four hundred pounds or three hundred and fifty or three hundred was considered a good day's work, but on the Burleigh place many picked five hundred pounds. All had to be picked free of trash. No one could do this who had not been trained in childhood. To get five hundred pounds a picker had to use both hands at once. Those who went into the cotton-fields after they were grown only knew how to pull out cotton by holding on to the stalk with one hand and picking it out with the other. Two hundred pounds a day would be a liberal estimate of what the most industrious could do in this manner. A very tall and lithe young woman, one of mammy's "brer Billy's" children, was the best cotton-picker at Burleigh. She picked two rows at a time, going down the middle with both arms extended and grasping the cotton-bolls with each hand. Some of the younger generation learned to imitate this. At Christmas Nelly's share of the prize-money was something over seventeen dollars. Her pride in going up to the master's desk to receive it, in the presence of the assembled negroes, as the acknowledged leader of the cotton-pickers, was a matter of as great interest to the white family as to her own race.

The negroes were helped in every way to gather the cotton, not being interrupted or broken down by any other work. Some of the men were detailed to carry the cotton-hampers to the wagons that the pickers might lift no weights. Water-carriers, with buckets of fresh water, went up and down the rows handing water to the pickers. They would get so interested and excited over the work that they had to be made to leave the fields at night, some of the very ambitious ones wishing to sleep at the end of their rows, that they might be up and at work in the morning earlier than their rivals. The cotton was weighed three times a day, and the number of pounds picked by each servant set down opposite to his or her name on a slate. Quite a remarkable feat of memory was exhibited by one of the negro men one day in connection with this. His duty was to help the overseer to weigh the cotton. One day the slate was caught in a rain and the figures were obliterated. This man came that night to the master's desk and gave from memory every record on the slate, the morning, mid-day, and evening weights of each picker. The negroes stood near enough to hear if he had made a mistake in any man's figures. It was the more remarkable as he could not have expected to be called on to do this. In addition to the cotton crop, corn was raised in such abundance that it was not an unusual thing to sell a surplus of a thousand or two bushels or more. A maxim with the master was that no animal grew fat on bought corn. In putting in his corn crop he made full allowance for a bad season, hence there was never a scarcity. A lock on a corn-crib was not known. After the mules and horses were fed in the evening the negroes carried home all that they cared to have. They raised chickens by the hundred. One of the chicken-raisers, old Uncle Isaac, estimated that he raised five hundred, unless the season was bad. Uncle Isaac's boast was that he was a child of the same year as the master, and that the master's mother had given to him in her own arms some of the baby Thomas's milk, as there was more of it than he wanted. He would draw himself up as he added, "I called marster brother till I was a right big boy, an' I called his mother ma till I was old enough to know better an' to stop it myself. She never tole me to stop."

The negroes sold all the chickens they did not eat. They were taken to Raymond or Cooper's Well in a four-mule wagon, provided by the master. As he paid the market price, and as there was some risk of their getting less than he gave, there was not often a desire to send them off if he would take them. And he had need to buy all he used after the death of our faithful Granny Harriet. Different servants were given the care of the poultry, and all failed so signally that Aunt Kitty, who was renowned for success in her own poultry-yard, was placed in charge. She was given all the conveniences and facilities she asked for,—chicken-houses, coops, and separate enclosures for young chickens. The result of all this outlay was not a chicken the first year, and only one the second. The history of that one deserves to be recorded. It was hatched out in the hedge and raised by its mother hen without the aid of our accomplished hen hussy.

The thrifty negroes made so much on their chickens, peanuts, popcorn, molasses-cakes, baskets, mats, brooms, taking in sewing, and in other little ways, that they were able to buy luxuries. Some of the women bought silk dresses; many had their Sunday dresses made by white mantua-makers. Of course they had the clothes of the master and mistress in addition; and in later years, as the house grew full of young masters and young mistresses, theirs were added. As the family knew that the servants liked nothing so well as the well-made clothes that they laid aside, they wore their clothes but little. They justly considered that those who had labored for them had rights to them while still fresh. Under these circumstances it did not seem wasteful for a daughter of the house to distribute, at the end of a season, as many as a dozen or more dresses that had been made up but a few months before. It was quite funny to see among the gallants three or four swallow-tail coats of the master's come in at the gate for the grand promenade on Sunday evenings, escorting the colored belles in all their bravery of hoop-skirts, and ruffles, and ribbons, and flowers. Mammy Harriet gives me this account of the management at Burleigh:

"De men had twelve pounds o' meat ebery two weeks an' de women ten pounds. Viney, my brer Billy's daughter, had as much as a man. You see she was a hearty eater. An' dey had 'lasses too 'cordin' to dey famblys,—a water-bucketful. Den some on 'em let dey meat gin out an' come for mo'. Marster git 'em mo' meat out o' de house, an' den he go out to de smokehouse an' cut mo'. I hab see marster out in de fiel' after breakfast an' Headman Charles say to him, 'Marster, some o' dese people ain't got nothin' to eat.' Den he ride back an' hab a bushel o' meal sifted, an' git a piece o' meat, an' tie up de salt, an' ride back an' say, 'Charles, let those fellows get a plenty of oak bark and cook these things. Here is a plenty of meat and meal and salt.' Den dey set on sometimes a dozen pots an' bile water to make up all dat bread.

"Dyar warn't no chile born on dat place widdout no clo'es to put on. Missis had 'em made in de house. I know I myself mik' clo'es for Nelly chile, eben to de bonnet. I mik' de bonnet out o' a piece o' missis dress. She gib five pieces to ebery chile at a time. She had two made in de house, de udder three she say, 'Make yourself. You ought to know how to sew for yourself.'

"Ebey udder Sunday was draw day. Dey draw de meat an' missis lay aside all her clo'es an' her chillun clo'es to gib 'way,—a pile on 'em. She say, 'Maria, send the servants to me in the house,' an' she gib de clo'es to 'em. I heard her say to marster one day, 'There is a beggar-woman here.' 'Well, have you something to give her?' 'No; I have too many servants to give my clothes to beggars. Give her some money.' He say, 'Very well.' An' he gib de 'oman money. She nebber 'fused her people nuthin'; nobody warn't 'fear'd to ask her for anything."

One day a great lubberly, stupid negro woman stalked into her room and said, "Missis, gib me a dress." The woman was uncouth and rude. The little girl sitting with her mother saw her get up at once and hand a pretty woollen dress to the woman. "She did not even thank you," the child objected, when the negro had gone out. "And don't it teach her to beg to give her the dress when she asks for it?" Time has not obliterated the memory of the gentle rebuke. "Poor thing, she has no one to teach her manners, and she has so little sense, and no one to ask for anything but me. I was very glad, indeed, that she came and asked me for something."

For some years the master accompanied every wagon loaded with cotton that went to market from his plantation. He slept on these journeys under the wagons, and sometimes on awakening in the morning he found that his great-coat, in which he was wrapped, was frozen hard to the ground. His negro drivers were more heavily clad than himself, each one being provided with a thick woollen great-coat that reached to his heels, home-knit woollen socks and gloves, and an enormous comforter for the neck. No illness resulted from the exposure. In the morning a hot meal, cooked by one of the negroes—and all the race are admirable cooks—was shared by the master and his men.

Until over seventy years old, he was singularly indifferent to cold or heat, or to discomforts of any sort. But he felt compassion for his negroes. He knew that the warm African blood in their veins was not fitted to endure what he could stand. He never regarded the weather for himself, but was very careful about sending them out in bad weather, and never did it unless it seemed a necessity. On such occasions he wore an anxious look, and said that he could not go to bed until his servants had gotten home safely. They were always sure of finding a hot fire and a warm drink ready for them on their return.

Every other year he distributed blankets on the plantation, giving one apiece to each individual. Many of the families were large, and as the fathers would move off under a load of twelve or fourteen blankets, some, whose quivers were less full, would be heard to exclaim over the good fortune of the lucky ones. There were usually a dozen or so left over in these distributions, and they were thrown in for good measure to those who had the large families. "Poor things, they have so many children," seemed to my dear mother a sufficient explanation for special favors that she often bestowed on those who had no other claim. Some of the negro men with the big families of children had a funny little affectation of feigning not to know either the names or the number of their boys and girls. "I disremember, missis, dyar's so many on 'em," with a little pleased laugh, was considered a sufficient answer to inquiries on the subject on every-day occasions. But not so on the days when blankets were to be given out. Then their memories were fresh. Then the babies that had not been in their cradles more than a few days, mayhap hours, were remembered and mentioned in due turn, with no danger of being forgotten or overlooked because there were "so many on 'em."

In addition to the blankets, comforts were quilted in the house by the seamstresses for every woman who had a young baby. The every-day clothes of all the negroes were cut out and made in the house; two complete woollen suits for winter and two cotton ones for summer. For Sundays, a bright calico dress was given to each woman. The thrifty ones, and, with scarcely an exception, these negroes were thrifty, had more than they needed, and the clothes were in their chests a year before they were put on. The woollen socks and stockings for both men and women were knit in the cabins by old women, and in the "great house" by young girls. These last were set a task by the mistress, with the privilege of holiday the rest of the day when it was done. This had the desired effect of making them quick and industrious, and so interested that they would be at their work betimes in the morning. The clever ones sometimes get through with the allotted task before breakfast.

On rainy days all the plantation women were brought into the house. Then Mammy Maria, who was in her way a field-marshal on such occasions, gave out the work and taught them to sew. By word and action she stimulated and urged them on, until there was not on the Burleigh plantation a woman who could not make and mend neatly her own and her husband's and children's clothes.

Poor mammy! She dreaded these days of teaching and worrying over her big scholars. It gave her the headache, she said: some seemed so hopelessly dull and stupid and lazy,—so unlike herself. Hers was a case both of greatness thrust upon one and of greatness achieved. She had grown up at my mother's feet, having been about her ever since she could remember, and had come to love the white family better than her own blood and race. She resented their being deceived and imposed on by her fellow-servants, and did not fail to inform them when such was the case. This confidence was considered as sacred, but of course it grew to be known that Mammy Maria was a "white folks' servant."

She was far more severe in her judgment of misdemeanors than the master and mistress. The place that she had made for herself was one that would, in a character less true and strong, have brought on herself the hatred and the distrust of her race. But they knew her to be just, one who never assailed the innocent, and with so warm and compassionate a heart in real trouble that none were afraid to come to her. From being a confidential servant she grew into being a kind of prime minister, and it was well known that if she espoused a cause and took it to the master it was sure to be attended to at once, and according to her advice.

Her independence and fearlessness in the discharge of her duty, both to the master and to her fellow-servants, won for her the affection and esteem of both. In consequence of her popularity with her own color, her namesakes became so numerous that the master had to forbid any further increase of them, on account of the confusion to which it gave rise. This her admirers evaded by having the babies christened Maria, and another name adopted for every-day use.

My brave, good mammy! Who that knew thee in those days, when thy heart was gay and bold as a young soldier's, could think that the time would come when that faithful heart would break for the love of thy old master!

CHAPTER VI.

PLANTATION MANAGEMENT.

Thomas owned more negroes than could work with advantage on one place. He was advised to put a part on a second plantation, but he refused to let a consideration of profit induce him to place his servants where he could not personally attend to their welfare. All the negroes were encouraged to come freely to the house to see the master and mistress, and they were very fond of making visits there, even when there was nothing more important to say than to ask after the young masters off at college, and to send their how-d'ye to them. They had their favorites among the growing-up sons and daughters, and chose their future owners, and spoke of themselves as belonging to the ones selected. It was a great grief to those who had chosen Charles Dabney when he was cut off at the threshold of his life, and I never heard of their making a second choice.

The master and mistress taught the negroes truthfulness and honesty, as they taught their own children, by not tempting them, and by trusting them. It was a maxim with the master that it made a child honest and truthful to believe its word. He was by nature so unsuspicious that it required no effort to carry this out in his daily life.

On one occasion one of his daughters was at a reception in New York given to the House of Bishops. The honored guest of the evening was that great missionary, Bishop Selwyn, of Litchfield, who had come over from England to our General Convention. Among other subjects the dishonesty of the negro race was discussed, and some one asked if all negroes were thieves. Thomas Dabney's daughter felt diffident about speaking, but she regretted afterwards that she had not said that a very large proportion of her father's negroes could be trusted to any extent. The interrogator had probably confounded negroes who were trusted with those who were not. The confidence shown in them by the heads of her Southern home had taught the negroes so much self-respect that a thoroughly thievish negro was put under the ban in his own little world. Thomas had the control of about five hundred of them. About two hundred were his own, and on the Burleigh plantation. The others belonged to his wards, and were nearly all family negroes, closely related to his, and living on neighboring plantations. He had the management of four estates belonging to minors. It was a saying in the family that the estates of his wards were better managed than his own, and their property increased faster than his. "Of course, I put the best overseers on their plantations," he said. "You see, I am here to look after my own." The negroes of these came to him as to their master, and he treated them as his own.

He bought a cook, one of his mother's negroes, after he went to Mississippi, at the same time making the arrangement to buy her husband. For some reason both did not go out together. A cook was always a belle on a plantation, and this young Alcey soon had all the unmarried men at her feet, among others a young fellow named Bob. One Sunday evening, as the rival suitors were sitting with her, Bob, who was thought to be a favored one, got his jawbone caught back in an unfortunate yawn, and spent several hours speechless, with his mouth wide open, while a messenger was despatched for the doctor. But this did not seem to disillusionize the object of his addresses, for she wrote a letter to her husband in Virginia that quite decided him not to join her. He also, it was said, had been casting his eyes around for a more congenial mate. When Mrs. Chamberlayne spoke to him of going out to Mississippi, he answered that Alcey had given him an account in a letter of the terrible ocean that had to be gone over on the way. Mrs. Chamberlayne said that if a woman could stand the journey a strong man certainly could. "Yes, Miss

Marthy, but Alcey know more 'bout dem mysteries dan I does."

When Alcey was spoken to on the subject, she said, "Tell marster not to bother 'bout sendin' for him. He lazy an' puny an' no 'count." Bob's charms had triumphed.

On wedding occasions, in addition to the materials for a cake, the bride always expected a good many gifts, and some of the master's family to be present. The mistress's big prayer-book was taken over, and the marriage service read by one of the young masters. They would not be satisfied unless the bride and the cake were duly complimented. The children of the house-servants were married in the dining-room at Burleigh, and it was a saying in the family that these turned out to be happy marriages.

At one of the weddings the bridegroom did not respond when his time came. "Solomon," said the young master, "say thou wilt." "Thou wilt," repeated Solomon, in his most solemn voice. The marriage ceremony went on.

"Courtenay, wilt thou have this man to thy wedded husband, to live together after God's ordinance in the holy estate of matrimony? Wilt thou obey him, and serve him, love, honor, and keep him in sickness and in health; and, forsaking all others, keep thee only unto him, so long as ye both shall live?"

"I does," responded the bride.

The nurse who took care of the women when their babies were born received a fee each time. The mothers themselves looked on these seasons as gala times. They were provided with flour, sugar, dried fruit, and often meals from the table, and a woman to do all their cooking, washing, and house-work for a month. During the rest of the year they did little more than take care of the babies. Their cabins were clean and orderly, their beds gay with bright quilts, and often the pillows were snowy enough to tempt any head.

When we children were allowed to go to see some of the servants, they delighted in setting out a little feast. If they had nothing else, we were not allowed to go without a new-laid egg or two. Once at Christmas Mammy Harriet gave a "high tea" to us children. I was at that time about fourteen years of age, the oldest of the invited. A friend of my own age, Arabella Foote, the youngest daughter of Henry S. Foote (Governor and United States Senator), was spending her Christmas holidays with me. Mammy felt some modesty about inviting the young lady into her house, but I took Arabella, and she enjoyed it as much as any of us. Mammy had made a nice cake and hot biscuits and tea for the occasion, set out in her choicest cups, some of rare old china, and with sugar in the sugar-bowl that she had inherited from her mother. She gave us besides, sweetmeats, nuts, raisins, fruits of several kinds,—indeed, a delightful tea. And she stood behind us waiting on the table, her bright bandanna kerchief towering aloft on her head, and she looking so pleased.

The children delighted in teaching the house-servants. One night the whole family were formally invited, the master, mistress, governess, and guests, by a twelve-year-old school-mistress to hear her pupils recite poetry. She had about a dozen of the maids, old and young, Mammy Maria among them. One of the guests was quite astonished to see his own servant, whom he had with him spending several months at Burleigh, get up and recite a piece of poetry that had been learned with pains for this occasion.

Some of the sons taught those of the plantation negroes who cared to learn, but very few were willing to take the trouble to study. Virginius was successful with his scholars. Five of them learned to read so well that they became preachers. For this service he got one dozen eggs a month; or occasionally in lieu of this he received a pullet at the end of two months. He taught in the kitchen by the light of pine torches. His method of enforcing discipline on these middle-aged men was truly ludicrous. As his tutor, being one of the old-fashioned sort, did not spare the rod in the morning, so at night Virginius belabored the backs of his sturdy fellows. His beatings were received with shouts of laughter, the whole school would be in an uproar, the scholars dodging about to escape the young pedagogue's stick, and the cook and other on-lookers roaring with laughter. One of his graduates asked his advice as to a course of reading, suggesting history as the branch that he wished to pursue. The youthful teacher promptly advised "Robinson Crusoe," and lent his own handsome copy to this promising pupil. After reading one hundred pages Joe came to him and said, "Mars Virginius, did you say dat book was history?" Virginius explained as well as he could what fiction was, on which Joe said, "I bin mistrustin' all 'long dat some o' de things what Robinson Crusoe say warn't true."

With negro slaves it seemed impossible for one of them to do a thing, it mattered not how insignificant, without the assistance of one or two others. It was often said with a laugh by their owners that it took two to help one to do nothing. It required a whole afternoon for Joe, the aspirant for historical knowledge, and another able-bodied man like himself, to butcher a sheep. On a plantation the work of the women and children, and of some of the men also, amounted to so little that but small effort was made to utilize it. Of course, some kind of occupation had to be devised to keep them employed a part of the time. But it was very laborious to find easy work for a large body of inefficient and lazy people, and at Burleigh the struggle was given up in many cases. The different departments would have been more easily and better managed if there had been fewer to work. Sometimes a friend would say to the master that he made smaller crops than his negroes ought to make. His reply was that he did not desire them to do all that they could.

The cook at Burleigh had always a scullion or two to help her, besides a man to cut her wood and put it on the huge andirons.* The scullions brought the

---

* The cook's husband, who for years had looked on himself as nearly blind, and therefore unable to do more than work about her, and put her wood on the fire, sometimes cutting a stick or two, made no less than eighteen good crops for himself when the war was over. He was one of the best farmers in the country. S. D. S.

water and prepared the vegetables, and made themselves generally useful. The vegetables were gathered and brought from the garden by the gardener, or by one of the half-dozen women whom he frequently had to help him. A second cook made the desserts, sweetmeats, etc. As children, we thought that the main business of the head cook was to scold the scullion and ourselves, and to pin a dish-rag to us if we ventured into her kitchen. Four women and a boy were in charge of the dairy. As the cows sometimes wandered to pastures several miles away, this number did not seem excessive. The boy brought the cows up, sometimes with one of the women to help him. Two of the women milked; the third held the semi-sinecure office, taking charge of the milk; and the fourth churned.

There were no blooded cattle on the plantation for many years, but thirty cows in the cowpen gave all the milk and butter that was needed for the house and plantation, and a good deal of butter was sold. The pastures were so good that the cattle increased rapidly and were sold, a hundred at a time. Southdown sheep were imported from Kentucky and pigs from England. Everything looked well and fat at Burleigh. The master was amused on being asked by a neighboring farmer if he would let him have some of his curly-tailed breed of pigs. The man innocently added that he noticed they were always fat, not knowing, as Thomas used to say, in repeating this, that corn would make the straightest tail curl. His beeves were fattened two years, after they had worked two years as oxen to make the flesh firm. One year they ran in the corn-field before the corn was gathered, and the next they were stalled. As all the oxen were fattened for beeves after two years of work, no old ox was on the place. He killed every winter eight or ten of these stalled oxen. The stalled sheep were so fat that they sometimes died of suffocation.*

---

* "It was just one week before Christmas. . . . The stall-fed ox nodded over his trough; the broad-backed Southdowns clustered together in a corner of their shed, basked in the sun and awaited a return of appetite; a remnant of sturdy porkers, left over from the November

f

One day, on the occasion of a large dinner, the master was hastily summoned to the kitchen, to see there a huge saddle of Southdown mutton that had by its own weight torn itself from the big kitchen spit, and was lying in the basting-pan.

During the spring and summer lambs were butchered twice a week, or oftener if required. That did not keep down the flock sufficiently, and a great many were sold. The hides from the beeves almost supplied the plantation with shoes. Two of the negro men were tanners and shoemakers. A Southern plantation, well managed, had nearly everything necessary to life done within its bounds. At Burleigh there were two carpenters in the carpenter-shop, two blacksmiths in the blacksmith-shop, two millers in the mill, and usually five seamstresses in the house. In the laundry there were two of the strongest and most capable women on the plantation, and they were perhaps the busiest of the corps of house-servants. Boys were kept about, ready to ride for the mail or to take notes around the neighborhood. There was no lack of numbers to fill every place; the trouble was rather to find work for supernumeraries, as already intimated.

One of the overseers, who was ambitious to put in a large crop, begged to have some of these hangers-on

---

killing, that blinked at you from out their warm beds, and grunted when requested to rise, suggested sausage; while over on Charley's farm, and under Aunt Sucky's able management, aldermanic turkeys, and sleek, plump pullets, and ducks, quacking low from very fatness, and geese that had ceased to wrangle,—all thought themselves, like man before Copernicus, the centre of the universe. . . .

"And can you not detect the odor of apples issuing even from that locked door? There are great piles of them stowed away there; and cider, I suspect, is not lacking. And above, the store-room showed shelves weighed down, since the arrival of the last steamer, with such things as Elmington could not supply. Boxes and bags and bundles gave forth the mellow fragrance of raisins, the cheerful rattle of nuts, the pungent savor of spices,—the promise of all things dear to the heart of the Virginia housewife. On every whiff floated mince-pie,—mince-pie embryonic, uncompounded; with every sniff there rose, like an exhalation before the imagination, visions of Plum-Pudding,—of the Plum-Pudding of Old England,—twin sister of Roast Beef,—and with Roast Beef, inseparable attendant and indispensable bulwark of Constitutional Liberty."—*Don Miff,* pp. 153, 154.

The above passage was inspired by the Burleigh Christmas.

sent to the field. There were twenty-seven servants in the service of the house, he said.

The land in cultivation looked like a lady's garden, scarcely a blade of grass to be seen in hundreds of acres. The rows and hills and furrows were laid off so carefully as to be a pleasure to the eye. The fences and bridges, gates and roads, were in good order. His wagons never broke down. All these details may seem quite out of place and superfluous. But they show the character of the man in a country where many such things were neglected for the one important consideration,—the cotton crop.

He never kept a slow mule; all must be fast and strong. They were sold as soon as they failed to come up to these requirements. Thomas bred all his own mules and nearly all his own horses,—his thoroughbred riding-horses always,—and frequently he had more than he needed of both. The great droves of mules and horses brought annually from Tennessee and Kentucky to less thrifty planters found no sale at Burleigh unless the master happened to need a pair of carriage-horses. Two teams of six mules each carried off his cotton crop, going to the station every working day for months. It was only ten miles off, but the eight bales of cotton, that weighed nearly five hundred pounds apiece, and the heavy, deeply cut-up roads, made it a day's journey. As the returning wagon-drivers came up in the evenings they were met by other men, who took the mules out and cared for them, and loaded up the wagons for the next day. It was not considered right by the master that those who occupied the responsible position of drivers should have these labors to perform. They had nothing to do but to go to the house to deliver the cotton receipts, get a drink of whiskey, and some tobacco too, if the regular allowance issued had run short, and then home to supper and to rest, ready for a fresh start in the morning.

Hog-killing time was a high carnival on the plantation. There were usually about a hundred and fifty or a hundred and seventy-five hogs, sometimes more. They supplied the house all the year round, and the negroes for six months. He had taken out to Mississippi the Virginia art of curing bacon. His hams were famous among his friends and guests, as were the chops and saddles of Southdown mutton, the legs of venison, wild or from his park, the great rounds and sirloins of beef, and the steaks cut with the grain.

It was no waste or useless lavishness that these great roasts of beef or mutton were seldom put on the table a second time, or that the number of chickens in the fattening coops were in the season not allowed to fall below sixty, or that during the winter and spring turkeys were on the table twice a week. Not only the house-servants, but usually several sick and favorite ones, were fed from the table. In addition to these, there were almost always the servants of guests and neighbors in the house.

It was customary on many plantations for boys to drive the mules in the cotton-gin. Under them the mules did not thrive, and had frequently to be changed. On the Burleigh place the most experienced and trustworthy of the drivers had charge of the gin-mules. Under them the same team ginned out the entire crop, working at it every day for months. At the end of the season they were as fat and well as at the beginning.

Fodder-pulling was looked on with dread by most planters, as the hot work among the corn-stalks gave the negroes chills and fevers. The master of Burleigh guarded his negroes against sickness by providing two barrels of whiskey for this season. Every man and woman came for a cup of it when the day's work was over. The wag of the plantation, Uncle Beverly, was always given two cups, because he had a very funny way of opening his enormous mouth and throwing the contents of the cup into it as if he were throwing it into a bucket. Everybody laughed when he did it, the master enjoying it as much as any of them.

The heart-warming laugh with his master seemed to be the best part.

Indulgent as he was when he thought his servants needed liquor, he was equally strict in forbidding them to touch it at other times. It was his boast that he was always obeyed in this, and also that under his system he had never had a drunkard on his plantation. Our friends and neighbors were not sure at Christmas and other festive seasons that the dining-room servants would not be intoxicated. At Burleigh the servants knew that the eggnog-bowl and the other things would be handed to them at the proper time, and they felt a pride in not displeasing the family by bad conduct. Likewise, his wagon-drivers were put on their good behavior as long as they had the wagons and teams under their care. The servants who went with the carriage to dinner-parties and at night about in the neighborhood had the lives of wife and children in their keeping, he used to say, and he chose them for their steadiness, and was never deceived or disappointed. In connection with this, his children and a number of young people, guests at Burleigh, were near meeting with an accident one cold winter's night. The roads were heavy, having been cut up by the cotton-wagons, and it was thought unsafe to go over five miles of a bad road on a dark night in anything less substantial than a six-mule plantation-wagon. There was great glee and fun in the getting off. It was at the Christmas season, and everybody felt in spirit for enjoying the Christmas-parties at the country-houses. There had been a series of them. As the wagon was loaded up with its gay, living freight, there was some talk of firing off some of the children's fire-crackers in order to put mettle into the mules. In the lightness of his heart the master called out to the steady Lewis, his trusted driver, "Lewis, don't bring them back till you have upset them twice." And with that parting speech, which was received with cheers, he went back into the house. He did not dream that Lewis, who had never disobeyed him in his life, did not mean to disobey him this time. We thought that Lewis was surely intoxicated, from the manner in which he brought us back home. But we had not had time to tell papa of our grave suspicions before Lewis's honest face appeared at the door with his apology to the amazed master. "I do my ve'y bes', marster, to tu'n dat waggin ober, sir. I run it in all de gullies I could fin', but I couldn't tu'n it ober, sir."

Southern children were taught to call the colored people aunt and uncle as titles of respect. They resented being called by their names without the title, and considered that it spoke ill for the manners of a child who would do so rude a thing. They called each other "brer" and "sis." This referred, not to the natural relationship, but to their relationship in the church. On formal occasions they were "Mr." and "Mrs." Ignorance of this led me into sad disgrace one night with my usually indulgent Mammy Maria. She had taken me to see her brother married. I heard her address him as Mr. Ferguson, and at once asked, "Mammy, what makes you call Henry Mr. Ferguson?" "Do you think 'cause we are black that we cyarn't have no names?" was mammy's indignant reply. She could not be angry more than a minute with "her white chillun." She never went to wedding or party or quilting without bringing to us an apple or a cake or a bouquet,—whatever was given to her there. I do not think that her own children fared as well. The mistress had wet-nurses for her babies, chosen from among her negro servants. The devotion of the nurses to these foster-children was greater than their love for their own. One of them, with a baby at home very sick, left it to stay with the white child. This one she insisted on walking the night through, because he was roaring with the colic, though the mistress entirely disapproved, and urged her to go home to her own child, whose illness was more serious, if less noisy, than the white nursling with its colic.

CHAPTER VII.

STILL WATERS AND GREEN PASTURES.

THE summer of 1836 was spent by the Burleigh Dabneys in Virginia. They returned home in October, and two weeks after reaching the plantation Sophia gave birth to her sixth son, Edward.

The Burleigh plantation was regarded as a healthful place. Thomas left a belt of trees around his house of a half-mile to nearly a mile in width, that no upturning of the soil in the cultivation of the crops might endanger the health of his family. He spent the summer of 1837 at home; but he sent Sophia and her boys to Raymond, to her father's. She spent the next eight summers there, the winters being passed on the plantation, which lay ten miles south of Raymond.

A great sorrow came to the household in the summer of 1838. Thomas was at Mount Prospect on a visit to his mother, when a letter from Mr. Lewis Smith informed him that his six-year-old James and his Christmas boy, Thomas, ten years of age, both died within one week. James died on the 9th and Thomas on the 15th of July. Years after this Thomas said that his heart had sunk lower in his body from the day that he heard of the loss of his two fair boys. James died first, and Sophia, dreading the effect on Thomas, allowed no one to tell him that his playfellow was gone. In dying Thomas called out, "Oh, I see Jimmy! Oh, gold all around! So beautiful!"

The two weeks of weary journeying and anxiety on the way from Virginia to Mississippi, during which his fears were for the worst, at length came to an end. Thomas Dabney approached the home in which he had left Sophia and her five boys. He dreaded lest his whole family had been swept off by the disease that had taken away two. Great, indeed, were his relief and thankfulness when Sophia, in her white dress, with her Mississippi baby, Edward, in her arms, met him at the gate. She and three children had been spared to him.

Thomas and Sophia found great comfort and enjoyment in the near neighborhood of her favorite sister Emmeline and her husband, Mr. Smith. The brothers-in-law were very congenial. The Smiths lived on the adjoining plantation of Midway, and the families spent the Sundays alternately at Burleigh and at Midway.

Augustine Dabney had established himself in Raymond. He soon made a reputation for knowledge of the law and for brilliant literary attainments. He made no less a reputation for singular simplicity and unworldliness of character. He was of so tender-hearted a nature that he charged no fees of any widow. It mattered not if she were far richer than he was. Of course, this became known, and all women, and men, too, in distress and trouble came to him for the advice and ready sympathy and assistance which they were sure to receive. The kindly nature was imposed on sometimes, but he did not resent it, and was ready the next time he heard a tale of distress to give all the comfort in his power. The brothers were in nearly every characteristic very different, but in their faith in human nature they were the same,—nothing could shake that. Both, in their different ways, had been deceived in people, but they put such cases out of their lives, considering them exceptional. The two hearts held not one drop of bitterness. Augustine was judge of the Probate Court of Hinds County for eight years, the result of four biennial elections by the people. He was a Whig. The Democratic party offered no opposing candidate from November, 1851, to November, 1859, during which years he held the office. Governor A. G. Brown, for many years one of the leaders of the Democratic party in Mississippi, said that it would have been useless for any one to run against Augustine Dabney.

It is recorded of him that no decision of his while on the bench was reversed by the Court of Appeals. His hospitality and lavish generosity impaired his estate.

But his simple home in Raymond was the centre of all that was most attractive. It was the resort of his brothers of the bar, and of the bishop of the diocese and the clergy, and all distinguished visitors in the county.

He was usually very quiet, but when a congenial theme was started, he was a charming talker. He was so scrupulously truthful in the smallest details that one felt condemned who had been betrayed into speaking in an exaggerated style in his presence. Mrs. Augustine Dabney was an invalid, with a nursery full of young children. She led the conversation at her table, unless Augustine happened to be in the talking vein. In this case she added to the charm of the entertainment by her witty sallies, not taking the talk away from him, but rather stimulating him. The intercourse between Mrs. Augustine Dabney and Sophia was always of the most delightful kind. They loved each other like sisters. The children of the brothers, under such influence, grew up in the closest intimacy, more like brothers and sisters than cousins. It was hardly an exaggeration to say that the dearest friend of each child was to be found in the other family. They paired off according to their ages, which fell nearly together. A life of Thomas could not be written if Augustine and his family were left out. The two households, in the somewhat isolated life in Mississippi, were more intimate with each other than with any other relations on either side.

In the early days of Mississippi the Choctaw Indians had not yet been moved to the Indian Territory. They soon learned to know that they had friends in the family at Burleigh. They fell into a way of camping for two weeks during every autumn on the Tallahala Creek. The name Tallahala is itself a Choctaw word, signifying owl. The lands along its banks, and through all that region of country, were once the hunting-grounds of the Indians. Many of their stone arrow-heads are yet to be found scattered through the woods, and many are upturned by the ploughmen in the fields. Less than four miles from Burleigh is a spot where their arrow-heads were evidently made. Bits of the flint lie scattered as they were left by them. Arrow-heads are there in all stages of construction; on each one can plainly be seen the reason why it was abandoned: an unlucky or unskilful blow had chipped it in the wrong place. Some were merely outlined in a rude way, some had one side well shaped, some were nearly completed, when an unwitting stroke spoiled them. Some were plainly the work of the veriest tyro, probably of some little brave, who was learning already the noble arts of the chase and of war. Three and a half miles southwest of this spot is a battle-field, where, in these early days, these arrow-heads were thickly strewn. In the midst is an Indian burial-mound, where, tradition says, the slain warriors who fell in that battle were interred. Not fifty yards from the door of the Burleigh house, on a hill-side, two very curious specimens of Indian stone-work were found by the children,—one a highly polished and beautiful hatchet. The Choctaws loved the Tallahala Creek. Its banks were clothed with thickets of cane which the men used for making their blowguns and arrows, and the women for making their baskets. Their peculiar way of selling their baskets was interesting. A certain basket would have as its price as much sugar as it could hold, another coffee in the same proportion, and others flour, etc. This arrangement was never departed from, so far as we know.

It was quite impossible to get a "coffee-basket" with sugar, or a "sugar-basket" with coffee, I think. Presents of clothing or of anything else were promptly subjected to a scrutinizing examination under the eyes of the donor. If a torn place or other defect could be found, it was pointed out with equal interest and naïveté. They were an innocent, inoffensive people, and never forgot a kindness. They were so scrupulously honest that they burned only the fallen and dead boughs that they found decaying on the ground. The master's fences and his woodpile were not molested. They came in the cotton-picking season, and the planters were always glad to have them, as they picked carefully and got no trash in their bags. They did all work well that they attempted at all, tanning buckskin, blowgun-making, and basket-weaving. On one occasion a baby was born in the Tallahala camp on the very night before they had arranged to depart for their homes. This did not interfere with the plan of march. The mother and the little "pooscoos," as the Choctaws call their babies, were set up on a pony, and in this manner they went off. The voices of the Choctaw women are low and sweet,—more like the cooing and chirpings of birds than like the human voice of any but some young children.

Mr. Lewis Smith was a true friend to the Indians. It was said that he could not refuse any request made by them. One day an Indian man cast admiring eyes on a red cloak that Mr. Smith had provided for the winter, and on an intimation that he desired it Mr. Smith took the cloak off and handed it to him.

It was with genuine regret that their white friends saw that year by year their number became fewer. At last the gray-headed chief led to the "nation" the last of the Choctaws of Hinds County.

Not more than three years had elapsed since Thomas had made his home in Mississippi when he received a letter from John Tyler, who aspired to the office of Vice-President of the United States, requesting him to use his personal influence with the prominent men of Mississippi to bring about this result. He wrote at once, saying that by reason of his brief residence in the State and limited acquaintance with the people any assistance which he could give would be of necessity small and almost valueless, but that he would do his utmost. It so happened that Mississippi was one of the first Southern States in which a convention was held for the purpose of discussing the names of Whig candidates for the offices of President and Vice-President of the United States. The main question before this convention was whom to nominate for President,—the question of whose name to put forward for Vice-President not being considered of much moment at that time.

This convention was held at Jackson, the capital of the State, twenty-five miles away from his plantation. As Thomas was not a public speaker, he requested his brother Augustine to present the name of John Tyler to the convention for this office.

On the last day of the convention, Thomas, feeling some solicitude, mounted his horse and rode to Jackson, arriving there just as the house was on the point of going into nominations.

He asked at once, "What are the chances for John Tyler?"

Augustine replied, "I have not done anything in that matter, and fear that it is now too late." After a moment's reflection he cried out, "No, it is not too late; let us speak to Sharkey, Poindexter, Chilton,— any of these gentlemen will second the nomination." So the brothers made their way to the seats of these gentlemen, and advocated the claims of their Virginia friend. His name was accordingly introduced in due form, but in the midst of the proceeding a voice called out, "John Tyler won't do. Who vouches for him?" Governor Sharkey at once replied, "Colonel Dabney does, and that's sufficient." Without further question or discussion the balloting began, and he received the nomination. And the State of Arkansas, holding her convention a few weeks thereafter, gave her votes to him whom Mississippi had endorsed. When the general convention of the party was held in St. Louis, it was discovered that John Tyler was the only candidate for the vice-presidency who had in advance any following; and when his own State came to his aid he was nominated without any serious opposition.

When, on President Harrison's death, Mr. Tyler became the chief executive of the United States many office-seekers put in their claims. Among others a Mississippi name was sent up. "Not a single appointment for Mississippi until Colonel Dabney is heard from," was the President's answer. But, as is well known, Mr. Tyler did not long adhere to the principles of the Whig party. The mortification to Thomas Dabney was excessive. He felt almost as if he were himself compromised, and his feeling against John Tyler became bitter. He refused to answer any letters or messages from him. Once during Mr. Tyler's term of office he went to Washington, intending to spend several days there. Mr. Tyler's son happened to be at the station, and recognized him as he was getting off the train. He seemed unconscious of the existing state of feeling, and was for taking Thomas at once with his luggage to the White House. Thomas could not explain to the affectionate young fellow, and left Washington on the next train, as he saw no other way out of the embarrassing situation.

Many years after this the ex-President, John Tyler, wept as he spoke of the loss of the friendship of Thomas Dabney, and tried to bring about a renewal of intercourse. They had not only been friends but were allied by marriage, as Thomas's first wife was a cousin of Mr. Tyler's. He wrote to beg that their children might visit each other, and invited the Mississippi family to come to Virginia to see his. But the subject was yet too sore with Thomas. He could never mention Mr. Tyler's name without emotion.

As time went on comforts and conveniences grew up around the families in the new country. But it was at times difficult to provide for so many. In June, 1837, Mr. Hill wrote to a sister in Virginia, "There is a great scarcity of provisions in this part of the State. Cornmeal is worth two dollars and fifty cents a bushel, and flour seventeen dollars a barrel."

Mr. and Mrs. Hill had chosen Raymond as their home. This little village was situated on an elevated ridge, and had been noted for its healthfulness. Several other Virginia families who moved to the far South at this time decided on making their homes in Raymond. They formed an agreeable and cultivated society.

In the autumn of 1838 (November 4) Sophia's first daughter was born. She was joyfully named Sarah by her father. About a year later Sophia wrote to her aunt in Virginia, "Little S. begins to step about."

In 1839, Mr. Charles Hill died. He was on his way to

visit Virginia, and had not gotten beyond the bounds of his adopted State when the fatal illness seized him. It was his request that no mourning should be worn for him, and no stone set up to mark his last resting-place. His family respected his wishes, and he lies in an unmarked grave in Holmes County, Mississippi.

The following are the last lines written in his journal before his death. They were penned on this journey: "When will men agree to differ,—to allow each other perfect freedom of conscience? Not until they love each other and become Christians. Not until they set no value upon worldly distinction but as a means of doing good and making others good, and therefore happy. Not until they act upon the truth that the least in the kingdom of God is greater than George Washington on earth in all his glory."

Those who knew him said that he lived up to these high views of the responsibilities of life. He was stern with his children, who were a good deal afraid of him. He threw a handsome doll in the fire that Sophia and Emmeline were disputing over. Sophia said it had the desired effect, as she never again said an unkind word to her sister.

When a very young man he had met his future wife, when she was a girl of only fifteen years old, and had lost his heart with her. We children delighted in making her give an account of the courtship. It took place as she was walking home from school with her books on her arm. It was, like everything about him, direct. "Miss Susan, give me your hand." The answer to this was that the little girl frankly placed her hand in his. He saw that she was unconscious of his meaning. "And your heart too," he added. This time she understood, and the hand was not withdrawn. Her mother had died when she was but two hours old, and her home with a step-mother was an unhappy one. This woman, in her father's absence, would take her by her long hair and throw her out of the house, and the little step-brother was set above her in every way. The harsh treatment brought out the patience and gentleness that endeared her to all who knew her in after-life. The step mother herself became attached to her, and at her death divided her property equally between her own boy and her step daughter.

In the summer of 1840 the second daughter, Susan, was born to Sophia. She was welcomed as a companion to Sarah, and a month after her birth, which took place in Raymond, she was taken to the plantation on a pillow. "May she be a blessing to all who love her," her grandmamma Macon wrote. In the winter of 1842 the third daughter was born, and was called Sophia, after her mother, who had gotten her name from Goldsmith's charming heroine. The next child, Benjamin, lived only eight days. In the autumn of 1845 Sophia gave birth to her eleventh child, Emmeline.

Our grandmother Hill's youngest daughter had married soon after her father's death, and the widowed mother in a few years resolved on giving up her home in Raymond. After several changes she fixed on the house of her favorite son-in-law, Thomas, as her home. The large number of young children made the house too noisy for her delicate nerves. Thomas, ever solicitous to be a true son to her, built a cottage for her after her own plan. It was placed near the house, and contained two large rooms and spacious closets.

The years spent by this dear grandmother in the midst of the Burleigh household were among the happiest of our lives. She was lovely to look upon in her lace-frilled cap, and with her reticule on her arm. Each child looked on her as his or her special friend, and she was never tired of trying to make everybody about her good and happy. She was too delicate to walk much. But she had beautiful taste, and seemed to make everything prettier about the place. Under her care many fine roses, tulips, hyacinths, and other flowers flourished in the Burleigh garden. During the last years of her life she lay on a lounge, with her New Testament and Jay's "Morning and Evening Exercises" within reach of her hand. Other books, too, were near, and she spent much time in reading. Her room became the sitting-room of the family, she was so bright and sunny-hearted, and always so ready to be interested in everything. Over all there was a halo as of a spirit at peace with God and man. A few months before her death, which did not take place till May, 1854, a sorrow came that would have been a heavy affliction at another time in her life. She said that she had no tears to shed, because she felt so near the other world, where the loved one had gone. Her last few months were sad. A depression seized her that could not be shaken off. She bore it with her usual patience, seeing a Merciful Hand in all that was sent, yet begging her Heavenly Father to shorten the days. The gloom was not lifted. She passed away in much suffering, leaving the memory of a spotless life. It was said of her that she never knew any scandal. Her neighbors in Raymond could not look at her and tell her stories that all knew but her. The thought of evil to that white soul was like a physical pain. She could not bear to hear any one spoken against, and was ever ready to plead the extenuating circumstances that her eyes could see in each case, however black it might look to others. The first word that she taught her favorite grandson to spell was "good." She was an accomplished needle-woman, and so industrious that she did not like to be idle, even while sick. Mr. Hill forbade her sewing, and when she heard his step she hid her work behind her in her large chair. She gave away everything. With all her love for the beautiful, she seemed to have no desire to own anything that could give pleasure to another. When she died, as has been said of another lovely Christian character, her things were "touching in their fewness."

At the time that she decided on giving up her home in Raymond she divided not only all her household effects, but her property of all kinds, among her three daughters. Thomas was much opposed to this arrangement and endeavored in vain to dissuade her. She would need money, however, to buy her clothes, and said that each daughter should hand to her an annual sum for this purpose. The amount named by her was small. Thomas tried to make her double it, but she was firm, and would receive nothing beyond the sum first asked for. A large proportion of this was spent each year in presents to the servants and to other needy persons. She was at heart an emancipationist, whether from sympathy with the colored race or with their owners I do not know.*

In 1845, Thomas decided to look for a summer home for his family somewhere on the shores of the Gulf of Mexico. He heard much of the beauty and salubrity of Pass Christian, and of the delightful society to be met there. He visited the line of Gulf coast, and resolved on buying a place at the Pass. He got a very simple but airy and cool house, situated in a grove of shade-trees looking directly on the shining beach and the blue waters of the Gulf.

The little village of Pass Christian, situated about midway between New Orleans and Mobile on the Mississippi Sound (as that part of the Mexican Gulf is called), is a place of extreme beauty. The houses, embosomed in the shade of live-oak, magnolia, and other beautiful trees, were dotted along the beach for four miles. The residents or sojourners were, in the main, people of culture and wealth,—either citizens of New Orleans or planters of Mississippi and Louisiana, who came there to spend the summer months. Almost directly out to sea lies Cat Island, some ten or twelve miles away, the most western of a chain of islands which run parallel with this coast, protecting it from frequent and sudden storms which vex the waters of the open Gulf. Inside of this natural barrier the water is generally shallow, and the deeper parts or channels are called "passes," hence the name Pass Christian. Eight miles out from the shore is another pass called Pass Marian; and there, in place of a light-house, an old iron ship was anchored. On board this ship lived the light-keeper with his wife and one child, a daughter. I remember that our hearts were stirred with compas-

---

* A few Sundays ago one of her old neighbors laid upon the altar of the parish church in Raymond a memorial of Susan Fitzhugh Hill,—a handful of the fragrant white star jasmine. It grew in her garden on a bush that her hand had tended fifty years ago.

sion for this little family, thinking that their lot was very dreary.

Many gentlemen at Pass Christian owned fast-sailing yachts, and during the season fortnightly regattas were held, in which the entire population felt deeply interested, as almost every one owning a yacht entered it for the race. Thomas was the first president of the yacht club, and was, I believe, annually re-elected as long as he lived at Pass Christian.

SOPHIA TO THOMAS DABNEY.

"PASS CHRISTIAN, July 30, 1847.

... "I have another great comfort to add. The servants I have brought with me have behaved remarkably well. I never have to remind them of their duties. They all seem to anticipate my wants. I always thought I valued my servants very highly, but I never valued them enough. They all act towards me as they did when you were sick. They add much to my enjoyment. It does not take much to trouble me when you are absent. ... I would give a great deal to see Charley, but tell him that I am very happy in thinking about his coming next summer. Tell Virginius and Sarah not to forget me. I know Charley will not."

Thomas was in Virginia on a visit to his mother. He had taken, as usual, some of her grandchildren to "show to her."

It was a shock and grief to Thomas when the State of Mississippi repudiated her debts. He worked against repudiation with all his energy. When he found his efforts in that direction useless, it occurred to him that the honor of the State that was the birthplace of his children could yet be saved by private subscription. He offered to head the list by giving ten thousand dollars. It would have ruined him, for he was just beginning to get his plantation in order. He still lived in the old log house with the leaky roof. But, with heroic improvidence, he refused to consider personal consequences. His efforts were fruitless. He could not rouse the people in his State to join him in a plan that they looked on as a costly piece of quixotism.

In one of these years Chancellor Tyler's estate was settled up. By the laws of Virginia Thomas came in as one of the heirs. He wrote to his brother-in-law, Mr. Whittle, that he declined to receive his share of the inheritance. In reply, Mr. Whittle suggested that he probably was not aware of the amount that he was refusing,—about ten thousand dollars. But Thomas requested that this might be divided equally among the sisters of his deceased wife. Sophia also declined to receive a small legacy (about three hundred dollars) which came to her from a maiden aunt. At her request it was given to one of the other heirs, a cousin who was not prosperous.

Thomas always maintained that no preparation could help him to bear a trial, and that it was no true kindness to make concealment; and he made none in his intercourse with those with whom he was thrown. He said that if he were condemned to be hanged, he should not wish a reprieve. A characteristic incident took place when he went with a young girl, the only daughter of Emmeline Smith, to have an operation performed on her eye. The oculist told her that it would give her no pain at all, and begged her to quiet herself. But she got into floods of tears, and had no courage to submit to the operation. In her distress she turned to Thomas,—

"Oh, Uncle Dabney, will it hurt very much?"

"Yes, my child," he said, "like the very devil."

The girl knew that he had told her the truth, and it braced her nerves for the pain. Putting her two hands in his, she asked him to hold them, and she submitted to the oculist without any more remonstrance.

In the early spring of this year (1847) a sad change came for the neighborhood. Mrs. Lewis Smith, while superintending the planting of a large garden for the plantation negroes, stood too long on the damp ground and took a cold which soon developed into pneumonia. The disease terminated fatally after a short illness. Our mother said of her that she was the best mistress whom she had ever known. She would add, in her humility, that she was a much better woman than she was. Our dear mother said that of many people. The loss of Mrs. Smith was much felt, and led to another scarcely less. Mr. Smith was so wretched at her death that he could not be roused, and he died in a few months of a broken heart. The two children, Campbell and Olivia, were committed to the guardianship of Thomas. When Mr. Smith felt himself dying, he asked Thomas to promise never to give up his son Campbell. Not even to a dying man, and one to whom he was tenderly attached, would Thomas make that promise. He told him that he could not make a promise that he might have to break, but he would do all that he could for the boy. After the funeral he took him home to Burleigh. From there he was sent in a few months, in accordance with Mr. Smith's expressed wishes, to school in Virginia.

In 1849, Thomas wrote to his ward, H. Campbell Smith:

. . . "I hope you are making good progress in your studies; for, if you flinch now, you can never make it up. Apply yourself to the extent of your powers, so that you may be well prepared to enter the university next October. I entertain no doubt about your competency to achieve it if you will but determine upon it. Do it, then, and it will be a source of gratification to you to the end of your life; but if you permit any circumstance to divert you from it, you will never forgive yourself."

Sophia to her aunt, March 7, 1847: "Our house will ever be a home to Olivia if she will be willing to come and live with me after she has completed her education. It will afford me great pleasure to have her with me as my *own*."

Olivia lived at Burleigh up to her marriage, and was ever an affectionate daughter of the house.

The home at Midway was broken up. The family at Burleigh turned more than ever to the Raymond Dabneys.

CHAPTER VIII.

MANAGEMENT OF SERVANTS.

The house-servants were never required to sit up later than ten, and only the cook and dining-room servants were detained till then. No grown servant slept in the house. Sixteen living children—nine sons and seven daughters—were born to Thomas and Sophia Dabney, and, though she was not strong, she managed to take care of her babies at night unassisted. Two young negro girls slept in the house, but were rarely disturbed. One of these girls, now a married woman with great girls of her own, relates to me a touching instance of the kindly simplicity of the sweet mistress: "I asked missis to button my dress for me one mornin'. I didn't know no better. An' missis buttoned it up for me."

A little incident will throw some light on the life of the mother who during thirty years was never without an infant in her arms. One night one of the little girls had a dream that frightened her, and ran to her mother's bed to wake her up. "Let us light the candle and play with your doll-babies," mamma said; and the two crouched down by the corner where the dolls slept, and planned over them and dressed them until the child was willing to go back to her own bed, the dream quite forgotten. There were several children in the nursery younger than this one at the time.

She did not allow the maids to be kept up at night to undress her daughters or to be called on to do many things that the body-servants in other households were expected to do. "They are not machines," she said to her children; "they are just like you, made of the same flesh and blood." When one of the children, old enough to dress herself, held out her foot to have the shoe and stocking taken off, she said, "Do it yourself. You are just as able to do it as Milly is."

She also impressed lessons of industry and economy on her children. She could not expect, she said, that they would always be as well off as they were then, and she did not know which one might be destined for poverty. Wastefulness was a sin, she said, apart from the bad habits that come in its train. She impressed these lessons the more earnestly as the father was inclined to be extravagant.

In cases of sickness where nursing at night was required she sent those servants who performed this part to bed the next morning. The parents themselves did most of the nursing. During the fifty years that Thomas spent in Mississippi he was very ill only once, and the kindness and devotion of his negroes—"his people," as they still call themselves, though they have been free twenty-one years—were often in after-life referred to. He could not bear a sound. As the house could not be kept quiet with so many young children about, the nursery was moved to Mammy Harriet's. Here we spent three weeks. We were too young to feel the anxiety of the time. We thought it no end of fun to keep house with mammy, and to play with her black cat that knew how to shake hands, and to hear her boy Ike ask riddles at night when he came home out of the fields. Our nurses were so wisely chosen that we never heard a ghost-story from one of them during the whole course of our childhood, nor anything else that the most careful parents could object to.

Thomas had quite an amusing experience when he attempted to set two of his servants free. A man who had been very lazy and unreliable in every way all his life,* asked the master one day to let him hire his time from him and live in Raymond. He thought that he could make a great deal of money in Raymond, blacking gentlemen's boots and waiting on them.

Uncle Abel's feet were so large and set at such an angle as to be damaging to the crops as he walked between the rows, and for that reason he was not

---

* This man had been sold by his former master for half a dollar, and had come into Thomas's possession through a mistake.

allowed to work in the fields. His sole business was to ride over the plantation, calling up the hogs and feeding them. He liked to hold gentlemen's horses at the gate, too, after a hostler had saddled them, but this was a voluntary addition to his duties.

The master's answer to Uncle Abel's proposition was that he should charge him nothing for his time; on the contrary, he would present him with twenty-five dollars and set him free for life. He added the stipulation, however, that Uncle Abel should never return to him. Uncle Abel made no reply, but nothing more was ever heard of his desire to make a fortune. The woman who had charge of the Pass Christian house also was opposed to plantation life, and did not wish to return to it when the master sold the summer place. She had been born on the water, she said, and she wanted to die on it, and asked to be allowed to live at the Pass and support herself by selling chickens and eggs. The master consented at once, and told her that he should give her twenty-five dollars as a start in life, but she must first promise not to return to him when she had grown tired of working for herself. Her answer to this proposition was to pack up her things in all haste to return with him to the plantation, and she was quite in a tremor lest the master should desire to set her free against her will.

Thomas sold but four negroes. One of these was a violent and bad woman, who, after many attempts, succeeded one day in stabbing her husband to death. She was tried for her life, and would have been hanged if her master had made any attempt to save her. He thought she ought to suffer the penalty of the law and made no move in her defence, and this conduct influenced the jury to bring in a verdict of manslaughter in self-defence, and she was acquitted. But he would not keep a murderess on his plantation, and she was sold. A kind man bought her, knowing her history. Another case was that of a man who attempted to kill the overseer. He was the son of our beloved nurse, Mammy Harriet,—Ike, who knew so many delightful riddles; and it was a sad day in the master's house when it was known that one of that family was to stand a trial for his life. As in the former case, no counsel was employed by the master to save his property, and, as in that case, Ike. was acquitted. He was sold, and we never saw him again. A third case was that of a girl who was so thievish that the plantation negroes petitioned the master to sell her. Nothing was safe in their houses if they were left open. They were afraid to leave their hampers in the field lest Indian Mary, as she was called on account of her straight black hair, should rob them. Instead of picking cotton herself she went from hamper to hamper filling her bag. As the negroes were paid for picking cotton this was no light grievance, and finally got to be unbearable and led to the above result. So Mary was told that she must choose a good master for herself. She chose a man who lived alone and had no other servant. There was no chance of stealing, for she was welcome, the man said, to everything in his little cabin. For years she came over on Sundays to her old home to tell how well she was getting on. One of the little girls in the house was much attached to her, and learned to knit that she might knit a pair of stockings for Mary's baby, and begged for pudding that she might send it to the old favorite.

The last case was that of a woman who had no family ties on the place that she cared for, and desired to be sold to a man who owned no other negroes. She also came over on Sundays to visit her friends both in the house and in the quarters.

Thomas disapproved of hiring out servants; it broke up families, he said. At times he hired out one or two mechanics. He hired a young blacksmith to a good master in Raymond for some years, the man being very happy there. The price that was paid for him was five hundred dollars a year. Another man offered six hundred dollars, but Thomas refused it, saying that he did not wish his young servant to work hard enough to be worth six hundred dollars to his employer.

One of his visits to his mother at her Mount Prospect home was made at Christmas. A company of gentlemen spent the holiday week there on the same occasion. As they were all going away, Thomas, who was about to mount his horse also, said to them, "Gentlemen, there is one person who has contributed much to our enjoyment. I mean the cook. Let us not forget her. Here is my five-dollar gold-piece for her." In a minute every hand held out a five-dollar gold-piece, and twenty-five dollars were sent to the kitchen to the cook.

Sophia Dabney was once sent for to spend a day or two with her sister, Mrs. Moncure, who was ill and needed her care. When she came home she said that Mrs. Moncure was a better mistress than she was. She spoke of the attachment of the servants for her sister, and their anxious inquiries at the house of her condition. When breakfast and tea were over, she had been surprised at the line of cups and plates that had been placed for her to fill in the absence of the sick mistress from the table. In Sophia's housekeeping she had not attempted to give any meal but dinner from her table. In her humility she forgot that her establishment, both of white and black, made it impossible to carry out the regulations that could be practised in a smaller family.

Mrs. Moncure had inherited a number of negroes from her father's estate. It is recorded of her that she never allowed any of these servants to be punished for any offence whatever. "They are mine" was the mantle of protection that she threw over them and their descendants. Mrs. Moncure had inherited the old family nurse, Mammy Mary, to whom she and my mother were greatly attached. She was one of the most exalted Christians whom I have ever met. When some one asked if she, in her long years of confinement to her own cabin in her old age, preferred bright weather to rainy days, her answer was, "I am thankful for whatever the Father sends."

My mother took her an annual present, and the old nurse sent freely to her for anything that she needed. As long as the old woman was able to move about she was a regular visitor at Burleigh, coming in the carriage with Mrs. Moncure when she spent the day with her sister. When Mammy Mary grew too feeble to go out she expected to be daily visited by Mrs. Moncure and her children, and by all the family connections who visited her mistress. She was a devout member of the Baptist Church, and attended it in Mrs. Moncure's carriage. For years her trim, neat figure, her snowy cap, and rapt face was a familiar picture to the congregation as she sat on the steps of the pulpit, a seat allowed her on account of her deafness. The church was built for the white people of the neighborhood, but a large number of benches were set apart for the negroes. They were well filled on "meeting-days." The man who took up the collection handed the plate to the slaves as well as to the masters, and our George Page, among others, did not fail to put in his contribution. George was able to do this. He has lately said that he received as much as fifty dollars a year from visitors to his master's house.

Thomas was an accurate shot with a rifle, and was successful as a huntsman. He was devoted to both hunting and fishing. The deer, which abounded on the plantation when he bought it, grew fewer and fewer as year by year they were hunted and killed. In the neighboring county of Scott they still roamed in great numbers. The lands were lying out, and free to any sportsman who cared to shoot the deer. Thomas and some of his neighbors organized a hunting club to go each autumn to enjoy the Scott County hunting-grounds. For eight years they spent two weeks of every November over there. Thomas took along, besides the horse on which he rode, a mule that he called his hunting mule. "Annie" was trained to stand while he fired from her back; and when, in the heat of pursuit, he leaped off and left Annie with her bridle hanging as it chanced to fall, the sagacious beast stood stock-still till her master returned to the spot. He attributed much of his success in the Scott County hunts to the docility of this mule.

He had a pack of hounds that were rarely used except on these annual hunts. A wagon with four mules carried his servants and a marquee large enough for twelve men, bed, camp-chest, etc. Provisions of various sorts were stowed away in the wagon. This camping-out frolic was looked forward to by the club with the zest of boys. The deer were killed in numbers. Occasionally a wild turkey would be brought into camp, and add variety to the feast.

The deer were so abundant that the greater number of the huntsmen did not care to shoot at a doe or a fawn. But the excitable ones did not regard age or sex. The huntsmen used to agree that one of their number, Mr. Mount, saw branching antlers on every deer's head that started up before him, as he rushed wildly in the chase.

Thomas delighted in telling stories of these hunts. They were full of adventure. The gay huntsmen, leaving all care behind, were as full of practical jokes as school-boys. On the breaking up of the camp the deer were divided out and taken home, some of them in their skins and with antlers on.

Thomas was in the habit of throwing his gun across his saddle-bow whenever he rode out into his fields, with the hope of getting a shot at a deer or a wild turkey. One day a gobbler started up at a distance of about fifty yards in front of him, and ran down the road. He fired and killed him, the bullet running along the spine and through the neck. Thomas's eyes were strong and far-sighted. He could read the name of an incoming steamer at Pass Christian before any one else present could make out the form of a letter. His eyes were not readily forgotten by any one who had ever seen him. Madame Desrayaux, the head of a French "pensionnat" in New Orleans, said that she could not recall the face of any of the fathers of her young ladies except Colonel Dabney's. Some of these she saw every year. She had seen him but once, as his daughter was with her but one winter. But she could never forget his eyes.

CHAPTER IX.

A SOUTHERN PLANTER'S WIFE.

It has already been said that in 1845 Pass Christian was chosen as a summer resort for the family. Eight happy summers were spent there. Thomas and Sophia enjoyed the good society, and soon made warm friends among the residents. It was a sort of Paradise to the children. Books and studies were left behind,—very little was thought of but bathing and crabbing and fishing, rowing, sailing, swimming, picking up shells and "fiddler-crabs," and trying to gather the pale pink sand-flowers, that withstood so much tossing from the sea-breezes, but fell in pieces with the lightest touch of the human hand. In the long summer mornings we ran just as wild as we pleased. In the afternoons we must be dressed and be civilized. At the Pass we took our dancing lessons. Our mother took as many of us out airing as the family carriage, reinforced by two ponies, could carry. One of the children heard a neighbor say, as the carriage drove by with the mother in the midst of the little flock, that when Mrs. Dabney went driving she took the whole Dabney family with her. The mother was only amused, and filled her carriage as full as ever. When the Baroness Bunsen's tenth child was born, she felt that she had never loved a baby so dearly,—her motherliness had increased with each child that came. It was so in Sophia's case. She became so accustomed to the noise of young children that she seemed quite unconscious of it, but missed it painfully if separated from her children. Her motherliness extended over the whole plantation. She had a special eye and care for any neglected or unfortunate or ill-treated negro child, and would contrive to have such cases near her. One deformed, sickly girl, who was of no value in any sense, she took to the Pass one summer for the benefit of the sea-bathing. In the Burleigh household of servants there was usually some young negro so hopelessly dull that her own mother would not try to teach her to sew or to do other useful things. Under the sheltering wing of the mistress this girl would be patiently taught to do many things. Sophia was aware that this was not the way to have her household ordered in the best style. She was quite indifferent to the public opinion that required only fine-looking, thoroughly trained servants about the establishment of a gentleman. Many of her servants were intelligent, and filled their departments well, and the dull one was screened by being kept in the nursery and about her. The objects of her patience and kindness were devoted to her and proud of her favor. In many instances they became much better instructed than would have been thought possible by one less conscientious and full of faith than herself.

She felt for her house servants on Sundays, and allowed the cook and dining-room servants to put substitutes in their places, as they were more confined than the others. They had pride in their office, and instructed the substitutes so successfully that very little difference was perceived. But now and then a ludicrous mistake was made in the table attendance. One day Sophia asked one of these substitutes to give her a potato. A hand was promptly thrust across the table over the heads of the children, the potato seized, and then, without a misgiving, deposited on the plate of the mistress at the head of the table. She gave no sign of disapproval, receiving it as if it had been handed her in a proper manner.

She often found difficulty in controlling her laughter. It was contagious and very peculiar. She gave scarcely a sound. Everything about her was soft,—her voice, her manner, and her laugh was almost inaudible. But it was irresistible. Every one in the room joined in, whether they knew the cause of amusement or not. She frequently held one hand over her face, down which the tears were running. With the other she was making signals of distress.* Much as these occa-

---

* "The last remark was levelled at her mother, who had a singular way

sions were enjoyed by those around her, it was to herself a real regret that she was so childlike in her merriment. She learned to dread certain stories and allusions, as they invariably threw her into one of these fits of laughing. Her children and husband, who naturally most delighted in seeing her laugh, were cautioned by her not to bring these things up. She assured them with an earnestness that they felt obliged to respect that she suffered physically as well as mentally in her effort at self-control.* A constant smile was on the mother's face even when she was alone, and oftentimes continued when she was asleep.

Thomas's devotion to her and trust in her judgment increased with every year of their married life. He often said that her judgment was better than his even in business, and that every mistake of his life had been committed on the occasions when he had failed to consult her. When the children asked his consent to anything his invariable answer was, "Go to your mother." This was so well understood that the reply to this was, "Mamma sent me to you," as she did when in doubt. His delicate, chivalrous attentions to her were unceasing. He delighted in teasing her, too, because she looked so young and pretty when her blushes were brought up by his raillery. One unceasing occasion of blushing on her part was when he would playfully threaten to sing to their assembled sons and daughters, now growing to be great boys and girls, the song that had won her young heart. He called this a "Dieaway," and the first line was, "Sweet Sophy, the girl that I love." It seemed to be the paraphrase of some song that he had adopted to suit his needs when he saw that a rival lover was in higher favor than himself,

---

of laughing; to wit, shaking all over, without emitting the slightest sound, while big tears rolled down her cheeks. Alice was the idol of her heart, and her queer freaks of vivacious drollery often set her mother off, as at present, into uncontrollable undulations of entirely inaudible laughter."—*Don Miff*, p. 69.

* Sarah Dabney inherited her mother's laugh. "I try to think of all the dead people that I know, but I cannot stop laughing," the little child said, after one of these fits of uncontrollable laughter in school.

—this was the account that he gave of it, and he said that it turned the scale in his favor. After this prelude, which was delicious to the listening children, he would begin on the first line with every sign of an intention of going through to the end. But her violent blushes and entreaties always brought it to a close after the singing of the first line. He was tenderly solicitous about her health, and in a constant state of anxiety if she were away from home. He especially disliked to have her go out in the carriage unaccompanied by himself. When she went to Raymond,—to church or to spend the day,—his rule was to ride to meet her at the bridge, or before she reached the bridge, across the Tallahala Creek. This bridge, being on his land, was kept in good order. But she had once been alarmed on a bridge when the carriage-horses had stopped and run backward, and this left an unpleasant association in her mind. Often, when he found that the carriage had been ordered out by Sophia for some expedition, he would change all his own plans and go with her. He grew more and more tenderly anxious as years passed, and said that he was never easy a moment when she was away. He disliked to be in a carriage, and never got into one if he could avoid it. He rode by the side, putting his face to the window and talking to her, and bending to catch her answers. His wild thoroughbred Nimrod disliked this, and they had many battles over it. Nimrod would leap and spring off, and walk on his hind legs in a way that would have frightened most wives.

The journey to the Pass, a distance of one hundred and eighty miles, was made overland by Thomas and Sophia and the young children and servants. The older children, as time went on, were usually sent by the river by way of Vicksburg and New Orleans. The travellers by land were seven days on the road. For the first few years a camp equipage was carried along, and the whole party camped out at night. But Thomas became acquainted with the country people along the road, and found it more comfortable to engage supper and beds in the houses. This arrangement, so satisfactory to the heads of the family, was regretted by the children, who took the wildest delight in the camping-out experience. For them there was a charm in the long shadows of the tall pine-trees stretching away in the mysterious darkness like the pillars of some vast cathedral, in the soughing of the night-wind in the tree-tops, in the scent of the crushed pine-needles as we lay down to sleep, and even the far-away howling of the wolves, which we heard at one of our camping-places, had its fascination. Then it was full of interest to us to watch the pitching of the tent at night and the building of the great camp-fire, and to sit around the fire while the busy servants prepared the meals.

Thomas set out on this journey to and from the Pass on the same day each year. The country people knew when to expect him. A stranger passing through the country one of these years saw such extensive arrangements for supper going forward that he asked why so many chickens, etc., were being prepared. The answer was that Colonel Dabney and his family always came on this day each year. He was looked for at the Pass at about two o'clock on the seventh day of the journey. One day several gentlemen were conversing at the Pass; one of them looked at his watch, and remarked that Colonel Dabney would be along in about five minutes. He went on to say that he had not heard from him since parting with him at the Pass on the preceding summer; but he knew his punctual habits. He had scarcely gotten through saying this when the carriage and wagon and two or three outriders appeared in view, and Thomas Dabney was taking off his hat to the group. An old friend of his was boasting to him one day that he had never been too late for a steamboat or a train. Thomas said that he could say more, he had never been near being too late.

The most remarkable instance of his punctuality is in connection with one of his visits to his mother. He wrote to her that one year from the date of his letter he would be in Richmond. He did not mention this again in his letters to her. She knew his way, and on the day set she drove in from Mount Prospect in her carriage to meet him.

The people in the "piney woods" counties of Mississippi, through which the road from Burleigh to Pass Christian lay, were almost totally uneducated. They had but little use for money, subsisting on the products of their little patches, and cows, pigs, and fowls. They were frequently "squatters," living on government lands. They raised a bale or two of cotton each year to clothe the family and provide for other simple needs. They had no cotton-gin, but separated the seed from the lint with their fingers. The women spun and wove by hand; with bark and roots of different kinds they dyed the cloth intended for the men, but for other purposes it was left in its native whiteness. The women and girls, of whom there seemed to be a good many in most of the houses, dressed in white from head to foot. The beds were white, white hangings covered the wall in different places, and every shelf and dresser had its snowy drapery. They showed ingenuity in varying the patterns of the fringes and edges that bordered these simple decorations. The chairs were made of white wood, and were scrubbed until they were almost as snowy as the cotton fabrics. The effect was very neat and pleasing. One of these simple people said that Mrs. Dabney was her idea of how a queen must look.

The hair of the children was, up to the age of ten years, so light as to be almost white; it looked like the snowy, silvery hair that comes with great age.

One man, Mr. Holyfield, was so proud of the single letter that he had received in his life that it was posted up on the inside of his door. Here, year by year, we read it. They had a way of not undressing at night, and were quite startled at the first sight of a lady in a night-gown. It was our grandmamma Hill. One of her family was hastily summoned, and the inquiry made if the old lady thought that she was going to die. They thought that she was attiring herself in a shroud.

Our dear mother was known as a friend to the peddlers who come about the country with packs on their backs. They were disliked by many planters, but

Thomas let her have her way in helping them. One day her son Edward was in Vicksburg buying clothes, and gave his name to the shopkeeper. The man asked if he were a son of Colonel Dabney, and being answered in the affirmative, was warm in his expressions of gratitude. He had been a peddler, he said, and had been most kindly treated at Burleigh. He had heard Mrs. Dabney say to her husband, "This man looks sick. Why do you not give him a horse?" "Certainly, my dear," was the answer, and when he got ready to tie his pack up, a horse was given to him.

Another peddler who had been helped by her is now the owner of a piano-store, and loses no opportunity of trying to serve her children, expressing a grateful recollection of her kindness. One day a peddler offered her ten dollars for a blind mule that he had seen in the stable. The mule was never used, but was fed and cared for on account of past services. She told him that she would not sell the poor beast, but she would give him to him on a certain condition. This condition was that if he grew tired of him he would not sell him, but bring him back to her. The promise was given. But the mule was fat and strong, and a good price was offered by some one, and the peddler sold him. He was a young German. It so happened that another German was in the Burleigh house at the time of this transaction, engaged in papering the walls. He was incensed that the lady's kindness should have met with such return at the hands of one of his countrymen. He resolved to vindicate the honor of the Fatherland by beating the recreant peddler every time that he met him. Mrs. Dabney remonstrated seriously, and plead the cause of the peddler. But it was of no avail.

The paper-hanger gave the peddler two beatings, and tried to beat him a third time. But the peddler turned on him, and gave him such a drubbing that the man was content to let him alone in the future. Several years after this two of Thomas's daughters were at Cooper's Wells for a few days. Finding that they needed some ribbons and other trifles, they sent their maid out to buy them. She returned with the things, and all the money that had been handed her. The shopkeeper had asked who her young mistresses were, and on hearing their name, had refused to receive payment. No one of that family could pay for anything in his shop, he said. On investigation, he turned out to be one of the peddlers whom our mother had helped.

When the fields were burned, in preparation for another crop, the fires, unless well managed, sometimes did mischief. Not infrequently, too, the negroes in their coon-hunts left their half-extinguished torches about, with no thought of the dangerous proximity of valuable property. One Sunday the cry was raised that the fences were burning. The master hurried to the fire with the men who could be called, and after a hard fight it was put out. Edward, who was now quite a lad, had run to the fire. He perceived that another part of the fence was afire and that it was fast running along the dried grass to the ginhouse. There was no time to get help. He beat it out and subdued it unassisted, and was nearly fainting when his father found him. He sent him back to the house, while he and the negroes completed the work. Edward did not tell any one of what he had done. When his father came, he said that the boy had saved ten thousand dollars for him a few hours before, at the risk of his life. Thomas did not readily express his affection for his children at this period of his life, but a few words, "That was right, my son," or "my child," with the fond, lingering touch on the head, were felt to mean far more than the words expressed.

CHAPTER X.

A SOUTHERN PLANTER.

PERHAPS no life was more independent than that of a Southern planter before the late war. One of the Mississippi neighbors said that he would rather be

Colonel Dabney on his plantation than the President of the United States.

Managing a plantation was something like managing a kingdom. The ruler had need of a great store, not only of wisdom, but of tact and patience as well.

When there was trouble in the house the real kindness and sympathy of the servants came out. They seemed to anticipate every wish. In a thousand touching little ways they showed their desire to give all the comfort and help that lay in their power. They seemed to claim a right to share in the sorrow that was their master's, and to make it their own. It was small wonder that the master and mistress were forbearing and patient when the same servants who sorrowed with them in their affliction should, at times, be perverse in their days of prosperity. Many persons said that the Burleigh servants were treated with over-indulgence. It is true that at times some of them acted like spoiled children, seeming not to know what they would have. Nothing went quite to their taste at these times. The white family would say among themselves, "What is the matter now? Why these martyr-like looks?" Mammy Maria usually threw light on these occasions. She was disgusted with her race for posing as martyrs when there was no grievance. A striking illustration of this difficulty in making things run smoothly occurred one summer, when the family was preparing to go to the Pass. The mistress made out her list of the servants whom she wished to accompany her. She let them know that they were to be allowed extra time to get their houses and clothes in order for the three months' absence from home. Some of them answered with tears. It would be cruel to be torn from home and friends, perhaps husband and children, and not to see them for all that time. Sophia regretfully made out a new list, leaving out the most clamorous ones. There were no tears shed nor mournful looks given by the newly elected, for dear to the colored heart was the thought of change and travel. It was a secret imparted by Mammy Maria to her mistress that great was the disappointment of those who had over-acted their part, thereby cutting themselves off from a much-coveted pleasure.

Thomas was never an early riser. He maintained that it did not so much matter when a man got up as what he did after he was up. He woke up in the morning as gay as a boy, and when Sophia, fully dressed, informed him that it was time to get up, received the announcement with one of his liveliest tunes. That was the only answer usually to the first summons or two. She could not help laughing; no one could who heard him. When she remonstrated he sang only the more gayly.

Every one knew when he was awake by the merry sounds proceeding from his chamber. He did not go in to breakfast till he had danced the Fisher's Hornpipe for the baby, singing along with the steps and drawing an imaginary bow across imaginary strings. All the nursery flocked about him at the signal, one or two of the little tots joining in the capering. This habit he kept up to the end of his life, and his grown children would smile as they heard the cheery notes sounding through the house on his awaking. Then he walked with his quick, half-military step, the laugh still on his face, into the dining-room, where breakfast was already in progress. It was not a ceremonious meal he maintained. Dinner was a ceremonious meal in his house. Every one was expected to be ready, and sitting with the family in the hall or drawing-room or dining-room not less than five minutes before the last bell was rung. If there was a lady guest, the master of the house handed her in to dinner. If the guest was a gentleman, he was expected to hand in one of the ladies, as Thomas showed by offering his arm to one.

He was the life of the company, as he sat at the foot of his own table. Many of his most amusing anecdotes and stories, as well as those of deeper meaning, are associated with the dinner-table. No one could fill his place when he was absent.

He was often absent, being called from home by matters of business or duty or pleasure. In addition to spending some time every other summer with his mother in Virginia, and going occasionally to New York, and two weeks every fall on the deer-hunt, he made frequent visits to New Orleans, Vicksburg, and Jackson, and occasional visits to other places. He rarely spent a week without passing a day with Augustine.

In travelling on steamboats, if alone, he always selected for himself the state-room just over the boiler. If the boat were to blow up, he said he should prefer being killed outright to running a risk of being only half killed, or of being maimed for life. It need hardly be added that he found no difficulty in securing his chosen state-room.

His interest in public affairs sometimes called him off to distant cities.

January always found him in New Orleans for a three weeks' visit. After attending to his business with his commission merchants and buying the plantation supplies, he enjoyed the pleasures of this brilliant city. He was a member of the Boston Club, and he there met the most interesting and distinguished citizens of New Orleans. One of the chief attractions of this place was the game of whist to be had there. He was considered authority on whist. A game that he once played at the Greenbrier White Sulphur Springs, in Virginia, was considered remarkable. His old friend, Mr. John Tabb, of Whitemarsh, Gloucester County, had invited him to a game of whist in his cottage at the Springs. Three whist-players of known skill were invited to play with him, and a company invited to witness the game. During the evening a singular incident took place. Twelve cards had been played out of each hand, leaving each gentleman with his thirteenth card only. At this point Thomas Dabney said to them that he wished to call their attention to a singular coincidence in the fact that every man present held in his hand a nine. When the cards were laid on the table this was seen to be true, to the surprise of all. One gentleman said he could show a more remarkable thing than that, it was the man who knew it.

He was never but once a candidate for any office in

Mississippi; that was for the State Legislature. He was defeated by one vote. The contest was strictly a party one, and all the candidates on the Whig ticket were defeated by their Democratic opponents.

Thomas Dabney was enthusiastic in his admiration of Henry Clay, and followed his career with the deepest interest. He seemed almost to know Mr. Clay's speeches by heart, and delighted in talking of him and quoting his brilliant sayings. "I had rather be right than President" was a great utterance, he said. He contracted a warm personal friendship for him, and was anxious to accept Mr. Clay's invitation to visit him at Ashland. But my mother objected. She knew that the great statesman had his failings as well as his virtues. She had a very gentle way of objecting, but her gentle way was a law to him. He yielded, and did not go. He greatly admired S. S. Prentiss, and enjoyed having a visit from him at the Pass Christian house.

The *National Intelligencer* was the most ably conducted paper in the United States, in his opinion. He kept it on file. In sending on his subscription his custom was to send twenty-five dollars at a time.

His lively interest in public affairs made him write a good deal for the public press. Unfortunately, the many papers stowed away with his articles in them have been destroyed.

Tutors were employed to teach in the family until the boys were old enough to be sent off to college. In order to make the boys study with more interest, the children of the neighbors were received into the school. When the three sons were sent off to college, a governess was employed to teach the daughters. The teachers at Burleigh were treated like guests and friends. Thomas said that he did not wish any but ladies to have the charge of his daughters, and they should be treated as ladies. Miss Dyott, the beloved governess, who lived in the house five years, loved the family like dear relatives. When Mrs. Moncure's daughter was taken as a pupil along with his daughters, he handed to Miss Dyott, in addition to her salary, the money paid for this child's tuition. She objected, and said that another pupil or two would really make her school-duties more interesting to his daughters and to herself; but he was firm, and she had to receive the money.

During her stay at Burleigh, when there was company to dinner, the master of the house took her in on his arm. At her death, many years later, the Burleigh family stood around her grave with her family as mourners.

It may be said that all honest men who had business transactions with Thomas Dabney became his personal friends. It was evident that he did not wish to get the advantage of any one. Several of his overseers soon became able to buy farms of their own, and grew to be rich men. He was so liberal in his dealings with them, that it was said they made as much in fattening and selling their riding-horses as their salaries amounted to. He was often cheated and imposed upon. Instead of worrying over it, he said he was very glad that he had found the scoundrels out.

The first tutor in the family was a young Virginian of high culture. He taught the sons—Charles, Virginius, and Edward—for nine years, and during the last few years some of the older girls went into the school-room along with their brothers. Thomas regarded this young man almost like a son. Always unsuspicious, he was slow in perceiving that he was falling into dissipated habits. He was attached to Thomas, and valued his good opinion so much that he was able to control himself when with him. But he found that the love of drink was getting too strong for him. He joined a temperance society, hoping to get self-control in this way. In an hour of weakness he broke his pledge. He no longer had respect for himself, and resolved on self-destruction. But he could not carry it into effect while under the influence of the strong character of Thomas Dabney.

When the time came for the household to go to Pass Christian, whither the tutors and governesses were always pressed to go as guests, he steadily refused to accompany them, as he had done in the preceding summer. He had made every arrangement to kill himself as soon as Thomas should be gone. "I have too much respect for Colonel Dabney to kill myself in his house," he had said to a gentleman in the neighborhood. He went to a neighboring plantation and cut his throat that night. The body was sent to Raymond for interment, and was put by the side of the two boys, Thomas and James Dabney. At once, on hearing of this, Thomas wrote to Augustine to have the remains of the unhappy man taken up. No suicide, he said, should rest by the side of his pure children.

It is a singular coincidence that the suicide of another teacher in his family, a German music-teacher, took place during his absence, and it was thought that if Thomas Dabney had been at home it would not have occurred. This man became so much attached to him as to be hardly happy out of his house. His visits to Burleigh became more and more frequent and longer, until finally he had his trunks brought with him. Thomas was passionately fond of music. He had in vain tried to persuade an accomplished Belgian violinist to move to Burleigh with his wife and child to live there. The hundred-dollar bill that accompanied the invitation had its effect, and he spent some weeks there. It is possible that he would have prolonged his stay but for being afraid to play on his violin on Sundays. He consulted the German governess in the family on this point in his native language, the French, in the hearing of some of the family, who understood French. The governess advised him not to play on his violin. So Sunday got to be a long day with him, and he and his wife and little "Carlito" went away. Sophia was not sorry to see him go, although when he played with the tears running down his face, she herself felt moved by the divine music which seemed to come from his very heart. All the more she felt that her husband and children were getting too much absorbed by it. Sometimes the artist improvised for hours, walking up and down the room, his eyes rolled upward in an ecstasy,—then exhaustion followed, and strong coffee was called for to steady the overstrained nerves. At these times the whole house was absorbed in the musician and his music. It was all too exciting and intoxicating for every-day life.

The violin was Thomas's favorite instrument. The German music-teacher did not play on the violin, but he was a brilliant performer on the piano and a good backgammon player. These two accomplishments, with a quiet, unobtrusive manner, made him a welcome inmate of the house. He was careless and indolent in his music lessons, and these had ceased long before he came to the house to live. But he was ready to play when music was wanted in the evenings, and was never tired of the mid-day game of backgammon, when Thomas came back from his rides on the plantation.

One summer, when the whole family went to Virginia, he concluded that he would stay on at Burleigh rather than give up his room. He explained once, when invited to spend the night away from Burleigh, that he could not sleep well except at "home." The family stayed longer than he expected in Virginia. They were detained by the yellow fever, which was raging in some of the cities through which the route home lay. The man grew morbidly anxious to see Thomas, the only human being for whom he was ever known to show affection in America. He went to Vicksburg to meet him, and there heard that there was still further delay, as the fever had broken out afresh. He became despondent and began to drink. When Thomas reached home he had been dead two days. He had blown his brains out with a revolver.

Charles, the eldest son, was ready for college in the fall of 1846. He was at this time sixteen years old. He was sent to the college of William and Mary in Virginia. In the following winter Thomas had the only serious illness that attacked him during the fifty years that he lived in Mississippi. On February 13 Sophia wrote to her son:

"MY DEAR CHARLEY,—This day I have received two letters from you, one dated the 20th of January to me and the other the 1st of February to Virginius and your papa. I have been uneasy about you, for I had not received a letter from you for three weeks. But your papa had more philosophy than I had. He said he was not at all uneasy. . . . Your papa is a good deal better. To-day he ate two doves at dinner, and he and Mr. Garlick drove out in the carriage. He has a very great appetite. He is not allowed to sit at my table. . . .

"I am afraid you will be disappointed when you see Sarah. She is at an ugly age. Sue has improved very much. I think she is equally as pretty as Sarah is now. But you have not the least idea how perfectly beautiful Emmy is. When Mr. Dimitry first saw her he was astonished, and exclaimed that she was a magnificent child. I never saw such a pair of eyes. Her skin is very fair, her cheeks rosy, and her countenance all amiability. She is very much caressed. Sue talks more about you than any of the children. She dreams about you occasionally. She dreamed a few nights ago that you had come home and brought a wife with you. She was quite disappointed when she opened her eyes and found it was a dream." . . .

Before this letter was sealed Sophia was bidden to add a postscript:

"Dear Charles, I have now something to write for your papa, as he is not able to write. He says that he is dissatisfied with your way of going on. You are spending too much money. You speak of the one hundred and eighty-seven dollars lately received with a levity that shocked him exceedingly. You say that it will last you some time. He says you are right, for it will last you till next fall. Are you aware that you have had about nine hundred dollars from your father? Do you think that he can afford such sums to you and do justice to his other children? If you do you are mistaken. But you know better. Be wise, therefore, and retrace your steps before it is too late. Your father will write as soon as he can. Your devoted mother,
"S. D."

It must have cost the mother-heart a pang to write thus to her dutiful, affectionate boy. Not until more than two months had passed was this matter explained.

T. S. D. TO HIS SON CHARLES.

"RAYMOND, 19th April, 1847.

"MY DEAR SON,—Your mother's letter to you of the 15th was read by me and approved. This is probably as much as you would wish me to say, but I shall say something more, as it is due to you. To begin with your mother's postscript, written at my dictation. I made her say that the one hundred and eighty-seven dollars would last you some time; 'Yes, it shall last you some time; until next fall.' Your reply to this is in these words: 'Now, my dear father, I will certainly make it last as long as I can. It will last me unless I have a doctor's bill to pay, which I hope will not be the case. I know how hard you work for this money, etc., etc.,' and, after saying other things, you conclude with, 'If I have been too extravagant this year, I will not be so again.' This reply does you more honor than any act of your life. It is a perfectly dutiful, respectful, and affectionate reply to a cruel and unjust injunction from your father, carrying with it an equally cruel and unjust imputation. But you were not unmindful that it came from your father. I will now explain. During my illness I was kept for many days under the influence of opium in large quantities. But I slept not. On the contrary, my imagination was haunted by horrible visions. I took up strange fancies having no foundation, but firmly believed in, notwithstanding. I thought of you, my absent one, when all others were freed from their earthly cares by sleep. During this time letters accumulated; and your mother asked me one day (it appears to have been on the 13th of February by your letter) if I would like to hear any of them read. I told her to read yours to me, but none others. One of yours acknowledged the receipt of the one hundred and eighty-seven dollars, with the remark that you would not have to call for any more for some time. Now, although I well knew before I was taken sick that you would want this one hundred and eighty-seven dollars by the time you could get it from Gloucester, and although I entertained great doubts about its sufficiency to carry you through the session, yet, at that moment of a distempered imagination, your remark above quoted struck me as extraordinary. I thought you had had a great deal of money. I confounded what I gave Christopher with what I gave you,—that you had each received two hundred and fifty dollars, and that you had received a like sum from your grandmother. This fancy of a sick brain became a fixed idea, and remained so even after my recovery; for it never occurred to me that it was false, and, consequently, it could need no investigation. I never knew better until I read the statement in your letter of the 2d instant. I have now acknowledged my fault; not esteeming it as a degradation for a parent to acknowledge his faults to his children. On the contrary, I should hold that parent irretrievably disgraced who should make the futile attempt (it must ever be futile) to conceal them by boldness or by an affected obtuseness.

"Under all the painful circumstances of the two letters from your mother and the one from me of the 1st of March, I cannot blame you much for your propositions concerning the army and navy and West Point. These propositions, coming at the time they do, and coupled with the assurance or remark that should you get to West Point you will not want me to give you anything more, looks as though you apprehended I might feel you to be burdensome. Now, my dear child, how you have mistaken me if this is, or ever was, for one moment your idea. You know but little of your father, of the depth of his love for you, of the vigils he has kept, is keeping, and expects to keep, till the last pulsation of his heart, on your behalf if you think this of him. No, my dear child, you never were a burden to me. The day you are felt to be such, or the day on which any of my children are felt to be such, will be a sad one in their poor father's house,—for poor he will then be indeed!

"I never *made* any objection to your going to West

Point, because I consider it a good school, where a good, though not a perfect, education may be acquired. I therefore acceded to what I believed to be your wish, and made an effort to get you in there. This I did because I am not one of those who think that parents know everything and children nothing. But the feature in it which would exempt me from paying your way is a positive and very great objection with me. It was not necessary that I should say so at that time, and I did not, because I did not choose to object *in any way* to promoting your wish. I will not make the objection insurmountable now, but will keep a standing application there in your behalf if you wish it. I will make it my business to interest General Foote, one of our Senators, in your behalf if it be possible for a Whig to find any favor with the present administration. As to what you say about the navy or getting a lieutenancy in the army, I cannot think of such a thing, my dear son, as your education would be nothing if arrested now, as it would be in such a case. Indeed, I hope that those notions have been put to flight by what I have already written.

"I shall not wish you to be more economical than you have been. You might have spared the assertion that you lost none of it at cards, as neither your mother nor myself ever doubted your honor for the millionth part of a second. You will not sit at cards during your college life, because I asked you not to do it. With the degree of A.M. in your pocket you can do as you wish in this respect.

"Unless you expect me to be more unfortunate in my efforts than I have been, I see no reason why you should say that you will want nothing more from me than a good education. I expect to educate my children without impairing my property. If I do this, they will divide what I have and what I may hereafter acquire (if any) equally among them.

"If you would not mortify me you will not let me find you next summer without an ample supply of seasonable clothing and every other thing proper for a gentleman. Reward such servants and others as de-

serve rewards at your hands. Do not leave Williamsburg without impressing it indelibly on the recollections of all with whom you have had associations that you are a gentleman. It is too late now for me to make any remittance to enable you to meet these views, but you can call upon your grandmother for any sum that may be necessary, and I will return it to her on the 1st of July.
"Your ever devoted father,
"THOS. S. DABNEY."

In the summer of 1846 Sophia wrote to her husband:
"PASS CHRISTIAN.

"I do want to see you very much, but I want you to remain a little longer with your friends, your mother particularly, you have not seen her for such a length of time. I know how I should feel when so long separated from a beloved son. . . . I do not like to make you unhappy one moment. I tell you all my grievances and all my joys."

She had made some allusion to the drunkenness of the tutor. Her English gardener had given her trouble in the same way.

On the 4th of November of this fall (1846) the seventh son was born. It was the anniversary of the birth of Sarah, now eight years old. She had received the name of her father's mother, and the infant boy was called Benjamin, after his father.

The Mexican war fever was running high now. Thomas had given his epaulettes and his two-yards-wide silken sash, that could pass through a lady's finger-ring, to the captain of the Raymond Fencibles. Even the little children in the nursery cried out that the Mexicans were firing when the fire crackled. Charles had a leaning towards a soldier's life, and his ardor was inflamed. His pleadings to be allowed to follow a military career were so earnest that his parents yielded a reluctant consent. The Mississippi Senator, Governor Henry S. Foote, was a personal friend. Application was made through him to the War Office, and the appointment for West Point came in due time. Charles knew that at heart his parents were unwilling for him to go into the army, and after receiving the commission he felt that he could not conscientiously act in opposition to their known wishes. He decided to throw up the appointment, thus sacrificing his ambition to filial obedience.

A letter written before he had made up his mind to this sacrifice is not without interest, as it shows the enthusiasm of the boy, and we can the better understand the effort that it cost him to give up all hope of being a soldier:

CHARLES TO HIS FATHER.

"WILLIAMSBURG, April 9, 1847.

"According to the most disinterested accounts I have seen of the battle of Buena Vista, our gallant regiment has covered itself with laurels that will never fade. Taylor, too, has shown himself to be one of the ablest tacticians the world has ever produced. Twelve months ago you thought him one of the most egregious fools that ever headed an army. I recollect saying to you at the time that there was no officer, in my opinion, who could better represent the true character of the American soldier. Our volunteers, too, how much were they hooted at, and particularly their commanding officers! The mortality among our colonels in the late battle will show to the world that the highest compliment that can be paid to any soldier, whether regular or volunteer, is to say that he is equal to an American volunteer colonel. Out of six colonels that we had on the field five were either killed or wounded, and every one who was not instantaneously killed fought lying on his back. After this battle we may all be proud to say that we are Mississippians. Look at the veteran coolness with which they received the charge of the Mexican cavalry. Look at the Southern impetuosity with which they threw themselves into every dangerous position. The killed and wounded all go to prove it. Out of four hundred, one hundred and fifty were either killed or wounded, a loss almost unparalleled. Her glory has cost her much, but to have lost her honor would have been an expense far greater. The Raymond Fencibles, from the list of her killed and wounded, has suffered greatly, and may truly be said to have performed its duty,—nearly half either killed or wounded, perhaps more than half. I do not know how small it was at the battle. Judging from the regiment, which was nine hundred and thirty when I was at Vicksburg, and now only four hundred, I think that more than half were killed. Downing I do not suppose was there; perhaps for the best; he might have been killed. He distinguished himself at Monterey, so much so that General Taylor mentioned him in his despatches. Your epaulettes and sash could not have been intrusted in better hands. . . . Vera Cruz is reported to be taken; if so, we will certainly get to Mexico now, unless the Mexicans sue for peace very shortly. General Scott is pushing ahead very rapidly. We are certainly a land of soldiers. . . .

"I have already told you, I know, my dear father, about the war news, and told you only those things that you knew. But you must excuse me. I know that had I been with you I should certainly have talked in the same way. I have no one here to talk to me about the Mississippi regiment, and therefore I have to write you whatever I want to say about it. Perhaps the *Raymond Gazette* may contain a more detailed account of the conduct of the Raymond Fencibles. If you have it I would be very glad for you to send it to me. You have no idea how much interest I take in everything connected with that company. . . .

"I do not think that I will ever come here again. There is too much frolicking and too much to attract one's attention. There are three or four, or sometimes fifteen, drunken students here a day. As far as the faculty is concerned, it is second to no college in America, but a great deal more depends on the student than on the professors. It matters not how learned the professors are, if the students frolic they will not learn much. . . .

"I wish most seriously that I had gone as a private in the Raymond Fencibles. . . . I can learn how to be a fine soldier, which is all that I want to be." . . .

CHAPTER XI.

HOME LIFE.

It was just after the close of the war with Mexico—in the summer of 1848—that General Zachary Taylor, who had been nominated by the Whigs for the Presidency, and was travelling from point to point, came to Pass Christian.

Our father's well-known and stanch Whig principles clearly entitled him to take a leading part in the political demonstrations which were here held in honor of the victorious general; and he was, accordingly, made chairman of the committee of reception. After meeting him at the boat, he brought him in his private carriage to his own house, which was at that time one of the largest in the village, and singularly well adapted (with its veranda stretching seventy feet along the front and proportionally wide) to accommodate the throng of people who were to come on the morrow to be presented to General Taylor. The following morning at an early hour the visitors began to arrive, of both sexes and of all ages,—in carriages, wagons, on horseback, on foot, and in boats. All day long as they came, they were received by Thomas and introduced to the general, and after a little time had been allowed for conversation, were invited to the refreshment-tables.

With unflagging zeal throughout this summer's day he looked after the welfare and saw to the comfort of all who came. If he singled out any one and showed him any special attention, it was the humblest there, —a lad, whose poor old mother dwelt in a dilapidated hut, and whose worldly possessions could well have been represented by zero. Him he led up to the general, saying, "Allow me to introduce to you ——, the son of my old friend, Mrs. ——. Who knows but what he, too, may not be a candidate for the highest office within the gift of the people?" General Taylor, after cordially shaking hands with the lad, put his hand on his head, and in the kindest tones said, "Yes, my son, to him who earnestly strives all things are possible."

The hero of many a hotly-contested battle won the hearts of us children (for most of us were children in 1848) by his guileless ways and simple, unaffected manners.

There came with him his suite, consisting of Colonel Craughn, a gray-headed veteran, who, when a young officer, at the head of but forty men, had obstinately and victoriously held a log fort against the repeated assaults of hundreds of hostile Indians, and Major Garnett, then a brave and handsome young soldier, who afterwards, having risen to the rank of general, fell fighting gallantly for his section in the late civil war. And in addition to these two, his own son, Captain Richard Taylor, who, in the same war, rose to eminence by reason of his gallantry and ability.*

Thomas had all the nursery, as well as the older children, to go to the pier to see General Taylor land. Some of the little ones became alarmed at the crowd and the shouting and began to cry. Thomas took a child on each arm, and, with a third clinging to his leg, received the hero of Mexico. The old soldier had a father's heart under his rough exterior. He kissed the little trio amid the waving of hats and cheers of the hundreds gathered to welcome him.

During his visit to Thomas an incident occurred that amused him.

He served one of the little girls sitting near him at table to butter, on which she frankly informed him that her mamma had forbidden her to eat that butter, that it was intended for him. The good-natured general led the laugh that followed this little disclosure.

---

* The above account of General Taylor's visit was written by Edward.

He was reminded by this, he said, of a little scene that he had witnessed at a house in which he was a visitor. Happening to look out of his bedroom window before going down to breakfast, he saw a lady explaining to her child how she was to behave herself, "for General Taylor is here," she said, and she was emphasizing her instructions by shaking a switch over the youngster's head.

During the week in the Pass Christian house he said many interesting things. One day he spoke of the impossibility of satisfying people in this world, and illustrated it with an incident in his own experience. Hearing an old and favorite negro servant of his say that she would be perfectly happy if she had a hundred dollars, he gave a hundred dollars to her. As he left the room, he heard her say regretfully, "I wish that I had said two hundred."

MRS. MACON TO HER SON THOMAS DABNEY.

"MOUNT PROSPECT, October 5, 1848.

"That you have been highly complimented by General Taylor's marked attention to you there can be no doubt, and I congratulate you on the event. But, my son, take care. Flattery is an intoxicating draft: we all like it; but, although sweet to the taste, it sometimes leaves a bitter behind it. Cardinal Wolsey said too much honor would sink a navy. Dryden said honor is an empty bubble. So that too much importance should not be attached to it."

MRS. MACON TO HER SON THOMAS DABNEY.

"MOUNT PROSPECT, November 25, 1848.

... "I congratulate you and my country on General Taylor's election, and trust and hope our halcyon days are returning. ... The longer I live the less I think of earthly honors. General Taylor is a great man, and I hope he will honor the Presidency. It will not honor him, I think, after the scoundrels that preceded him. Only think of the changes in our country! I lived in the days that wise patriots ruled. Such men as we have in high offices now are not fit for door-keepers for them. In my day the suffrages of the people was a sure sign that the person voted for was worthy the trust given him, and now it is only a sign that the people are corrupt, and choose one of their own sort to help them out in their corruption.

... "I want to know the name of your daughter."

It was not surprising that one who had known General Washington personally, and to whom he was "Cousin George," should find the times degenerate under some, at least, of his successors.

The little girl referred to was Ida, born this fall.

CHARLES TO HIS MOTHER.

"UNIVERSITY OF VIRGINIA, All-Fools' Day, 1849.

... "I think father did precisely right in not recommending any one to General Taylor; for to recommend a person, however worthy he may be, to another upon whom you have no claim is a very delicate thing. I suppose Mr. Mayson is getting on well with the children. You have not mentioned anything about them of late. Tell the boys if they study hard now they will not find much difficulty at college. Just get their minds in good training and half the battle is accomplished. There are many young men here who have very good minds who cannot study. It is all owing to their not mastering their minds when young. That is an advantage which I have over many. My mind has always been completely under my control and well trained, though most unprofitably and unphilosophically employed while I was at school. ... Remember me to old Grannie Harriet. I know that it will please the old lady to know that I often think of her."

Some time after this Mrs. Lewis Chamberlayne wrote to Charles: "Your father has just written me of the death of old Harriet. He wrote of it as of the death of an old friend."

The almost fatherly feeling of this young brother of

nineteen for his younger brothers and sisters is shown in his letters at this period.

CHARLES TO HIS FATHER.

"Montrose, August 2, 1849.

"I promised that you should hear from me again on the same subject, and that I would endeavor to give some reasons why boys should be sent to a public school a year or two before entering college.

"First of all, confined at home as I was, and as I suppose my younger brothers will be if they follow the same course, they must necessarily be ignorant of the world, and also inexperienced in resisting the many temptations which await them when they come forth. They go immediately to college, the worst of all places, — a place in which vice appears in its most alluring and irresistible form. The transition is too sudden, — from a *nursery* to a *college* where they are treated as men, and where they feel it incumbent on themselves to act as such. Mistaken though in what they think becomes a man, how can it be expected that in ninety-nine cases out of a hundred they will not be guilty of the most foolish excesses? By what I have said I merely intend to give you a faint conception of what my feelings were when I went to college. I was certainly very ignorant of many things, which the simplicity of my first letters plainly indicates, which things I would have known had I gone to a public school or mixed much in society.

"In the second place, boys educated at home never go as well prepared in their studies. You can rarely find a *single* person (one person) able to prepare boys in Latin, Greek, mathematics, and French sufficiently to enter a HIGH class in a college of HIGH STANDING. College is no place to learn the rudiments of anything. It is expected that the boys should know them before they go. Consequently, they are not taught with any particular care. I knew a good deal of Latin and Greek when I went to college, but the inside of a mathematical or French book I had never seen. Now, my dear father, you cannot but be convinced of the insuperable disadvantages under which I entered college; and you cannot fail to pardon the warmth with which I advocate the pursuit of a different course with regard to my brothers. However, if you detect any error in my reasoning I hope you will not fail to say so. I know that I am not infallible. I have often thought wrong and done wrong, and been utterly unconscious of it at the time. I hope you will not think that I mean to blame any one with regard to the course that was pursued by me. (Yes, I do blame Mr. G. for pretending to prepare me for college when he never had seen the inside of one.) I know that it was your overfondness for me which made you keep me at home as long as you could. I am sensible, too, that you spared no pains to have me prepared in the very best way, and that you conscientiously believed that the one you had marked out was the very best,—as it certainly was the most expensive. The great care, then, with which you have watched over my education,—the many hours of solicitude which I have cost you,—all these, my dear father, conspire to make me still more sensible of what I owe you, and to incite me to still greater exertions; but, should the realization of my loftiest hopes be attained, I trust that I shall not be so narrow-minded as to believe that my debt is wholly paid. Under these circumstances, then, you cannot fail to pardon me for so much deploring the many disadvantages under which I entered the grand arena of education, and for lamenting that I cannot prove myself as worthy as I would wish of your great confidence and affection. I shall make the attempt to come up to your expectations,—in such a noble cause defeat itself will be glorious."

CHARLES TO HIS FATHER.

"University of Virginia, September 29, 1849.

. . . "I am truly glad that Sarah has been put with a governess. I have not been as much pleased at anything in a long time. She ought to have every advantage. There is a magnificence, a loftiness of character about her that I never saw in a child, and I can hardly say in a grown person. She is bound to be a great

woman, though she may live in retirement. I think
that her traits of character are more prominent than
those of any child I ever saw. Let her, then, have every
opportunity; and do not think that because she is a
woman any kind of education will be sufficient for her
to keep house. I know you do not think this, yet there
are many who constantly say that a woman ought not
to be well educated,—that any kind of education will
be enough for a housekeeper, and that a very intelligent and accomplished woman is likely to make a bad
wife. Of course those who say this possess the most
narrow, grovelling, and contemptible souls, which will
never soar beyond their own self-importance. And if
an educated woman does not make a good wife, it is
because the man who received her hand was unworthy
of it, and because it was the hand of a slave, and not
of a wife and an equal, that was the object of his desire.
My thus defending the fair sex will be ascribed to my
age. I have no particular one in view."

CHARLES TO HIS FATHER.

"UNIVERSITY OF VIRGINIA, March 5, 1850.

"I was not introduced to General Taylor. It would
have afforded me great pleasure; but he was to be there
so short a time, his presence was such a novelty, he
had done so much shaking of hands, and must have
been so tired, that I could not force myself into his
presence under the belief that there was a possibility
that the addition of any company whatsoever would
be agreeable. Dr. Chamberlayne was introduced to
him on the night of the 21st inst., and the old general
spoke of you, mother and the children with enthusiasm. . . . I have noticed the Whig and Democratic
parties very narrowly for the last month, and have come
to this conclusion without hesitation, viz., that THERE
IS NOT ANY DIFFERENCE at all between them. If you
ask a Democrat why he had rather Cass should have
been elected than Taylor, he will say, Because he is
safer on the Wilmot proviso. If you ask a Whig, he
will say that Taylor is the safer. The United States
Bank is dead forever. They differ, you see, only with

regard to men. . . . Those two men,* should there be a dissolution, will obtain the direction of affairs in the Southern republic. Calhoun has been at the point of death for some time, but I believe and sincerely trust that he is now better. He is the greatest statesman in America, and Lord Brougham says that we can only do him justice if we say in the world, not such an orator as Henry Clay, but as far above him as the great orb of heaven is above the glow-worm,—in purity resembling Washington, in intellect Jefferson. I am so glad that you have a portrait of him."

In May of the year 1850 the last son was born, and received his father's name, Thomas Smith.

SOPHIA DABNEY TO HER SON CHARLES.

"October, 1851.

"I shall enclose Sarah's last letter to you. I know it will please you, although it is not as good as some of her other letters. You must write to her occasionally, and give her your best advice, both as to her studies and as to her conduct in society; advice from an older brother always seems so interesting. Sarah will highly appreciate any advice from you, she is so much attached to you."

SOPHIA DABNEY TO HER SON CHARLES.

"January 14, 1852.

. . . "Busybody is sitting by me, every now and then putting the cork in the inkstand and begging for candy."

SOPHIA DABNEY TO HER SON CHARLES.

"Burleigh, May 4, 1852.

"I am truly thankful that I am able to write to you. . . . I was so unwell before the birth of my baby that I did not think it prudent for me to write. I had a great deal of headache, and it was increased by

---

* Jefferson Davis and John C. Calhoun.

writing. Often I felt a great desire to tell you what was going on here, for I knew that none of them knew how interesting it would be to you as well as I did. Nobody knows you as I do. I know you as well as I know myself. . . . Ben says he loves his brother Charles better than all his brothers. He says that he intends to live with you. . . . I must tell you that Sarah and Sue waited on me with so much kindness, kept everything so quiet, that enabled me to get well so quickly. I can go to the table now. My daughters have been great comforts to me. I do not think I shall regret that the youngest is a daughter. I call her Lelia."

SOPHIA DABNEY TO HER SON CHARLES.

"May 27, 1852.

. . . "The girls and boys have not returned from Mr. Mayson's wedding. No doubt they will have a great deal to write to you, for your papa returned yesterday, and seemed perfectly charmed with everything and everybody. He says that Sarah and Sue looked very well, and a great deal of attention was paid them. They were perfectly at their ease, like young ladies, at the same time as modest as possible. They were dressed beautifully,—that is, plain and elegant. They had their hair dressed by the hair-dresser at the hotel. . . . The bride's mother said to your papa that she hoped Mr. Mayson would like her family as much as he did ours. I suppose that Sarah and Sue have given you an account of the old bachelor, Colonel Hemingway. He seems to know everybody. Mr. Dabney says that he stuck to the 'two misses,' as he called Sarah and Sue, and paid every attention that was necessary. . . . I have been very nervous and weak since the birth of my little daughter, but I think I am getting better. I am driving out every day; that will restore me very soon."

T. S. D. TO HIS SON CHARLES.

"BURLEIGH, 30th May, 1852.

. . . "The children returned from Jackson yesterday in high glee, having been sufficiently attended to even had they been grown. They were called upon by the governor's family, but were unfortunately at Mrs. Saunders's boarding-house at the time. They called at the governor's mansion, and were equally unfortunate then, for the ladies were paying their respects to the bride at that hour. I will mention one more circumstance in connection with your little sisters of a very pleasant character. Mrs. Foote said that she wished me to introduce her to my daughters (this was at the wedding), to which I replied that they would highly appreciate the honor; and I was about to go after them, when she stopped me, and insisted upon being taken to them, they being in the other room at the time. She accordingly ran her arm through mine, and was conducted by me to them and introduced. The governor made me take him to them also, and he did not omit to express his admiration of them in very marked terms.

"I am happy to say to you, also, that the brothers were no discredit to the sisters. I had sent the boys to Vicksburg to rig out for the occasion, and they did not fail to do it *brown*. . . . And they conducted themselves with sufficient ease for boys of their age."

This wedding of our favorite tutor, Charles Mayson, was a real episode in our childhood. It was our first experience of going from home to anything like an evening company. Mr. Mayson had come from Jackson expressly to beg that his former pupils might be allowed to attend his marriage, as he felt that on account of their youth an invitation would hardly be successful if sent by letter. As he had foreseen, our mother was unwilling to trust children brought up in so secluded a way at a large fashionable wedding. But, to our delight, he overruled all objections, and we were allowed to go. These letters give a quaint description of the appearance and behavior of the party seen through the medium of our parents' eyes.

CHARLES TO HIS FATHER.

"CAMBRIDGE, June, 1852.

"The late nomination of the Whig party is such that it must strike the mind of every one. It shows a disposition on the part of the Northern Whigs which I had hoped did not exist. It was the triumph of section over section,—of Northern majority over Southern minority. It has thrown a gloom over the face of nearly every Whig student in college, and nine-tenths of the students, I believe, are Whigs. All, I may say, deplore the nomination of General Scott as the ruin of the Whig party and as the forerunner in all probability of new internal difficulties. All that remains now for us to do is to try our best to defeat him. I was proud to see the South so united in her opposition to him and in her advocacy of Mr. Fillmore. While she continues thus in harmony the worst that can happen will be at least unattended with dishonor. On the first ballot you remember the South was unanimously for Mr. Fillmore with the exception of ONE vote from Virginia for General Scott. She held on to her favorite up to the forty-eighth ballot, when Scott gained four from the South,—two from Virginia (making three in all from that State) and two from Missouri. Then it was that the nefarious game was decided. Even on the final ballot there were only thirteen from the South that deserted a cause which should have had no deserters. The infamy which those men deserve who insisted in forcing upon the country a man whom I may say one-half of it unanimously opposed, cannot be heaped upon them sufficiently high by one generation, but the work must be left unfinished, and the completion of it bequeathed as a legacy to posterity.

"It is my opinion, as well as that of many others, as I have already stated, that the nomination of General Scott portends evil to the country. God save us from his election! The Northern abolitionists and Western Freesoilers advocated him because they are in hopes that, in case he is elected, he will be made a tool of by some of their party. They are dissatisfied with the just administration and unconquerable impartiality of Mr. Fillmore. For them he has no sympathy, with him they have no influence. But here is a man whose individual conceit and vanity will make him believe anything provided it is accompanied with flattery.

With him, then, there is a chance—more particularly as it was they who supported him—of succeeding in all their plans, of alienating one section of the Union from the other. General Scott a compromise man! I doubt that most considerably, notwithstanding his having accepted the platform. And even if he is, he resembles a vast majority of the people of the United States. It was certainly not on account of his favoring the Compromise more than all others that he was selected. Millard Fillmore is a compromise man,—a strong compromise man. He has given every evidence of it, and the South has shown its gratitude and its high appreciation of his services by clinging to him so long and with so much unanimity. Then it must be that the Freesoilers and abolitionists believe at least that by means of General Scott's weakness they can get possession of him and take the government into their own hands. They could not advocate the dropping a man so firmly adhering to the compromise on any other grounds. *If Mr. Fillmore is not as popular as General Scott it must be because his cause is not popular.* If his cause is not popular, farewell to the Union. Millard Fillmore and the Union are one. If he has been guilty of partiality to the South, the South will always continue to demand that partiality, let the President be who he may. If it is not accorded, why, the South must withdraw that authority which it has delegated.

"The news of the nomination was received in Boston with hisses, groans, and oaths. I shall send you a paper containing an account of it. But with these Webster Whigs I have no sympathy. They could at any time have thrown the scale in Mr. Fillmore's favor. Instead of that, they were constantly sending despatch after despatch to Boston saying that the Fillmore men were all *wavering*, and that in a short time they would unite with the Webster men; that one hundred and thirty-three men were going to abandon their favorite—their idol—to advocate another man who only had twenty-nine votes! *and not a single one from the South.* Did you ever hear of anything so absurd, so preposterous, so unfounded, so unreasonable? With the fact staring them in the face of one hundred and thirty-nine or thereabouts supporting Mr. Fillmore, and continuing to support him for upwards of forty ballots, they were still infatuated enough and foolish enough to think that the Fillmore men were going to desert him and advocate their man; a man who never saw the day when he was popular,—a man who never saw the day when he could create the least excitement or enthusiasm in the nation, unless it was when he met and overthrew Hayne, of South Carolina, on the floor of the Senate. I do not say that he created any excitement or enthusiasm then, but I say that if he did not do it then, he never has done it at all. When I say that Mr. Webster 'never saw the day when he was popular,' I mean that he never saw the day when he was the first choice of even a *tolerable* portion of his party. Was not I right, then, in saying that reason did not reside among the New England, and especially among the Boston, people? Was I not right in saying that the publication of the letter of a reasonable man, a patriot and a Whig, would be of no avail among such a people? I deeply regret that I proved so good a prophet,—so far am I from congratulating myself. At the time that I said what I did about the Boston people I was excited, and intended acknowledging it to you as soon as you had received that letter. The reason of my being excited was the fact, if I remember rightly, of my having just been to a large abolition meeting in the loyal city. Hearing such violent disunion and disgraceful speeches,—seeing such a tremendous and orderly audience of citizens,—and that in the daytime,—for if a Yankee deserts his work you may know he is interested,—I could not help being convinced that the disaffection towards the laws and the country was much greater than we in the South are apt to suppose. Now I see that the opinion I formed under excitement is the true one. You will agree with me too, I think.

"Your letter of the 8th June was received yesterday morning, containing your address to the Whig delegates of Mississippi. I agree with you in everything you say. I not only agree with you, but think that you ought to have said what you did say and in the manner in which you said it. The delegates from Mississippi acted just as you wanted them to act; whether it was in accordance with your advice, or with their own sound judgment and patriotism, or with both, is a matter of no consequence at all. You are satisfied, whichever way it may be, I know. I showed your address to several of my friends, and they liked it very much; said that it was exactly what it should be. We could not help being amused, though, at your comparing the Presidential candidates to a party playing loo or set-back euchre. They all concurred that your illustration was capital, and that you showed an intimate acquaintance with the game. . . . I knew before you mentioned it that Mr. Fillmore was the first choice of the Whigs of Mississippi, and believed that Mr. Webster was the second, but it was with great unwillingness that I believed it. I had rather see him President than General Scott; but take out the general and there is not a Whig living who stands on the Compromise that I would not rather see President than Daniel Webster. In making an assertion like this I am not to be understood as meaning *any* Whig, *wherever you may find him*, but any Whig who has sufficient capacity to occupy the office, and sufficient determination to act his own way, regulated by a sound judgment. As a *manufactured* orator, as a man of learning, and as a lawyer, I admire Mr. Webster; but I do say that he is GREAT in no sense of the word, unless allusion is made to his corporeal dimensions. He can follow when others lead, and follow with considerable effect, but he cannot lead. He has not that decision of character and judgment, the necessary ingredients of all great minds. Put him under the control of a determined man, and Daniel Webster will appear to be great; he will make great efforts; but remove that control, and his efforts will be like the flounderings of a wounded whale, destitute of judgment and equally injurious to friends and foes. With a mind capable of comprehending anything, he can originate nothing. In other words, Daniel Webster

would have made a capital tool in the hands of a
tyrant. In my 'long letter' I said that I thought Mr.
Clay looked upon Daniel Webster as a rival. I said so
because Mr. Clay has *never* come out and advocated
Mr. Webster's pretensions to the Presidency, at least
as far as I know. You are much more familiar with
Mr. Clay's history, and of course know whether he has
or not. I do not speak positively under such circumstances. You say that you do not believe that Mr.
Clay has ever honored mortal man so highly as to
regard him as a rival. That is a matter of opinion,
and cannot be determined either one way or the other.
I do say this much, though, that if he has ever regarded Mr. Webster as a rival his jealousy was misplaced. There is no comparison between the two men.
God Almighty made Henry Clay; Daniel Webster made
Daniel Webster. The greater workman has made the
greater man. I think that Mr. Clay is the only great
man now living in America. When he is gone we will
all be on a level. There cannot, in the nature of things,
be many great men at a time.

"I acknowledge myself in error in saying that 'Mr.
Clay favored General Scott in preference to Mr. Fillmore.' I do not think that I said that exactly. As
well as I remember it was this: that 'Mr. Clay favored
General Scott.' I did not mean at all to throw out the
insinuation that he was opposed to Mr. Fillmore, but I
meant that he had no objection to General Scott. Some
years ago he recommended the general in a letter to some
one or some convention. I do not remember the occasion. He has spoken of General Scott frequently as being
a fit man for the Presidency. In his letter, published
some six or eight weeks ago (I have not seen it), he rec-
ommends, so I am told, Mr. Fillmore, because he has done
his duty and given satisfaction; because he thinks it
right to 'let well enough alone.' But for these circumstances I am certain, as far as a man can be of such a
thing, that General Scott would be Mr. Clay's first choice.
That letter of Mr. Clay's, to which I have just alluded,
gave mortal offence to the Webster Whigs about here.
I have heard them allude to it. They think that it was

written to break down the Webster party, and that but for it Webster would have been the nominee! That is another one of the Massachusetts absurdities.

"In my last letter to you I predicted four things. Three of them have already come to pass: First, that Mr. Webster would have scarcely any supporters at the convention out of New England. On the first ballot (which is the proper one for this purpose) Mr. Webster had only twenty-nine votes, twenty-four of which were from New England,—eleven from Massachusetts. Second, that the South would go for Mr. Fillmore to a man. She did so, with the exception of one vote. Third, that General Scott would get the nomination by means of the Western and Northern States. The last prediction remains to be verified, viz., that the general will be beaten, and that his defeat will be a victory to his country. You see I am quite a prophet, notwithstanding I do not read newspapers much.

"I was at first just as much shocked at the nomination of the Democratic convention as I am now at that of the Whig, but I am now entirely changed. For General Pierce I have the highest admiration. Next to Mr. Fillmore, whom we have tried, and whom we know, I had rather have General Pierce. I had the pleasure of being in General Pierce's company without knowing it. When he received the news of his nomination he was in Boston. So many persons called on him that the report was started that he had gone to Baltimore, whereas he had only come out to Cambridge. He played the incognito admirably. He went to the hotel where I board, took a seat nearly opposite to me at table, and, as a matter of course, we discussed him in his presence. Not one word was spoken in his favor. All were Whigs with the exception of two,—myself, who claim no party, and a young fellow by the name of States Right Gist, of South Carolina. His name reveals his politics. But I was struck forcibly by the appearance of an elderly gentleman who sat nearly opposite to me, a thing which has not seldom happened to me. I thought at the time of sending a waiter to him to attend to him——"

The letter ends abruptly here, the other sheet on which it was continued having been lost, along with many valuable papers and other property, when the family left Burleigh, as refugees, during the war.

Charles did send his own waiter to attend to the stranger, and did not know till he had left the table that he was Mr. Franklin Pierce.

CHARLES TO VIRGINIUS.

"CAMBRIDGE, June, 1852.

... "A few days ago a fellow in the Freshman class was expelled for ringing some church-bell. He hired a splendid carriage and four gray horses, and was driven around and through the college yard,—had his hat off like some distinguished stranger,—met all the students as they were coming out of the chapel from prayers, and they gave him three tremendous cheers. That looks very much like bearding the devil. It requires considerable audacity to do such a thing in broad daytime and in the middle of a town. ... There is one thing of which I feel quite certain, and that is that this place will cost you about a thousand dollars a year, including vacations. It will require the most rigid economy not to exceed that sum."

DR. J. A. SMITH TO CHARLES.

... "For no one ever arrives at eminence in this world, or, at any rate, the exceptions are too rare to be taken into the account, without proposing to himself some great object of which he is to think every day and nearly all day,—filling, it may be, his dreams at night. He must passively submit to every needful privation and actively surmount for weeks, nay, perhaps for years, every obstacle which may perhaps successively arise to foil his aspirations. And this is the key to the success of enthusiasts, who are thus enabled, when guided by good sense, to overcome difficulties which to ordinary minds appear absolutely insuperable.

"An intense desire, then, to attain the end you seek is to be the constantly impelling motive, not only to urge you on and to solace your toil, but *to strew your path with flowers.*

"For, once thoroughly embarked and speeding onward, you will enjoy, so far as external pursuits are concerned, the greatest happiness this world affords. I speak from some little experience, more observation, and much reading. . . .

"Your affectionate uncle,
"J. Aug. Smith."

CHARLES TO HIS MOTHER.

"Cambridge, July 24, 1852.

. . . "We, of course, saw the risk of having our rights challenged, but we determined to encounter it in order to hear such a man as Winthrop. I was amply repaid for my trouble. He delivered the finest oration I ever heard. It was classic in the extreme. He took a masterly view of the different systems of philosophy in the world, and their practical effect. He showed the great influence of educated men in forming and controlling 'public opinion,'—the great power of an unfettered press, and its results according as it is in the hands of good or bad men. Assembled around the speaker were the different grandees of the land; there were Greenleaf and Shaw, of great legal reputation; Everett, Sparks, Quincy; Thornwell, the president of South Carolina College, and John S. Preston, brother of William C. Preston, of that State; the governor and staff, and a host of others, who occupy the highest civic or educational positions in the country. . . . I went close to the speaker's chair. I heard Edward Everett. He is the most graceful and elegant man I ever saw in my life. His gesticulation and pronunciation of language excelled even my ideal of what it should be. With a tall and commanding figure, light complexion, and brown hair, inclined to curl, his movements were as graceful, as smooth, and as noiseless as the rolling of an ocean after a storm. After Mr. Everett spoke Chief-Justice Shaw, of Massachusetts. His speech was legal in its nature. He eulogized his calling and demonstrated the great benefits which resulted to society from hanging a man. After Judge Shaw spoke Dr. Fuller, a preacher of Baltimore. He fired away at the chief-justice's speech, and showed that hanging a man was not the best use to which he could be put,—that it was the object of society to prevent and not to punish crime. Then came the South Carolinians, Thornwell and Preston. Both delivered good and patriotic speeches, and the audience gave six hearty cheers for South Carolina. There were several other speeches delivered,—good enough in their way, but not worthy of my taking notice of them here. Old Quincy delivered a very witty and amusing speech. As he is one of the distinguished men of Massachusetts, it would not do to pass over him."

T. S. D. TO HIS SON CHARLES.

"BURLEIGH, 29th October, 1852.

"The papers received last night bring the appalling intelligence of the death of Mr. Webster. Thus has the country lost its two giants in one year,—within four months, indeed. When Mr. Clay died, great as was the nation's grief, there was yet a consolation in the reflection that Mr. Webster was left to us. But who is left now? Truly, no one. There is not a living man who is capable of half filling the shoes of him of Marshfield. I cannot conjecture who Mr. Fillmore will appoint to the State Department, but have no doubt he will do his best.

"You cannot appreciate the force or truth of my expression that 'no one' is left to us, now that Mr. Webster is dead, unless you will look into the *Democratic Review* occasionally, and especially the number for this month (October). You will find there that 'Young America,' the 'Party of Progress,' is summoned to the polls to vindicate the principles that would not have discredited a French Jacobin of the last century. The Whigs are stigmatized as *small men with limited ideas.* Pierce, as the standard-bearer of 'American progress,' will, they are assured, *bring these matters right.* The matters to be brought right are not left for conjecture. They are the seizure of Cuba, the

Sandwich Islands, the Northern fisheries, Australia, Grenada, Central America, Mexico, and the West Indies! Young America is assured that nothing more is necessary than that they elect Pierce, and all of these fair possessions will be theirs. The editor says, by way of making the thing more interesting, I suppose, that we shall first have to whip (his term is that we shall be *involved* with) England, France, Spain, and Mexico; but he says that 'private enterprise' and 'a free people will do it.' It will be nothing but a wholesome exercise, it seems. The Whigs are small men with *limited* ideas because they cannot see their way out of such enterprises, and would not go into them if they could, may be added. These are but a few of the astounding propositions of this journal, and it is the leading Democratic journal of the Union.

"Who can lash this man and this party with scorpions, now that Mr. Clay and Mr. Webster are dead? They could make 'Young America' tremble, even when Young America held the helm. I should not fear these men much if Mr. Webster lived, because, in power or out of power, his words were listened to by the whole country as words of wisdom, and heeded as such. Whose words will weigh as much now?"

T. S. D. TO HIS SON CHARLES.

"BURLEIGH, 10th December, 1852.

... "We had a fair hunt under all the circumstances, having killed sixty-seven deer. I think they obviously diminish each year. . . . Sophy sends you a 'book-marker,' having worked it for you herself." . . .

CHARLES TO HIS MOTHER.

"CAMBRIDGE, December 12, 1852.

"Your letter of the 26th ult. reached me the day before yesterday, containing the painful intelligence that my father was sick. I am now most anxious to hear from you again, and have felt sad ever since the arrival of your letter. I hope that his sickness is nothing more than the result of exposure, and that his wonted good health will, long before this reaches you, have been entirely restored. I am glad, though, that you mentioned it, as I never desire anything of that kind concealed from me, for if it was I should never know when to repose confidence in the letters which I receive. I feel homesick to-night. I would give worlds to be with you now. But I must drag myself along through time until next summer, and have no companion to cheer me up in the arduous task save hope. I feel as if I could not possibly love you enough, but I feel that you know how much I do love you. But my heart bleeds when I think that my conduct towards you has not always been in accordance with the depth of my affection. My consolation consists, however, in knowing that you know me well enough to perceive when my conduct is at variance with my affection, and that you would not judge of the latter, which is infinite and eternal, by an act sudden and momentary.

"And my father, who, I trust, is now pursuing his wonted occupation, can I ever do enough to justify the confidence which I know he has always reposed in me? Can I ever approach anything like the realization of the expectations which he has associated with me? I am afraid not. When I think of this my heart almost bursts; and though from experience and study I have for the most part acquired the habit of controlling my feelings and emotions, yet tears will often fill my eyes when I am alone when I think of those to whom I owe so much,—whom I love so much, yea, love to distraction. As it is said that the chief happiness of parents when they become old consists in the contemplation of the welfare and affection of their children; and as you and he are now getting old, the main object of my future life shall be whatever will most conduce to bring about that happiness; and fortune, ambition, glory, shall all be neglected to attain it. I know that it is painful to you for me to be away from you,—to me it is utter wretchedness. I feel as if I would never be willing to endure another separation. There is more happiness to be found around the domestic fireside, in the conversation of those whom we love, than in gilded houses, exalted stations, the attentions and applauses of the multitude. You must forgive me for sometimes feeling lonely and desolate, considering I am so far from you, and for burdening you with a portion of my melancholy."

The oversensitive conscience of Charles accused him of faults which he did not possess. His reverence and filial affection for his parents were never known to fail. In the family life his example was without blemish.

T. S. D. TO HIS SON CHARLES.

"BURLEIGH, 19th December, 1852.

"Your mother and the girls are employed in making mince-pies and other good things, held to be appropriate for the approaching Christmas festival. And this reminds me that my whole family participated with me in this celebration last year. When will they do it again? Never, is the probable answer. Not that any of us are likely to die within the compass of a year, but the position or employments of some will, most probably, forbid it. Should we all live to see the sun make his next annual circuit, I suppose that all will be here except Virginius. How of the next? Virginius should not be here then. And the next? But we will pursue this theme no further.

"We expect a larger company than we had last Christmas, although something like half of our last year's company will be absent. Virginius and yourself, for example. —— —— will be here certainly. He will bring Colonel Vick with him, whom I specially invited. I also expect Mr. Wm. Moncure, having invited him a month ago, and Dr. Latimer, E. Lott, J. Shelton, O. V. and Wm. Shearer, Jennings, Lyles, Hal Smith, Hal's father, and Vernon. Edward will be here with one of his school-fellows, and it is probable that some will be here unexpectedly, as Summers has a friend with him, for example."

The whole family never met again. In nine months from the date of this letter Charles Dabney died.

CHARLES TO HIS FATHER.

"CAMBRIDGE, December 21, 1852.

"Tell Sophy that I thank her very much for the 'book-marker' which she made for me, and that it afforded me the greatest pleasure to see that she thought of me. I am glad also to see the progress she has made in needle-work, and to hear such flattering accounts of the studious habits of all of them. I shall indeed 'remember' her."*

T. S. D. TO HIS SON CHARLES.

"BURLEIGH, 18th January, 1853.

... "I have ordered one thousand dollars to be forwarded to you immediately by the Bank of Louisiana, which will give you a little surplus over your estimates; a thing well enough to provide, as it will enable you to bring some little presents to your sisters, which I always approve of, as the affections are cultivated in this manner as successfully perhaps as in any other single mode.

"You need not make yourself so uneasy about your expenses. I am perfectly satisfied with them myself, and it is lucky that I am, for I do not anticipate any reduction in them for some time to come. I hope you do not expect to support yourself from the start. I say I HOPE you do not, for I should be sorry to see you disappointed, and perhaps mortified. Immediate success does not depend on merit, but most frequently on the lack of it. But all this you know. Be satisfied, then, to bide your time, with but little fear of my becoming fatigued. . . .

"P.S.—There is not the least objection to your accepting Olivia's present, and I am gratified at her proposition. It would be impossible for me to accept any such thing of her, but it is very different with my children. I would not consent to her making them costly presents, but such as are merely complimentary, as in your case, gratify me very much."

---

* The motto of the little marker was, "Remember Me."

T. S. D. TO HIS SON CHARLES.
"BURLEIGH, 30th January, 1853.

... "I am very glad that you called my attention to Alexander Hamilton. Whether he was a greater man than either of the Adamses would be a very difficult point (but an unnecessary one) to determine. It may be enough that he ranks with Madison as a contributor to the *Federalist*, and with him also, and with Adams and Jefferson, as a statesman and patriot of the Revolution. Do you not remember the speech of John Adams upon the adoption of the Declaration of Independence? If a greater amount of patriotism, heroism, and eloquence is to be found in the same number of English words elsewhere than in that speech, I know not where to look for them. But still, it would be difficult to ascribe to me too high an admiration of and veneration for the genius and character of General Hamilton. I therefore write you to purchase for the Burleigh library all of his writings, the *Federalist* COMPLETE included. I also wish you to purchase Sparks's 'Life of Washington,' as a suitable companion for the other books. These are American works, and yet, in my poor judgment, they may safely be reckoned the classics of future ages. Entertaining these views of the great value of the principles inculcated by the writings of Washington and the Adamses and Hamilton and Webster, I think you had better procure them all in very substantial bindings: calf if you choose, but that may not be necessary.

"If you think it judicious, you may purchase books for yourself, during the year, to the amount of one thousand dollars. I do not name that sum as your limit by any means, but only as your *present* limit. It may be that it would be injudicious to purchase so many at once, but you will judge of that, and let me know, whenever you have made up your mind what sum you prefer to have for this object."

CHARLES TO HIS FATHER.
"CAMBRIDGE, February 15, 1853.

"Last evening I received yours of 30th January. Parts of it greatly moved me, and upon those parts I will touch first and somewhat at length.

"When I came to that portion in which you authorize me to purchase books to the amount of one thousand dollars my head felt giddy, my heart swelled. That is an outlay, that is a favor far beyond anything I had hoped. But you correctly suggest that it might be injudicious in me to buy as many books at one time and so early in life. The law books that I will want will be such as will suit the kind and the extent of practice which I have a right to expect, for I have not the right to think that I am going to get any very difficult cases, or any great number of them, for some time. It would be a useless expenditure therefore to buy a large number of law books unless I expected to enter immediately into a large practice, for law books are of that nature that as soon as a new book, or a new edition of an old one, comes out, those which preceded it are rendered almost entirely worthless. This last remark is of course general in its nature, and does not apply to 'reports,' for they are always good and necessary, but to treatises on legal subjects, text-books, etc. And, besides all this, I wish to buy my law books—that is, those that will not be immediately necessary to me as a capital to start on—with my own earnings. I am unwilling to put you to a greater expense than my prospects will justify, and of them I can only judge after I have entered upon the practice. Nor do I wish to bear more heavily on you than there is any need that I should. . . . But as I hope and expect to be something else than a mere lawyer, I will want some books of a historical, literary, and philosophical character, a moderate number of which, though enough to supply my wants for many years, will cost about two hundred and fifty dollars. But even this expense I would be unwilling to encounter all at once but for the likelihood there is that, after entering into business, I may be so engaged as not to have an opportunity for many years to come, perhaps, of getting books on as good terms and of making selections where there are so many to select from.

"Another reason is that I will have some time to read before I get involved in business (if I ever should become so fortunate) than I will ever have afterwards. Without the books I might be comparatively idle. My mind would rust, dimness would take the place of what is now freshness, and the wheels of intellect would roll backward. Although there is more to be learned in my profession than I ever will know did I study it exclusively every hour during the day, yet I do not wish it to be the only ladder upon which I am to climb hereafter. No lawyer pretends to know everything about law. If a lawyer wishes to be anything else than a bore to the jury he addresses, he must gather flowers and perfume in a poetic land. If he wishes to give anything more than a mere legal argument, he must gather wisdom and acuteness from metaphysics. If he wishes to be learned, he must rob history of its contents. It is on this account that I wish to possess somewhat of a miscellaneous library. Without it, as you know, I would be contracted in mind, uninteresting as a companion, and dull and disagreeable as a lawyer, and the groundwork which I have laid in my academic career, and the great expense to which I have been put to lay it, would all result in nothing except as far as it operated as a mental training. If you have any suggestion to make on this subject, or if you differ in your views from anything that I have here written, of course you will not fail to make known your opinions at length. It is needless for me to say that the older I get, and the more I learn, the more I am satisfied of the correctness of your views with regard to education and the method of attaining it. . . .

"I have, my dear father, written coolly on the generous and affectionate offer you have made me, but my heart has been filled to overflowing. To say that I thank you, that I am grateful, would be acting so coldly as to chill you. I am at a loss what to say, and it is therefore that my letter has somewhat the appearance of abruptness and disconnection. To say little, but to resolve high, will, then, be the best way by which I can show my high appreciation of it. You have thus indirectly shown me what you expect of me. My hopes and my efforts will all be enlisted on the side of your expectations. But do not rear them too high. Wait and see me fairly engaged in the contest of life before you assign them any definite proportions. I have hopes, yea, high hopes, but I never like to breathe them even to any one.

"There was one thing in your letter which hurt me; not because I thought that you intended it to do so, but because it showed me that, under excitement, I might have written foolishly and rashly on a former occasion. In speaking of the books which you wish me to procure for the Burleigh library you say, 'These are American works, and yet, in my poor judgment, they may safely be reckoned the classics,' etc. It was the word POOR. This word hurt me, not so much because it might be construed into a very mild and kind reproof, but because it has suggested to me that I did not address myself with that courtesy and respect which I owe you, not only from the relation, but also from the love and affection you bear to me. I know that I deserved it all, and I hope that you will think no more of it, and say no more about it. The lesson and the kindness with which it was given I will remember. I don't know that I ever told you that I confided in your judgment; that would have been as unnecessary as telling people that I loved you; but, I know this, that no excitement could ever make me either act or write in a manner intentionally disrespectful towards you. Could I be capable of such a thing, so far from meriting your love, I would taint the very atmosphere in which I breathe."

CHARLES TO HIS FATHER.

"CAMBRIDGE, MASS., 13th February, 1853.

... "Yes, Mr. Clay was the Golconda of the Whig party, in whom the rough diamonds were quarried, and Daniel Webster was the skilful artificer who polished them; but, like the artificer to whom King Hiero of Syracuse gave his gold that he might make him a crown, he robbed him of nearly all of it, and gave him in return an adulterated and worthless bauble. So has Mr. Clay fared in the hands of Mr. Webster, not in your day, for you know all about the two men, but in those days in which posterity shall live."

CHARLES TO HIS MOTHER.

"CAMBRIDGE, MASS., February 27, 1853.

... "But it has been a still longer time since I have received a letter from you. But I know how many cares and duties you have, how many interruptions you are liable to, and I therefore feel thankful and happy if I receive a letter from you once in six weeks. ... I send a little handkerchief to Sophy."

CHARLES TO HIS FATHER.

"CAMBRIDGE, MASS., February, 1853.

"In my last I promised that my next should have a continuation of the subject then under discussion; and accordingly I will now proceed to give my views upon the American mind. I will begin by saying that I never had a contempt for the American mind, and, so far as I can remember, I never intentionally expressed any; but, on the contrary, I have the highest admiration for it, and believe that it will attain an eminence equal, if not above, that of any other nation. But I do say, and think too, that since our separation from England we have not attained any height worthy the excessive praises lavished by our people upon their writers. It is a fact, which I think cannot be contradicted, that our greatest men and best educated men (public men, I mean, for of private men we know nothing) were born and raised subjects of the British throne. And all, or nearly all, had given evidence of their intellect before the Revolution had systematically broken out. Washington, Franklin, Jefferson, Adams, Henry, Hamilton, etc., were as much subjects of the king of Great Britain, up to 1776, as I am a citizen of the United States. In addition to these being the greatest men this country ever had, three of them, Franklin, Jefferson, and Adams, were the most learned. Franklin must have been near his seventieth year when he signed the Declaration of Independence. Mr. Jefferson, at thirty-three years of age, wrote the Declaration, which is of itself sufficient to satisfy any man of his learning and ability. Mr. Adams, about that time, made some speeches, which, in the opinion of many, equal anything in the English language. Now, I think the greatness of these men, up to the period of the Revolution, was no more owing to American (what is now meant by American) institutions than to the Chinese; but they were brought forth and matured under British institutions. It is true they differed somewhat from the institutions in the island of Great Britain itself; but, nevertheless, they were regulated by British laws, and governed by men appointed by the British throne.

"In point of respect and admiration for our Revolutionary patriots and sages I yield to no one.

"But the class of literary men and philosophers to whom I wish my remarks to apply are those who are essentially 'American,' those who have been born and reared since the birth of America. I think that this class is not only vastly inferior to our sages of the Revolution, but also very much inferior to the men of England and France produced during the same period. It may be said that great crises are necessary to bring forth great men. Great crises bring forth great heroes and great patriots; but, in my judgment, great scholars and great philosophers can be produced quite as well in the quiet monotony and stillness of the cell as amidst the turmoil of war and the upturning of the moral and political world. War gives occasion for the display of greatness of soul and readiness in meeting emergencies; but Peace is the mother of the Arts,—of those things which adorn society and make it more comfortable for its dwellers.

"The question will here arise, Have we done nothing? Yes, we have done a great deal,—vastly more than any other nation of the earth could have done. In 1776 civilization was bounded by the Alleghanies. All the territory beyond them was inhabited by the most worthless and determined of enemies. Since that time all of these enemies have been overthrown,—all of that territory put into cultivation. We have laid many thousands of miles of railroad, cut many long canals, built innumerable cities. Our steam marine exceeds that (I believe) of the whole world. And, what is more, we have put into practice the theories of liberty and government which heretofore only found existence in the brains of philosophers. Well may it be said of us, that, like the infant Hercules, we have strangled dragons in our cradle. But our destiny, I thank heaven, is higher: we have yet to slay the Lernean hydra and the Nemean lion and to lift rivers from their beds, which are the labors of manhood in full vigor. Looking, then, at what we have done, it is plain that our powers and energies have been directed to securing the comforts of life,—to the conquest of the asperities of nature,—that we have had no time to devote to the cultivation of the arts and refinements of life. We have manifested no backwardness in making application of those principles of mechanics which aid at all in taking obstacles from our path. We have put science to use wherever it could possibly have been done. In fact, in this we are superior to the rest of the world.

"Besides, we were born to the inheritance of a literature. The English literature, philosophy, and science, up to the period of the Revolution, belongs as much to us as to the English themselves. We never, therefore, felt the want of such things, and what people do not want they are not likely to strive hard to attain. But now we are a nation ourselves; and though we are capable of using whatever the English mind produces, yet it is not ours. Since our birth as a nation we have had so many obstacles in the physical world to contend with, that no time has been left us for anything else. Now that they have been removed, we may look for the dawn of a brighter day. The great encouragement given by our people to newspapers and periodicals of every kind is a happy omen. Our writers will not need the condescending patronage of crowned heads and conceited courtiers; but the honest approval and liberal rewards conferred by freemen's hearts and freemen's hands will amply supply their every want. I am glad that the government at Washington has held out so many encouragements to Lieutenant Maury."

THOMAS DABNEY TO HIS SON CHARLES.

"BURLEIGH, May 6, 1853.

... "I entirely concur in your proposition, that to slight a letter is to do an unpardonable thing."

CHARLES TO HIS FATHER.

"CAMBRIDGE, MASS., July 3, 1853.

"I will embark on the first ship that sails for New Orleans after the 8th. The diplomas are not given out till the 20th. At that time the academic honors are conferred. I will, of course, leave mine behind me, to be brought on by a friend. . . .

"I am quite bothered as to what sort of presents to buy for my little sisters, but I hope before I leave to think of something."

CHAPTER XII.

HOLIDAY TIMES ON THE PLANTATION.

A LIFE of Thomas Dabney could not be written without some reference to the Christmas at Burleigh. It was looked forward to not only by the family and by friends in the neighborhood and at a distance, but by the house and plantation servants. The house was crowded with guests, young people and older ones too. During the holiday season Thomas and his guests were ready to accept invitations to parties in other houses, but no one in the neighborhood invited company for Christmas-Day, as, for years, everybody was expected at Burleigh on that day. On one of the nights during the holidays it was his custom to invite his former overseers and other plain neighbors to an eggnog-party. In the concoction of this beverage he took a hand himself, and the freedom and ease of the company, as they saw the master of the house beating his half of the eggs in the great china bowl, made it a pleasant scene for those who cared nothing for the eggnog.

During the holidays there were refreshments, in the old Virginia style, of more sorts than one. The oysters were roasted on the coals on the dining-room hearth, under the eyes of the guests.

Great bunches of holly and magnolia, of pine and mistletoe, were suspended from the ceiling of hall and dining-room and drawing-room.

Sometimes, not often, there was a Christmas-tree,— on one occasion one for the colored Sunday-school. One Christmas everybody hung up a sock or stocking; a long line, on the hall staircase. There were twenty-two of them, white silk stockings, black silk stockings, thread and cotton and woollen socks and stockings. And at the end of the line was, side by side with the old-fashioned home-spun and home-knit sock of the head of the house, the dainty pink sock of the three-weeks-old baby.

Who of that company does not remember the morning scramble over the stockings and the notes in prose and poetry that tumbled out!

The children's nurses modestly hung their stockings up by the nursery fireplace.

Music and dancing and cards and games of all sorts filled up a large share of the days and half the nights. The plantation was as gay as the house. The negroes in their holiday clothes were enjoying themselves in their own houses and in the "great house" too. A visit of a day to one of the neighboring towns was considered by them necessary to the complete enjoyment of the holidays.

They had their music and dancing too. The sound of the fiddles and banjos, and the steady rhythm of their dancing feet, floated on the air by day and night to the Burleigh house. But a time came when this was to cease. The whole plantation joined the Baptist church. Henceforth not a musical note nor the joyful motion of a negro's foot was ever again heard on the plantation. "I done buss' my fiddle an' my banjo, an' done fling 'em 'way," the most music-loving fellow on the place said to the preacher, when asked for his religious experience. It was surely the greatest sacrifice of feeling that such a race could make. Although it was a sin to have music and dancing of their own, it was none to enjoy that at the "great house." They filled the porches and doors, and in serried ranks stood men, women, and children, gazing as long as the music and dancing went on. Frequently they stood there till the night was more than half gone. In the crowd of faces could be recognized the venerable ones of the aged preachers, surrounded by their flocks.

Christmas was incomplete until the master of the house had sung his songs. He was full of action and gesture. His family used to say that although he was in character and general bearing an Englishman, his French blood asserted itself in his manner. In his motions he was quick, and at times, when he chose to make them so, very amusing, yet too full of grace to be undignified. He was fond of dancing, and put fresh interest in it, as he did in everything that he joined in.

On Christmas mornings the servants delighted in catching the family with "Christmas giff!" "Christmas giff!" betimes in the morning. They would spring out of unexpected corners and from behind doors on the young masters and mistresses. At such times there was an affectionate throwing off of the reserve and decorum of every-day life.

"Hi! ain't dis Chris'mus?" one of the quietest and most low-voiced of the maid-servants asked, in a voice as loud as a sea-captain's. One of the ladies of the house had heard an unfamiliar and astonishingly loud laugh under her window, and had ventured to put an inquiring head out.

In times of sorrow, when no Christmas or other festivities gladdened the Mississippi home, the negroes felt it sensibly. "It 'pears so lonesome; it mak' me feel bad not to see no comp'ny comin'," our faithful Aunt Abby said on one of these occasions. Her post as the head maid rendered her duties onerous when the house was full of guests. We had thought that she would be glad to have a quiet Christmas, which she could spend by her own fireside, instead of attending to the wants of a houseful of young people.

In the presence of the guests, unless they were old friends, the dignity of the family required that no light behavior should be indulged in, even though it were Christmas. In no hands was the dignity of the family so safe as with negro slaves. A negro was as proud of the "blood" of his master and mistress as if it had been his own. Indeed, they greatly magnified the importance of their owners, and were readily affronted if aspersion of any sort were cast on their master's family. It was very humiliating to them, for they are all aristocrats by nature, to belong to what they call "poor white trash."

Our steady Lewis was often sent to take us to evening entertainments, on account of his being so quiet and nice in his ways. On one of these occasions he became so incensed that he refused to set his foot on that plantation again. Mammy Maria informed us of the cause of Lewis's anger. One of the maids in the house in which we were spending the evening had insulted him by saying that her mistress wore more trimming on her clothes than his young ladies did!

Hog-killing was one of the plantation frolics. It began at daybreak. Every man, woman, and child seemed to take a part. Even the one or two or three or four fat dogs that came along with each family seemed to know that the early bustle was the presage of boundless enjoyment, such as could only be brought about by unlimited fresh pork.

The servants made fires in every direction all over the frozen ground, and round each fire was a merry group. They made more jokes and laughed more gayly than on other days; for not only did they fry great pans of liver, and bake hoe-cake after ash-cake, and ash-cake after hoe-cake, and eat them the livelong day, but when the day was over there was the great bag for each man's shoulder, filled with tenderloin and liver, heads, and lights, and spare-ribs; and all these good things were not counted in the "'lowance," either.

The only night-work done on the place was the semi-monthly corn-shelling, in preparation for the Saturday's grinding. The mellow songs of the corn-shellers floated on the air during the hour required for this work. When they found an ear of red or blue corn, or a double ear, it was often laid aside to be given in the morning to one of the white children.

The church at Pass Christian was the first Episcopal church that we had seen. The organ up in the gallery and the singing up there behind us seemed mysterious and heavenly. The tall pines and the giant live-oak on the great Indian mound in front and the cedars that stood round it, made the church seem a place where the world and its thoughts could not enter. One day we were told that we were to be taken to the beautiful little church to be christened; all, from Edward down to the baby, Thomas, in the nurse's arms,—the eight Mississippi children.

We were baptized by the rector, the Rev. Thomas Staughton Savage, Mrs. Savage standing by our mother's side as godmother for the whole flock. Dr. and Mrs. Savage had both been missionaries to Africa, and only returned to America when his health had been shattered by the deadly climate. During his residence there he became known to the scientific world as the discoverer of the gorilla.*

Thomas was a man of strong prejudices. Later in life, when his character was softened by age, sorrow, and religion, he yielded readily to influence. There had been opportunities for the baptism of the children before, but because the characters of the clergymen were not altogether to his taste, he had refused to allow his children to be christened by them.

Dr. Savage was a man whose unaffected piety, joined to his many gifts, won his esteem, and the long deferred christening was arranged. An envelope containing a handsome sum for each child's name was put into the rector's hand when it was over. The church, he was

---

* See Huxley's "Evidence as to Man's Place in Nature," p. 33.

told, made no charge for admission into her folds. But he made his offering; it could be used in some way, any way that the minister thought best.

There was no Episcopal church in Raymond. He gave aid to the Methodists there, because he felt that he must help the cause of religion in his neighborhood.

He was always a strong believer in the doctrines of Christianity, and had great reverence for religion. But he was not a religious man. It was long years after this that he became a communicant and a true Christian.

Yet through all these years he did the deeds of a Christian. He was the most liberal of contributors to every enterprise that was gotten up to build up Sunday-schools or churches, or to support the clergy. His house was the resort and resting-place not only of the bishop and clergy of the Episcopal Church, but of the ministers of all denominations.

A Baptist preacher, who spent a day or so at Burleigh every time that his monthly Sunday came around to preach in the neighborhood, was so fond of staying there as to rouse the jealousy of his own congregation. He was a worthy old man, but unsuccessful, as far as earthly eyes could see, in his ministrations. When he was bidding his congregation good-by in a farewell sermon, he mentioned by name his friend, Colonel Dabney. "I have preached twenty years here," he said, "and have converted no one, not even Colonel Dabney."

Thomas once had an Episcopal clergyman and his family, consisting of his wife, five children, and two servants, to spend six weeks at Burleigh. At another time he had an Episcopal clergyman and his family of six in his house for two months. Other occasions might be mentioned when he had the care of clergymen's families during the absence of the parents.

Thomas was more than once spoken of as an "incomparable host." When a Louisiana gentleman expressed a desire to establish a school near Raymond, he received the family into his house, and they were entertained there for two months. This family consisted of the father and mother, their eight children and an adopted child, one negro and four Irish servants, and two horses. The gray-haired Creole negro had been strict in his observance of Friday as a fast day. But the mutton was tempting, and, as one of the Burleigh negroes expressed it, "Uncle Felix done tu'n, 'cause the mutton is too good."

CHAPTER XIII.

THE VALLEY OF THE SHADOW.

The summer of 1853 was an anxious one in the South, for the yellow fever was raging in New Orleans and in other Southern cities. It had never been known to reach Pass Christian, and the Dabneys felt safe there. But the New Orleans daily papers, giving the mortality at two hundred, and finally even three hundred a day, cast a gloom over all faces. A great many New Orleans people fled for safety to the Pass. The daily boats were crowded with refugees. Quarantine laws were unknown then.

In September it began to be rumored that the disease had broken out at the Pass Christian hotel, and that the victims were buried every night, lest people might be deterred from going there.

It was all too true. But scarcely any one believed it.

Charles Dabney had come home after two years of study at the Law School of Harvard University, having graduated there with honor. His mother feared that his having been so long in a Northern climate made him peculiarly susceptible to the fever. She urged on him this danger, and begged her husband to take the family away from the Pass. But he did not believe it possible that the fever could spread in that air. Charles was full of youthful spirits, and so happy to be in the home circle once more, that he could not be made to apprehend any danger. When the last week in September came, the fever was more deadly than ever in

New Orleans. This decided Thomas to take his whole family to Burleigh by the overland route. As before mentioned, he and the mother and the little ones and the servants had always gone by this way. His wagons were commodious, and he invited a number of friends to become his guests in this journey, and to remain at Burleigh until it should be safe for them to return to their homes in New Orleans. Quite a party accepted the invitation, and it was looked forward to as a delightful and novel excursion. But different things interfered, and all but one young lady found it impossible to accompany the family on the seven days' journey through the country. On the afternoon of the first day's travel she got out of the wagon to take a long walk. Charles was on his riding-horse. He felt ill at the time, as he afterwards told his mother, but he could not see a young lady, his guest, walk unattended by himself. He walked two and a half miles with her, when he found himself near fainting. They had now reached the house where the travellers were to spend the night. The next morning it was decided that he was not able to continue the journey that day; but no special anxiety was felt. Yellow fever was not thought of. It had been maintained that it could not be contracted on the Mississippi coast of the Gulf of Mexico

One of the children held back to say good-by to brother Charley, but the father said that there was no use in that; he had only a bilious attack, and would be up in a day or two. So Edward was sent forward with the charge of the children and wagons, and the rest of the household, amounting to twenty-one persons.

Thomas and Sophia, with the baby and nurse and a man-servant, remained behind with Charles. Thomas was not long in finding that the sickness that he had hoped was so slight was baffling his knowledge of disease. The symptoms were unlike any that he had seen. The situation was agonizing. Neither physician nor medicine was to be had in that country, not even a cupping-glass to relieve the throbbing temples.

Still, no thought of the yellow fever crossed the

mind of any one. Even if it had, the result, under circumstances so disastrous, could hardly have been other than it was.

They were not much longer to be in doubt as to the enemy that was battling with that young life.

A gush of black vomit let them know that their boy was dying of the yellow fever. He asked his mother to hand a looking-glass to him. She held it before his face, and he was shocked to see the blood on his mouth. At once he prepared himself for the death that could be but a few hours off. "Lord, have mercy on me," his mother heard him whisper. "Tell Virginius," he said, "to set a good example to his younger brothers and sisters; much depends on him, now that he is to be the eldest. No one knows how I have felt the responsibility of being the eldest, and how I have been weighed down by it. I have tried hard to set a good example. I felt the responsibility." Turning to his father, he said, "Do not expect so much of your other children as you expected of me. I was injured by that. I tried too hard not to disappoint you. I broke myself down. I am willing to die. But I am sorry not to be the eldest."

He spoke lovingly of each brother and sister by name. To his partial eyes they were all dear and good. Only that summer he had said that he would like to marry a wife like any one of his six sisters.

Then he sent a message of love and good-by to the nine absent ones, and kissed and caressed the baby sister, stroking her curls and admiring the "pretty head." Then he called his father to him and said, "Kiss me for Virginius, for Edward, for Sarah, for Sue, for Sophy, for Emmy, for Ben, for Ida, for Tommy;" and at each name the kiss was given. "Now kiss me for yourself."

The last kiss was given, and the poor distracted father rushed from the house and into the woods. It was more than an hour before he had regained self-control and could trust himself to go back to that bedside. Death seemed slow in coming. Unmindful of himself, even in death, the dying son sought by his last act to do what yet lay in his power to help his parents. He stretched himself straight and close to the side of the wretched room, and kept the position for more than an hour. "It is too hard," he said at last. "I cannot stand it. I tried to lie there straight, that you might not have any trouble in composing my limbs. Bury me here now, in these woods. But do not leave me here. In the winter take me up and put me by the side of my brothers."

When the sun rose on Wednesday, the 28th of September, it was all over. The father who, but a few days ago, knew that he had a son ready to take his place as the worthy head of the family, now felt that his staff had been taken from him. The mother's grief was quiet but crushing. Her health received a shock from which it never recovered.

His favorite place was at her feet, and no companionship was so sweet to him as hers. They laughed together like two happy children, and talked the long summer mornings through in the Pass Christian house. "Oh, smile again," he said to her in that last summer, his own joyous face beaming as he spoke. "You look so beautiful when you smile."

The poor, ignorant people in whose house they were staying were kind and sympathizing, and did all that they could to help my dear father and mother. They had a number of children, and Thomas Dabney spoke with regret to the father of the family at having brought a dangerous and contagious disease under his roof. The man answered that he was not afraid, and that even if there were danger he could not have turned a sick man from his door.

They laid their son there to rest among the pines till January. Then he was carried to Raymond, where he now sleeps beside his brothers.

He was twenty-three years old. Thirty-three years have passed since that time. But his birthday, the 3d of May, and the day of his death, the 28th of September, are tenderly observed each year by his favorite sister, Sarah.

The father and mother bowed their heads in submission to the blow. Sympathy came from all sides,—from the old professors at William and Mary and the college friends there, and from the professors and students at the Universities of Virginia and Harvard. He had warm personal friends among them all. Not the least gratifying message that came to them was from a poor and humble family living near the University of Virginia, whom he had helped. They did not know how to write to his family to express their sympathy, but friends of the Dabneys heard of their grief.

The winter of '53 and '54 was spent quietly among the home and plantation duties at Burleigh. The father's elastic disposition, joined to a strong sense of duty to others, prevented any outward show of grief. In the presence of her family our mother, too, was cheerful, and the smile was still on her face. It seemed a part of herself. But it was not the bright look that we had known before, and whenever she was found after being alone for even a few minutes it was seen that she had been bathed in tears.

In July a daughter was born, the last of a long line of sixteen children to whom she had given birth, nine sons and seven daughters. It was seen from the first that the child was too frail to live. Her young sisters named her Rosalie. She lived but two months. The weary mother, seeing one of the children in the nursery crying over the cradle, said, "Do not shed a tear for the baby. She is better off. I am thankful that she is gone. I was not able to take care of her."

It was now time to go to the summer-house on the sea-shore. But Sophia found that she could not bring herself to go to Pass Christian again; and in a year or two, as her aversion to the thought of ever going there seemed to increase, Thomas sold the place.

He had not thought it safe to keep his wife and children on the plantation during the hot months. The eighteen summers spent in Mississippi had all been passed either at Sophia's father's in Raymond, or in Virginia, or at the sea-shore. But this summer he decided to stay at Burleigh, as she wished it.

CHAPTER XIV.

SUMMER TRAVEL.

THEY found the Burleigh house well suited to the hot climate, as the halls and rooms were high-pitched and spacious. They spent many comfortable summers there, and did not suffer from any illness caused by climatic influences.

But the health of our mother was becoming more and more undermined. Two years after the great bereavement had come to her Thomas decided to take her to Virginia, among their relations and old friends, and to the White Sulphur and other springs, hoping that a complete change would benefit her. He kept her for two weeks in Baltimore that he might get the advice of Dr. Thomas Buckler on her case. Dr. Buckler could find no disease. There was none except that to which no earthly physician can minister,—the rooted sorrow that could not be plucked from the memory. But she was not without comfort. She found consolation in her religion. She had not forgotten her heavenly Father in her days of prosperity, and now in her time of adversity she leaned more and more heavily on that strong arm.

The Dabneys spent six months among the familiar scenes of Gloucester and at Montrose, and with other relatives and friends, and in the Virginia mountains.

Montrose—that charming, old-fashioned place with its smooth lawn and quaint box-bordered flower-beds— was the home of my father's sister, our dear "Aunt Martha." We had been taught from childhood to love and admire her, not without a little awe, too. We had not seen her, and she was only known to us as the writer of very beautiful and touching letters, which were read to us by our father with affectionate pride. He thought they possessed great literary merit, and often urged her to use her pen for the magazines. She was a woman of remarkable gifts and attainments, and charmed the young nephews and nieces by her delightful talk on a wide range of subjects. They became greatly attached to her, and her house was henceforth regarded by some of them as a second home.

The six eldest children were with their parents. The four little ones were left under the sheltering care of their good aunt, Mrs. Augustine Dabney, that the mother might have complete rest. She tried to enjoy it all and to get well. At times she did much enjoy the society of those whom she had loved and had not seen for many years. In Gloucester County the Exchange, now owned by Thomas's cousin, Mr. James Dabney, the only surviving son of Dr. James Dabney, was the house in which the large family of Burleigh Dabneys were entertained. The beloved uncle, Dr. James Dabney, had passed away years before.

James had married Miss Emory Tabb, the daughter of Mr. Thomas Tabb of the old estate of Toddsbury, Gloucester County. She was but a child when Thomas had moved from Gloucester, but she was ready to welcome her husband's cousins as her own. When he drove up with the carriages from the steamboat-landing, where he had gone to meet his kinsmen, his young wife was standing on the portico of the Exchange with both hands held out.

My mother's maid, Aunt Abby, brought our number up to nine, and a distant connection of my mother's, whom she had picked up in Baltimore, made our party ten in number.

The whole-souled mistress of the Exchange took no count of numbers, and made us feel that we were to be happy there as long as we chose to stay. The memory of that visit is among the brightest in the lives of many of that party. From the Exchange the Burleigh Dabneys visited in the old neighborhood. The style of living in Gloucester, which the younger generation had often heard described, was not changed. The six weeks spent there were passed in driving about the country, sailing and rowing on the river, and in attending dinner- and evening-parties. Music and dancing were in order, not only in the evenings, but in the forenoons as well. The sight of her children's enjoyment and the change of scene brightened up my mother. She thought that she could now enjoy the Virginia springs. But after going to several of the fashionable resorts she felt that they did not suit her taste. Her husband, who watched every look and feeling, at once looked out for a quiet spot. This he found at "Old Crow's," the breakfast house not far from the White Sulphur Springs. Here we spent some happy weeks rambling over the mountains and enjoying the delicious air. My father had keen relish for it all,—the visits to his old friends, the life at the Springs, and the weeks at Old Crow's. He used to say that when he set out to enjoy himself, even if it were only at a very poor circus, he always tried to see the pleasant things, and did not look out for faults. This bright way of going through the world made him a charming travelling companion. He wished our party to have the full enjoyment of the mountain scenery, and he chartered stages to take his family from one place to another. In this way we were never crowded, and the company in the stage was such as he selected. He frequently invited friends to go with us as his guests. An incident happened one day that amused the party. My mother's maid, Aunt Abby, and I (then in my fifteenth year) were sitting together on the front seat. We both got sleepy at about the same time, and her head fell on my shoulder, and my head rested on the top of hers. By and by I woke up and raised my head, but she was still sleeping. Papa was laughing heartily at the scene when I opened my eyes, and so was M. Pierre Soulé, our guest for the day. Aunt Abby was too dear an old friend to be disturbed, and she had her nap out. The good soul was quite embarrassed when she awoke to find how she had been violating the proprieties,— that was her view of it.

The father had no plan for that summer, except to follow the pleasure that seemed to present itself. One day we got off the train to dine at Staunton. The hotel was new and clean, the scenery lovely, and the dinner all that could be desired. We were in the humor to enjoy everything, and were eager in our expressions of admiration. "Shall I have the trunks taken off the train and stay here a week?" my dear father asked in his delightful impulsive way. The motion was carried by acclamation. I do not know what arguments he used, but he ran from the dinner-table to the baggage-car, and he got the luggage taken off. No one could easily refuse him anything, he was so good-natured,— it seemed contagious.

Some one has said that the name of one old Virginian to another old Virginian is as a trumpet to a war-horse. Our experience at Staunton and elsewhere that summer went far to prove the truth of this statement. Thomas met friends at Staunton, old and new. Some were friends whom he had lost sight of in the passing years.

The younger members made excursions about the country, and explored Weir's Cave, and filled up the week as they pleased.

One day we were going from Washington City to the White Sulphur Springs, and President Pierce and his wife and several members of his household got on the train. The conductor asked Mr. Dabney to bring his family to join the Presidential party in the car where Mr. Pierce and his family sat. So we went in. Poor Mrs. Pierce was a sweet-looking lady. She had lately lost her only child, a son, and was clad in the deepest mourning. She seemed overwhelmed with her grief, and we did not see her smile that day. Mr. Pierce was sad, too, and very tender in his manner to her. His manner to every one was kind and subdued and very attractive.

During the day one of Mr. Dabney's children became ill with a chill. Mr. Pierce showed his kind heart by trying to relieve her. He asked her father not to let her ride backwards, and in many little solicitous ways showed his sympathy. Thomas Dabney had been prejudiced against Mr. Pierce. This kind attention to his child removed the unpleasant impressions, which, after all, referred only to politics. The kindness reminded him of Charles's admiration of Mr. Pierce, and he never criticised him harshly again.

At all the towns through which the trains passed the people were gathered in crowds to see the President. But he sat in the corner of his seat in his quiet, simple fashion, and most of them went away without having been able to find out which was he. At one station, the eager face of a little boy attracted Thomas's attention. "Where is the President?" he was asking in an excited voice. Thomas put his hand out of the window and beckoned to the child. "Come here, my little fellow," he said, "I will show the President to you." But the crowd of men as well as the boy saw the hand waved from the window, and at once several of these rushed up and thrust their heads into Thomas's window. The lad had no chance. As he turned, and walked disconsolately away, he said, with a burst of tears, "I ain't going to lose my dinner again to see no more Presidents."

We had an ex-Presidential party at the Warm Springs,—the ——. Mrs. ——, for a reason which could only be conjectured, as it was neither useful nor becoming, wore a tiara of diamonds, curiously suggestive of a queen's crown. It was said that she never appeared in company without it. She certainly had it on when she alighted from the dusty stage at the Warm Springs. She spoke of —— always as "the President."

In travelling through Ohio that summer, the children of the party informed Aunt Abby that she was free, and that of course she was going to leave them, and they proceeded to seize her hand with loud good-byes. This was amusing to them, but Aunt Abby looked at it as anything but amusing. She burst into floods of tears, and her mistress put a stop to the teasing of the children. The master had to reassure her, by telling her what to say if any one should try to carry her off. In Cincinnati two men got on the train and went at once to her, asking if she were free. True to her master's instructions, she answered yes. "You are free as long as you are in Ohio," he had said. "You will only be saying what is true." She looked so frightened and wretched that the men did not believe her, and

plied her with more questions, but nothing could be
got out of her. She thought that they really meant to
drag her out and make her free whether she wished it
or not, as the children had said they would. She got
down on the floor of the car, and squeezed herself under
the seat on which her master and mistress sat, and
could not be persuaded for some hours to leave her
hiding-place. Another Mississippi family, Mr. and Mrs.
Hinton, were on the same train, and they also had a
servant with them. This servant and Aunt Abby had
formed quite a friendship on the journey, and sat together on the car. She answered the abolitionists as
Aunt Abby did, and the men left the train without ac-
complishing any other object than to give amusement
to the Southern travellers and to frighten the two
servants.

Friends and acquaintances attached themselves to
our party as we journeyed about the country, till we
got to be seventeen in number. One day my father
was marshalling us out of a dining-room, where the
train had stopped for dinner. He told the man at the
door that he had seventeen eating dinner, and he proceeded to count us as we filed out. As mamma came,
"There's my wife," he cried, " she counts for two."
The door-keeper, who up to this time had kept a close
eye on us, cried out, laughing, " Oh, sir, do not count
any more. It is all right, I know. I am satisfied."
And he took the money that my father put in his hand
without looking longer at the advancing column.

The mother seemed benefited by the long absence
from home and home cares. She wrote to one of her
absent children, after they were settled once more at
Burleigh,—

" I know that you will be glad to hear I am better
than when you saw me. I take a good deal of interest
in my housekeeping now."

It had been a grief to her that she took no interest
in anything.

The main interest in the life of the parents in this
winter (1855–1856) was the education of the children.
The father's ambition for his children was great. He

wished them to excel in everything, and was proportionally disappointed when they failed. The mother was not less in earnest about their education, but she did not expect impossibilities as he did. To her thirteen-year-old Emmy the mother wrote:

"I am making a wadded wrapper for you to study hard in. . . . I trust you and Sophy will go hard to work. You must always be at the head of your class. Let me hear from you frequently, and tell me exactly how you stand in your classes."

She had no ear for music, and understood that her children could hardly be expected to be very proficient in that. But Thomas desired and expected his daughters to perform like professionals. He was excessively fond of music, although he never learned to play on any instrument except the flute, on which he played very poorly, and he gave that up as soon as he heard better music from his children's fingers. He filled the house with musical instruments,—two pianos, and a harp, and a flute or so, and, later on, a melodeon for sacred music.

The daughters tried hard to come up to his ideal, and studied music and practised many hours for years. But only one, Sophy, realized his dream. Her music was a great delight to him and a source of almost unbounded pride.

Music with Virginius was a passion from his cradle. At the time that the Belgian violinist was at Burleigh he showed such a love for it, that his mother became seriously uneasy lest he should be unfitted for life by giving himself up to the study of the violin. He was allowed to buy a violin from the young musician, but he received no encouragement to apply himself to the study of it, and did not till he went to Europe, after his course at the University was over. It was a very uncommon thing in those days for the sons of American parents to be taught music.

The father expected all his sons to take the degree of Master of Arts at the University of Virginia. They might give themselves as many years as they chose to get it in, but they must bring that home eventually. They found mathematics the great obstacle, and gave up trying to get through on that. They had diplomas to show to him after each commencement, but he was never satisfied because they had not taken the whole course.

He was not a man to go by halves in anything. He could hate and detest as well as love and admire. His belief in human nature made him see the good in every man at first, and he thought well of even the most unprepossessing until forced to believe ill of them. When once he had seen anything mean or untrue in a man, it was wellnigh useless to try to make him see any good in that man afterwards. His prejudices carried him away as far in the opposite direction as his good nature had carried him in the man's favor. He was strong in all his feelings, and it was difficult for him to overlook or forgive such faults as arose from narrowness and dishonesty of purpose. His wife's influence was great, and she used it unceasingly to soften this disposition in him. She tried, too, to prevent him from expressing his adverse opinions of men and things as openly and imprudently as he did. He was incapable of dissembling or even concealing a feeling if he saw anything going on that he thought wrong. He could not even be made to see any virtue in restraining the expression of his disapprobation at such times. But he yielded his judgment to hers in many instances, because he could not bear to differ with her in anything, however insignificant.

He spoke as openly to people as behind their backs. It was often a subject of marvel that he was allowed to say what another man could hardly have done with impunity.

As an instance of this, he one day spoke sharply to Colonel McClung, the famous duellist of Mississippi. It was said that Colonel McClung had killed five men, and had grown reckless and bad-tempered and easy to take offence, especially when he was drinking. One day Thomas went up to Cooper's Wells, and on alighting saw Colonel McClung. He saw at once that he was intoxicated, and tried to avoid him, but Colonel McClung was fond of whist and fond of Thomas as a partner, and followed him, insisting on a game. There was no getting out of it, as the part of prudence dictated. Colonel McClung played carelessly, a thing annoying to his partner, and he spoke sharply. "Do you speak so to me, sir?" Colonel McClung asked, raising his eyes of fire, his whole frame quivering with suppressed passion. But his eyes of fire met the eyes of a lion. "I do, sir."

Colonel McClung saw that he could not daunt that man. He gazed at him a moment. "I thought that he meant to challenge me," Thomas said, in speaking of it afterwards. "Every gentleman there thought that he would challenge me. But he calmed down in a moment and, to the surprise of everybody, said, 'You are right, Colonel Dabney; I did revoke and play carelessly. I shall do better, sir.'"

"Did you ever have the feeling of fear in your life, papa?" one of his children asked one day. "I cannot remember, my dear, that I ever did," he said, in a musing way, as if he had not more than half heard the question and took no interest in it.

CHAPTER XV.

SUMMER-TIME—FALLING ASLEEP.

THE summers of 1856–57–58 were spent by the family at Burleigh. Indeed, from this time, the house was not again closed in summer. Occasionally some members of the family went to Mississippi City on the sea-coast for the change, or to the Hinds County watering-place, Cooper's Wells, or to the Virginia springs or farther north; but of so large a family, some were always at home after the Pass Christian house had been sold.

The summers grew to be the gayest season at Burleigh. The house was nearly always crowded with guests. Everybody in the neighborhood kept open house. Friends from towns and cities found it the pleasant time to visit the country, and there were other reasons for their coming too. It was safe from the yellow fever. In yellow fever summers entire households, including, of course, servants and children of all ages, were entertained. Sometimes for weeks, and even months, the white family numbered from twenty to twenty-five persons, and sometimes more. Music and dancing, charades and games, cards, riding on horseback, and wagon- and carriage-driving were the diversions. One yellow fever summer we got up a history class, and everybody had every morning to sit in a long line in the hall and answer in his or her turn a question or two in English history. Blunders gave more universal satisfaction than accurate knowledge, and it ceased to be a disgrace to be unable to answer very simple questions. One summer a church fair absorbed a great deal of time and thought. One winter we young people and our guests took up English poetry. It became a rage to study the best English poetry and recite it to each other on long walks. We learned several thousand lines before the enthusiasm died out. A lady who spent many weeks and months there in these years used to say that she had learned more at the "Burleigh Academy" than at any other that she had ever attended. A well-selected library of thirteen hundred volumes put all the standard authors within reach.

One of the best actors in the charades was our father. The only objection to him was that he was so amusing to the other actors that they could scarcely get through with their parts. Any one who excelled in anything that could entertain the company was called on to do it. There were few who did not catch the spirit of the house and join in whatever was on foot. One young friend, who danced the Fisher's Hornpipe and the Cachuca very gracefully, was dressed in fancy costume and made to dance her *pas seul* every time that she made a visit. In the garret were trunks of fancy costumes, masks, etc., for such occasions,—some were bought, but most of them were fabricated out of old finery. Poetry and speeches were declaimed, and songs sung by people who had not dreamed that they had so much in them before.

An English gentleman, an Oxford man, who spent a summer there under these happy conditions, said that the entertainment at Burleigh was like that in English houses. Sufficient attention was paid to visitors to make them comfortable, and to make them understand that their society was desired, but they were allowed to follow their own bent in disposing of their time. Mrs. Dabney's quiet dignity and her husband's high spirits and vivacious temperament were just the complementary qualities needed for a delightful home atmosphere.

Burleigh was loved almost like a home by some of the coming and going guests, and by one or two young boys who had lived there as members of the family,— the sons of friends or relations.

The summer of 1858 was one of the gayest known at Burleigh. During the summers of 1859 and 1860 some of the young members of the family travelled in the North.

Among the guests at Burleigh in these years none were oftener there, or contributed more to the happiness of the house, than the Raymond Dabneys. The brilliant band of sisters in the Raymond household were the most welcome visitors who came to Burleigh, and the brothers were looked on almost as sons of the house.

Thomas and Sophia felt a just pride in this charming family of four nephews and five nieces. In their turn they honored Thomas almost as a second father, and Sophia was the dearest of their aunts.

Thomas was the friend of young men, and encouraged and assisted all who applied to him. During their University days two of his sons, Charles and Virginius, wrote to him of worthy young men who were struggling to educate themselves and were in need of money. In both cases he sent a check for five hundred dollars to his sons, to hand to their friends as a gift. The following letter from a young friend will throw light on this side of his character:

. . . "Aunt S. told me the other day of something which I was glad to hear, because it makes me feel nearer than ever to you all. It was simply an act of generosity on the part of your father, which would stand without a parallel in the experience of those greatly older and more acquainted with life and human nature than I am. I suppose you have heard it, but may I repeat it?

"At the time of a commercial crisis in New Orleans, when three of my uncles, ——, ——, and ——, were thought to be embarrassed, your father heard of it and sent to them a blank check, stating the amount he had in bank (fifty thousand dollars or more, I think), and instructing them to draw upon it to the whole amount, if necessary to prevent their name from going to protest. I do not think the check was used, but the generous friendship of the deed remains."

The incident is true, except as regards the amount offered. It was not over twenty-five thousand dollars, or, at most, thirty thousand dollars, as he never had in bank more than the proceeds of the sale of a single crop, and his largest cotton crop brought thirty thousand dollars.

He sent a check for fifty dollars to every church that applied to him for aid, without regard to its creed.

He was so lavish in providing for his family that his wife and daughters learned not to trust him to make purchases, because he got so much more than was needed.

A few illustrations of this will show his ideas on such matters. Sophia asked him one day to buy a brooch for the eldest girl. He was so pleased with the commission that he bought six, two apiece for the three eldest. Another day she asked for two diamond rings; the two eldest daughters had practised their music faithfully and this was to be a reward. The next two she thought too young for diamond rings. He bought four,—it would not do to make a difference, he said. When one watch was sent for he bought three.

Sometimes his shopping experiences were really ludicrous. On his return from New Orleans one winter he brought in the place of a pink silk-tissue dress, that had been on his memorandum for one of the daughters, a quantity of some costly stuff for the entire family. It had struck his fancy, and he had gotten enough of it to make dresses for Sophia and each of her daughters. It was neither tasteful nor suitable.

But the dear mother, with that rare unworldliness and lack of ostentation that sometimes brought a smile to the faces of her friends, had the dresses made up—five or six of them—all alike.

And the dear father admired, and thought that we would always be willing to trust to his taste in the future.

He looked on it as a great sin in parents to show a preference for one child over another. It was unpardonable to feel it, he said, unworthy of a true father or mother. He said that he loved all his children alike, and he should feel like tearing his heart from his bosom if he did not. I never saw any one feel so strongly on this subject,—the cruel injustice of it struck him afresh when some instance came to his knowledge of some parent who felt otherwise than himself.

His children can testify, from full hearts, the unspeakable *comfort* of the *impartial* love of father and mother.

During all these years, since Charles's death, the mother's health had been failing. Her husband did everything that devoted love could prompt. They went on trips to pleasant places, and on visits to pleasant houses. Still, as time passed, she grew no better. It was now seven years since her great sorrow, but it seemed to bear her down more than ever before. She began to say that she was tired of bringing up her young children. "I do not bring them up as I did the others," she said. "I am not able to do it. My daughters could take better care of them." And when she was ill, and we worked to save her, she said, "Oh, why did you not let me die?" When she thought that she was dying her lips moved and a daughter's ear caught the humble prayer, "Bless my children. Make them useful members of society." She was spared to us some months after this.

The land began to be full of the talk of the coming war. Thomas was an Old-Line Whig, and that is as much as to say he was a Union man. He despised the "Blue-Cockade Men," as he called the secessionists, on account of the badge that many wore before hostilities began. He felt sure that they would not be the men to shoulder their rifles when real work had to be done. He did all that he could, in his neighborhood and through the press, to calm the excited feelings that the demagogues were lashing to a frenzy. He believed that the leaders were getting the war up to further their own ambitious schemes. From the first he doubted not that it would be a terrible conflict; it had been brewing too many years to be other than terrible.

He foresaw that in any event, whether conquered or victorious, the South would be ruined.

"If the South succeeds," he said, "this will be but the beginning of secessions."

He decided to sell everything that he owned and to move, before it was too late, to England with all his family.

When his plans were fully made, he spoke to Sophia one night,—

"My dear, I have made up my mind to sell our property and to get out of this country at once. We shall go to England. We have enough to enable us to live there with our children."

"Yes, my dear; but what will you do with Abby?"

The question was unanswerable. It opened up a whole vista of similar ones. "What will you do with Maria, with Harriet, with their children and husbands?" He could set one or two free and provide annuities, but if he tried to make all his servants comfortable whom he could not make up his mind to sell, it would be quite impossible for him to take his family to live in England.

That question of my good mother's settled forever his mind and the destiny of her house.

Thomas Dabney and his wife deliberately chose to go down with their country.

Has not their daughter, then, the right to say, as was said at the beginning of these memorials, that the tie between this master and his slaves was as sacred and binding, if not as near, as the tie of blood?

But the mother who almost forgot her own children that night on her pillow to stand up for her slaves, was not to see the desolation that was even now at her doors.

We did not know it then, but on the 9th of January, 1861, Mississippi was to throw off her allegiance to the United States government.

Three weeks before that 9th of January, one week before that last Christmas before the war, Thomas was standing in the dining-room, near Sophia, when she called to him suddenly. He threw out his arms just in time to catch her, and she sank on his breast.

She never spoke afterwards to him or to any one else. She fell asleep as he held her in his arms, and he took her to her bed.

She slept for nearly four days, while her physicians and her large family and many relations and friends gathered around her.

Thomas was with her day and night, sitting or lying by her side,—his fingers on her pulse,—scarcely hearing his children when they begged him to take some care of himself.

He felt the last pulsation of that loved heart. The breath had come more and more faintly, and at longer intervals, and he knew that the end was at hand.

"It is over," he said, as he rose to go towards his children.

Five daughters and two sons were there, the youngest child seven years of age. The two oldest sons only were absent, and one daughter.

Two of the children were married, and two others grown men and women, but to him they were all to be from this day his motherless children.

During our mother's lifetime he was sometimes a stern father. But from the day on which his lonely widowhood began he was never again other than the tenderest mother could have been. His whole nature seemed changed. He was father and mother in one. The wise, strong judgment and counsel of the man were there, but blended now with a pitying compassion and sympathy that were more than womanly. It was such tenderness as only the strong and brave can feel.

He missed so sorely the loving and congenial and ennobling companionship that for thirty-four years had been his, that he could not bear to see his children suffer any approach to what he felt. The constraint that he put upon himself to appear cheerful was the most touching part of his grief, and we feared at times that his heart would break. During that perfect union there had been not one jar or disagreement.

The only large wedding that took place in the Burleigh house was on the occasion of the marriage of Susan to Lyell Smedes. She had been engaged to him for two years, and her parents, who were much attached to him, warmly approved her choice. The servants long remembered the wedding-feast on this happy event; every man, woman, and child on the plantation was remembered in the wedding-cakes and other good things.

It was during the short married life that followed this event that our mother passed away. Lyell's presence was especially comforting to our father. His own children could not cheer him as the son-in-law did. But the dear father was unselfish in his grief as in everything else.

"Do not stay with me," he said; "go and take your young wife in your arms and comfort her as I comforted her mother when she was young and when she was old." In a few weeks the household was plunged into a new and deep sorrow by the death of this husband of eleven weeks.

The following extract is taken from his father's[*] meditations on the morning's lesson for Sexagesima Sunday. It will throw light on a character of singular

---

[*] Rev. Aldert Smedes.

beauty and guilelessness, and on a life which passed so quickly from the home-circle at Burleigh:

. . . "We shall deduce but one lesson from this interesting story: it is, the honor in which God holds filial obedience! . . . Let the true moral, then, of the story of the Rechabites sink into every heart. It was their obedience to their father for which God held them in honor. 'Thus saith the Lord of Hosts, the God of Israel, *Because ye have obeyed* the commandment of Jonadab, your father, and kept his precepts, and done according to all that he hath commanded you: therefore, thus saith the Lord of Hosts, Jonadab, the son of Rechab, shall not want a man to stand before me forever.'

"In what precise sense this promise was fulfilled to the father of the Rechabites it is not our purpose to inquire. But to every Christian father of an obedient son the words assume a meaning as true as it is full of encouragement and blessing.

"That son may grow up before his father, the delight of his eyes, the pride of his heart, with all the innocence and graces of a childhood baptized into Christ, gradually developing under parental culture, blessed of heaven, into the traits and virtues of a boyhood and youth, eager and joyous in every active sport, sedulous in every appropriate duty, and restrained from every excess of riot. Having won in this incipient stage, by amiability, docility, and a habitual preference of others to himself, the good will and esteem of preceptors, companions, and parents, he may be sent with trembling, but with trust, to the ordeal of college life. Amid the temptations which there beset the young he may be enabled to hold fast his integrity. Every letter from himself, every report from the authorities, every testimony of his many friends may cheer the anxious hearts of the circle at home, with evidence that he has not forgotten the precepts of his father's house nor forsaken the law of his mother's lips. At length, carrying with him the honors of his college and the hearts of all who shared his labors in its halls, he is launched upon the business of the world.

An independent and successful career opens almost immediately upon him, but it is one exposed to many and great dangers. Yet, though now of age to choose his own path, he does not forsake the paths in which he has been trained. He obeys a father's wishes by becoming an aid to his pastor in the Sunday-school and in the choir; he is regularly present when the sanctuary opens its doors; on all occasions and in every company he evinces his reverence for religion and for sacred things. A stranger in the place where his business has led him, he soon makes in every one of its inhabitants a friend.

"At length the time arrives when, after years of absence, he is to be held once more to the bosom which pillowed his infancy. He brings back to his home a form matured, indeed, into the fullest and firmest expression of manly vigor, but a countenance flushed with the same rosy innocence and beaming with the same sweet smile which rendered his infancy attractive.

"It was impossible to see his expanded chest, his elastic but firm step, his appearance of health and manly vigor without the conviction that his body was a temple which no foul excess had defiled. While the cheerfulness, amiability, and kindness that made his face shine almost as an angel's and were expressed in every gesture towards those with whom he conversed, were the same tokens of a heart as loving and guileless as a child's.

"But his brief reprieve from business expires, and he hurries to his adopted home to claim the dearest prize this earth contains for man. God has crowned the mercies of a life unusually blessed by giving to him the bride whom his heart had chosen. One brother performs the sacred service, another assists as his nearest friend. A crowd of relatives and friends, with tears and smiles and warm congratulations, attest their sympathy and joy. The bride and groom in the bloom of health and youth and beauty stand, happiest of the happy, in the midst of a circle as full of kindness, gayety, love, and hope as ever such an occasion assem-

)led. Surely the father of a son so placed, though realizing the scene only from a great way off, might be excused if, amid other thoughts it suggested, this one should stand prominently out, 'that he should not want a man to stand before God forever.'

"But a cloud soon passed over this cheerful sky! It was shrouded in the blackness of night! In his mysterious wisdom and goodness it pleased the Almighty Being, who had made this young man so lovely and given him so much to love, to remove him by a swift disease from all that he held dear, from all who held him dear. His manly form lies low in the dust. His beauty is withered like the flowers which, from many hands, were scattered profusely over his bier. And now what remains for the afflicted ones he has left behind? For the widow in her speechless, tearless grief? For the mother, who goes mourning all the day long and waters her couch with her tears? Shall no light rise upon their darkness? Nay, rather in the recollection with which their memory is stored, of the Christian graces of his childhood, youth, and manhood, in the testimony which comes to them from so many quarters, even from the companions of his gayest hours, from young and old, from man and woman, from high and low, of his generosity, his disinterestedness, his purity of thought, and word, and deed; shall they not hear the whisper of 'the voice from heaven,' saying, 'Blessed are the dead who die in the Lord,' and shall not his father feel in a sense, highest, holiest, and most blessed of all, that 'he shall not want a man to stand before God forever!'"

We placed him by the side of our mother, among her children. On the simple slab of Italian marble that marks the spot are his name and age—twenty-five years—and the words:

"Blessed are the pure in heart, for they shall see God."

CHAPTER XVI.

SLAVES AND WAR-TIMES.

On the day after our mother's death one of the daughters went to the kitchen to attend to the housekeeping. She found the cook in a flood of tears. "I have lost the best friend that I had," she said. She spoke the truth, for few besides the mistress who was gone could have had patience with Alcey. She was the cook who had been bought from Mr. Dabney's mother's estate, and had been treated with marked kindness on account of her being a stranger; but she seemed to be vicious and heartless, and nothing but the untiring forbearance and kindness of this mistress had touched the hardened nature.

When one hires servants and they do not give some sort of satisfaction, redress is at hand. The servant is dismissed. But with slaves, at Burleigh, and with all the good masters and mistresses in the South,—and I have known very few who were not good,—there was no redress.

It may be thought that Southerners could punish their servants, and so have everything go on just as they pleased. But he who says this knows little of human nature. "I cannot punish people with whom I associate every day," Thomas Dabney said, and he expressed the sentiment of thousands of other slave-owners. It was true that discipline had sometimes to be used, but not often, in very many instances only once in a lifetime, and in many more, never. George Page, who in his youth, and in his middle age, was about his master's person and knew him well, said, "Marster is a heap more strict with his children than he is with his servants. He does not overlook things in his children like he does in his people."

Apart from the humane point of view, common sense, joined with that great instructor, responsibility, taught slave-owners that very little can be effected by fear of punishment.

Fear and punishment only tend to harden the rebellious heart. What, then, was to be done with a grown servant who was too lazy or too ill-tempered to do half work, with abundant and comfortable support insured whether the work was done or not? It is clear that unless the moral nature could be appealed to, that servant had to be endured. It would not have answered to set that one free; that would have made dissatisfaction among the others. Very many slave-owners looked on slavery as an incubus, and longed to be rid of it, but they were not able to give up their young and valuable negroes, nor were they willing to set adrift the aged and helpless. To have provided for this class, without any compensation for the loss of the other, would have reduced them to penury.

Now that the institution is swept away, I venture to express the conviction that there is not an intelligent white man or woman in the South who would have it recalled, if a wish could do it. Those who suffered and lost most—those who were reduced from a life of affluence to one of grinding poverty—are content to pay the price.

Good masters saw the evil that bad masters could do. It is true, a bad master was universally execrated, and no vocation was held so debasing as the negro trader's. Every conscientious proprietor felt that these were helpless creatures, whose life and limb were, in a certain sense, under his control. There were others who felt that slavery was a yoke upon the white man's neck almost as galling as on the slaves; and it was a saying that the mistress of a plantation was the most complete slave on it. I can testify to the truth of this in my mother's life and experience. There was no hour of the day that she was not called upon to minister to their real or imaginary wants. Who can wonder that we longed for a lifting of the incubus, and that in the family of Thomas Dabney the first feeling, when the war ended, was of joy that one dreadful responsibility, at least, was removed? Gradual emancipation had been a hope and a dream not to be realized.

It may not be out of place to give an illustration of how one of the Burleigh servants carried her point over the heads of the white family.

After the mistress had passed away, Alcey resolved that she would not cook any more, and she took her own way of getting assigned to field work. She systematically disobeyed orders and stole or destroyed the greater part of the provisions given to her for the table. No special notice was taken, so she resolved to show more plainly that she was tired of the kitchen. Instead of getting the chickens for dinner from the coop, as usual, she unearthed from some corner an old hen that had been sitting for six weeks, and served her up as a fricassee! We had company to dinner that day; that would have deterred most of the servants, but not Alcey. She achieved her object, for she was sent to the field the next day, without so much as a reprimand, if I remember rightly. We were very sorry, for she was the most accomplished cook whom we had had in Mississippi. But what was to be done? No master could have made her cook unless by making a brute of himself, and using such measures as would lower him in his own eyes. Her master merely said, "Choose any one whom you like as your cook, and let Alcey go out to the field."

Those were days of trial and perplexity to the young mistresses. The old house-servants, though having at heart an affection for them, considered or pretended to consider them too young to know what they wanted.

Besides, had they not known these young ladies ever since they were born? And did not they call them mammy or aunt in consideration of superior age?

If complaint were made to the master, his answer was, "If you cannot get along with the servants, and they will not recognize your authority, choose any others that you think will do better." Several had to be sent to the fields before some of the old trained servants, who had never worked out of the "great house" in their lives, saw that there was to be a head to the house, even though that head was set on young shoulders.

In this time of change and discouragement Mammy Maria's strong, true love for the house showed itself, and was indeed a help and support. She had never in her life received what could be called an order from any younger member of the family. To her everything was put in the form of a request. She was too much beloved for any one of her " white children" to wish to alter this relationship now. But mammy decided herself on changing her manner to us. Instead of her independent way of letting us know her views, and expecting us to follow her advice, she addressed her young mistresses in a manner marked by the most studied deference. The slightest expressed wish, though couched as ever in the form of a request, was a command to mammy, and was obeyed with more punctilious exactness than if it had come from the father or mother. She and they had been *bons camarades* many a year together, and understood each other,—there was no need to obey strictly, or to obey at all, if she saw a better way. But here was a different state of things, —here was upheaval and rebellion. The servants hardly meant it so; most of it was thoughtlessness on their part, but the result was discomfort and perplexity to mammy's "white children." Her loyal heart showed her this way of giving comfort to us.

After the war actually began, Thomas Dabney espoused the side of the South with all the enthusiasm of his nature. As has been said, he did nothing by halves. He at once organized his household on a more economical footing that he might have the more to aid in carrying on the war. He said that we at home ought not to live more luxuriously than our soldiers in camp, and he himself set the example of giving up many luxuries which were yet abundant in the land. It was considered unpatriotic to plant cotton, and he urged his neighbors to turn all their energies towards sustaining the Southern soldiers. They planted half crops of cotton; but not a cotton-seed was allowed to be put in the ground on the Burleigh plantation. Every acre was planted in corn, that the army should not lack food for man and beast. He gave his money with both hands, and his sons as freely. He was most restive at not being in the army himself. He was on the point of enlisting many times, and did enlist once, when special troops were called for to go to Columbus, Kentucky, where heavy fighting was expected.

His daughters were in despair at seeing him at the age of sixty-two preparing to go into the trenches. No argument on the subject of his age could move him when this uncontrollable longing to go into the army got possession of him, as it did from time to time. His daughters came around him and reminded him that all their brothers who were old enough to handle a musket were at the front, and he ought not to run the risk of leaving them without a natural protector. Perhaps the strongest argument used was that he could best serve his country by remaining at home and giving his personal supervision to the fields which were to feed the armies. He finally yielded to their wishes and stayed at home.

His fourteen-year-old son, Benjamin, caught the war fever, and his father gave his consent for him to go into the ranks. He sent a trusted body-servant with his sons.

"William," he said, "I wish you to stand by your young masters, and to look after them as well as you can. And if they are killed, I want you to bring them home to me."

"Yes, marster."

"And here is my sword, William. I give it to you to take to the war. You can fight with it, too, if you see a chance."

"Yes, marster, I will show them the English of it."

And William, who was about six feet two inches in height, threw his head back and looked proud of the trust. (See *Addendum*, p. 342.)

William was armed with the master's own sword, which he had had sharpened before handing it to him. It had been his when, at the age of fourteen years, he had gone to Old Point Comfort, where the British were expected to land. The edge had been ground off when peace was declared after the war of 1812, and it had not been sharpened till the Confederate war broke out.

Thomas wrote much for the papers in these days, urging every Southerner to take care of the soldiers in the field. Five young men, who were guests at Burleigh in the first spring of the war, were fitted out by him and sent off with one hundred dollars apiece, and directions to have their bills charged to him. Gray cloth was ordered up from New Orleans, and uniforms cut out and made by the dozen in the house and sent to the camps. Blankets were not to be bought in any Southern market, and he decided to give every one that he owned, but his daughters begged to be allowed to keep some, and he compromised on giving away nineteen of the largest size, about half. He wished us to cut up the carpets to put on the beds. Great boxes of food and wine were sent off to the hospitals. He sent his carriage for sick soldiers, and took care of them as long as they were allowed to stay, treating each private as if he were the commander-in-chief of the army.

He greatly enjoyed a dinner that he gave to General John C. Breckenridge and a brilliant party of officers and friends in September of 1862. It was the last entertainment given at Burleigh before the tide of war swept over it. There were about eighteen guests, among them some friends from New Orleans,—Mr. Needler Jennings, Mr. George W. Ward, and Mr. Violet, Andrew Jackson Polk, of Tennessee, and the Hon. Senator Gwynn, of California. Two of our own soldier boys were there on furlough, Edward Dabney and Augustine Dabney's son, Thomas Gregory Dabney.

Everybody was full of hope. None then realized the true state of things, that Vicksburg would fall and all our part of the country be overrun. Vicksburg had stood two sieges, and we thought that little city impregnable, and the gay company assured the ladies that they should be defended, and should never see the war more near-by.

General Breckenridge had been called the handsomest man in the United States when he was a candidate for the Vice-Presidency a few years before. It would be impossible to exaggerate the beauty of his person or the grace and courtesy of his bearing. His face was one of classic beauty, and his figure worthy in its proportions to bear the massive head, so superbly set upon the shoulders; but to see him mounted on his warhorse, riding as if he and the charger were one, the long black plumes of his hat nodding with every movement, his eye fired with enthusiasm, this was the most impressive picture that had met our eyes. As we stood on the porch the next morning watching the receding cavalcade, they waved their hats and saluted till the bend in the road shut them from our view.

The Burleigh family had cause to remember the second siege of Vicksburg. One of the daughters, Sophy, lay halting between life and death. Her physician informed the family that any excitement would probably be fatal, and on no account must the impending siege of Vicksburg be alluded to in the sick-room. We had heard every gun of the first siege, and this one was expected to begin every hour.

Presently a dull, booming sound was heard; it announced that the siege had opened. The watchers hoped that the patient slept. A moment more and another and another gun broke the stillness.

"What is that?" she asked.

"Isn't it thunder?" somebody suggested.

"Thunder does not sound at regular intervals. The siege of Vicksburg has begun."

But it did not excite her, as we had feared it would, and though every shot seemed to go through the loud-beating hearts of the father and sisters during those long days of suspense, she did not seem to attend, and got well as fast as if there had been no siege of Vicksburg.

The plantation life went on as usual. The servants went about their duties, we thought, more conscientiously than before. They seemed to do better when there was trouble in the white family, and they knew that there was trouble enough when all the young men in the family were off at the wars. They sewed on the soldiers' clothes and knit socks for the army, and packed the boxes with as much alacrity as the white people did. They were our greatest comfort during the war.

When hostilities began, the younger children were taught by a tutor who had been in the family for several years. Mr. Dabney had not thought of sending him away, though he was a Northern man, and, it was to be supposed, with Northern sympathies. He was so quiet that we at Burleigh rarely thought of his sympathies, for he never seemed to speak if he could avoid it. But the neighbors had a report that he was a spy, and Mr. Dabney was informed of it, with a request that Mr. T—— should be dismissed. This was communicated to the tutor in the kindest manner, and the man was moved to tears as Thomas talked with him.

Thomas Dabney originated the scheme for the Confederate government to raise money by getting out bonds on the basis of the cotton then in the hands of the planters. The cotton bonds supplied the sinews of war during the early part of the struggle.

At a trial of strength between himself and five young men who were guests in his house for a month or two before they went off to the war, he held out at arm's length a weight that was too heavy for them to hold out.

One day after his beloved wife had been dead about a year, Thomas was lying on his bed in his chamber, one of his daughters and a niece sitting by him. He began to sing the song that had so often been begged for in vain by their children,—the song that had won their mother's heart.

He sang it from beginning to end. As he came to the last line, he struck with his clinched fist upon his breast,—

"Do they think that I can forget you! Do they think that I can forget you!" he cried.

Some one, little knowing the man, had spoken to him jestingly of marrying again in this early stage of his grief.

The Episcopal Church of St. Mark's, at Raymond,

had been built years before the war, and had been the parish church of Thomas and his family. The drive of ten miles did not seem inconvenient then. But it became impossible to get so far afterwards. The family fell into a way of reading the service at home, and the neighbors liked to attend, and the large household was frequently swelled to quite a congregation. Occasionally the bishop or one of the clergy were there, and were surprised to see the number that could be gathered together, almost without giving out any notice. In the afternoon the daughters held a service and Sunday-school for the negroes, and the large library was well filled by them. They delighted in the chants and hymns, and knew much of the service and the catechism by heart.

Many years after they were free, a brawny blacksmith sent a message to his teachers of these days, "Tell de ladies I ain't forgit what dey teach me in de Sunday-school."

Thomas never allowed anything to interfere with his attending the services. Oftentimes friends came in, or other things happened that made it an effort to break off. But when the hour came, he would say, quietly, "We always have the service at eleven o'clock on Sundays," and the guests were invited to join him. It was a surprise to many who knew him only as a charming companion, always ready for any sort of amusement that was not really wicked. Some persons who had not been in a church for years felt constrained to go in to these services. The quiet dignity of the head of the house made it difficult to approach him with a light excuse.

He did not himself lead the daily family prayers in his house, or conduct the church services on Sundays. His deep humility made him feel unworthy to take this part.

He loved to hear his daughters read the service and the prayers. If for any reason they were omitted, he would ask for them. When he was sick, we always had the services around his bed. He was not one to express his religious feelings, but no one felt more deeply or reverently. His faith was that of a little child, without a doubt, or shadow of one. He did not seem even to know what was meant by religious doubts. I do not believe that in the course of his life he ever questioned the truth of revealed religion for five consecutive minutes. The subject did not interest him, and he never took part in any conversation bearing on it.

And yet he was not a communicant, and he was passing through life with that error fixed in his mind, that one must feel worthy before one can without hypocrisy become a communicant. It was a happiness to him to see his children go up to be confirmed as they grew up. In his humility, he thought them better than himself.

One Sunday only himself and a daughter were left in the house; everybody else was away. She had not thought of going through with the services under the circumstances. But her father asked,—

"Will you not have the services, my child?"

"I had not meant to do it. I thought that we could read to ourselves."

"I want you to read the services, my dear," he said, in his humble, gentle way that always came when he spoke of these things. So they two went through the full service together.

When they were not far from the end, there came a knock at the door; a neighbor had come to spend the day. His daughter thought that Thomas would not ask her to go on, as the visitor was one who was not a religious man. But he said at once,—

"My daughter and I are having prayers."

And the visitor joined in with a very earnest face. He had not before seen this side of my father's character.

In the spring of 1863 Thomas Dabney began to feel that his children were in one of the worst places in the world for non-combatants, the neighborhood of a beleaguered city. He lamented that all his children were not sons. He longed more and more to go into the army as the fighting drew closer to us. He ordered an army uniform to be made for himself, and we feared that we should not be able to keep him with us. His intense sufferings from loneliness urged him, no less than his love for the military life, to plunge into the excitement now so near at hand. In his grief he said not infrequently in these days that it would have been better for him if he had had no children left him to take care of. All the men in the land who were men indeed were off in the army; the whole country seemed forsaken, except by the old men and the boys and the women and children. He envied every soldier in the ranks, and felt like a chained lion. Not to go into the army cost him, without a doubt, the greatest struggle of his life.

The rumor came that the whole country around Vicksburg was to be abandoned to the enemy. Already General Grant's troops were moving on Vicksburg, and that place would soon be in a state of siege. The citizens were fleeing in every direction. Thomas Dabney, feeling that he had a home and food to offer to these homeless ones, caused to be inserted in one of the Vicksburg papers an invitation to any and all citizens desirous of leaving the city to take refuge at Burleigh.

One family of Louisiana refugees had come to us before this. This invitation brought out an Englishwoman, Mrs. Allen, and her two children, and later on her husband.

At this juncture our hopes were raised by the arrival of an officer, sent out by General Pemberton, with orders to seize every pleasure horse in the country. A large body of men were to be mounted, we were told, and this body of cavalry was to patrol the country lying around Vicksburg; and even to relieve that place when the time came. The officer was astonished when he was hailed as the bringer of joyful tidings. Many ladies, he said, had shed tears when their carriage and other favorite horses had been carried off by him. He had gotten nervous, and hated to come among the women of the country with that dreadful order in his hand. Every horse in the Burleigh stables was brought out freely. One riding horse was exempted from the draft as a necessary part of the plantation equipment.

My father preferred to retain his buggy horse, Gold Dust, and he was allowed to do so.

Alas! in a few weeks Gold Dust was to be in the service of the enemy and pitted against his own master's son, and against the Burleigh carriage horses and other equine acquaintances of the stables and pastures. When last seen our carriage horses, powerful young roans, were on the battle-field of Big Black in the artillery service.

We now set to work to bury the money and silver. Some of our friends had buried their watches, and so destroyed them. We sewed up our watches and such valuables as would be spoiled by dampness in the form of a bustle, and gave it to our trusted Aunt Abby to wear. Mammy Maria was too nervous and cried too much to have any responsibility put on her. Large hoops were in fashion at this time, and we tied our silver in bags and put these under our hoops, and went out one May day a mile from the house to a rock-quarry. Here we dug a hole with the dinner-knives that we had secreted about our persons for the purpose, and in this hole we placed our valuables. Then we put over them the largest stone that six or seven girls could move.

As we were not in the habit of walking out in the hot sun, some one proposed that we should dig up a young holly, or something of the kind, and set it out on our return to the house. This would account, it was thought, to the servants for our walk. So we pulled up a shrub or two and set them out as soon as we got home.

Mammy Maria watched these proceedings in silence, and then said in her brusque way, and in her capacity of a privileged servant, "You needn't think you is foolin' me. I know you don't go out in de hot sun in May to set out trees an' 'spect 'em to live."

The children buried their treasures too; Tom, a powder-can, as the most prized of his possessions. It was of a brilliant red, and a late acquisition, and might be coveted by the enemy. Little Lelia buried her dolls and their wardrobes securely in a hole dug in the greenhouse. Lelia's nurse, who helped at the frequent exhumings and re-interments, as rumors of the war were cheering or alarming,—for we had a fresh rumor nearly every day,—was true to her, but Tom was less fortunate in his confidant, and that red powder-can was near costing the thirteen-year-old boy his life. Ida buried her chief treasure, a pair of cheap china vases, a quarter of a mile from the house, down the spring hill.

In the midst of all this Mrs. Allen's baby died. One of the plantation carpenters made a coffin, and the Burleigh family buried the little child. No clergyman was to be had. Many of them were gone as chaplains in the army. Our pastor led his company into the first battle of Manassas.

The baby was buried in the park under a small oak-tree. The deer, seeing the procession of the family and the coffin borne by the negro men come in, with the curiosity of their species drew near. The gentler ones mingled with the group around the open grave, one special pet licking the hands of her human friends and stretching out her beautiful neck to reach the flowers that the young children had brought to strew on the little coffin.

The rude coffin and the absence of the minister, and of any white man save one silvery-haired one, spoke of war. But it was a beautiful and peaceful scene. The setting sun threw its slanting rays on the deer as they stood in the background near the forest-trees, and on the little group gathered close to the grave.

A woman's voice was repeating the solemn ritual of the Episcopal Church for the burial of the dead.

CHAPTER XVII.

A WEEK WITHIN THE LINES.

THE next rumor that came was that we were left within the enemy's lines, and it was true. Thomas Dabney thought it best to stay quietly at home and take the best care that he could of his family, both white and black. But his daughters became nervous and alarmed about his personal safety under such circumstances. He had been conspicuous in helping the Southern cause in every way in his power, by money and hospitality, and through the public journals of the State. We had heard of rough treatment of aged men found in their homes by the Northern soldiery. We heard later of the murder of two unarmed old gentlemen, Mr. Sam Smith, of Mathews County, Virginia, and Mr. Hyde, of Louisiana. Mr. Sam Smith was hanged near his place, and Mr. Hyde was burned up in his own house.

We made up our minds that our father should not risk his life if we could prevent it. The Federal troops might now be looked for at any hour. We wept and entreated him to leave us, and finally told him that if he did not we should go out of the house ourselves and seek a place of safety, knowing well that he would not allow us to go unattended by himself. We represented to him that we should be far safer without him, and cited to him many instances where the Northern troops had been kind to the women who had no men to protect them, and very rough with those who had one of their own sex in the house. We entreated him by day and by night until he could no longer resist our tears and prayers. With a heavy heart he bade us good-by.

The neighbors were carrying their servants to the east side of Pearl River, within the Confederate lines. We urged him to take a part of his there. He was opposed to this, and justly so. It would show a lack of trust in them, he said. Besides, it would be too great a strain of their obedience to him if he ordered his able-bodied men and women to leave their families behind and follow him. But he yielded his own judgment in this case also.

Most reluctantly he called for his young men and women, and told them that they must prepare to go with him twenty-seven miles into the Pearl River swamp. They obeyed cheerfully, and he kept them there against their inclination and against his, under uncomfortable conditions, for a week.

Meanwhile, at Burleigh we breathed freely when we saw our dear father ride off. The overseer was an easy-going man, who had not, like him, helped to carry on the war, and he expected to pass unnoticed as an obscure person and a non-combatant. He was to have control of things in the master's absence.

It was not long before the news came that a company of eighty Federals, from General Grant's army, had reached the plantation, and had encamped in a field on the Tallahala Creek, only a half-mile from the house. They were near enough for us to hear the reveille in the morning and the tattoo at night.

Very soon some of them rode up, by twos and threes, and came into the house. At first they were civil, but each day they grew more and more rough, and finally they became violent. They went into every room from the garret to the cellar, and through every closet, wardrobe, bureau, and trunk, and carried off everything that struck their fancy. They found several hundred dollars in the iron safe, and thought it a fortune. They looked like the dregs of some city. We have thought they must have been the camp-followers of General Grant's army, and not his regularly enlisted men. They were scarcely in uniform; perhaps a blue jacket on one and trousers on another, the rest of the garb being of any hue or cut other than a military one.

When keys were not produced at once, they forced the locks. Lelia's doll-trunk, only a few inches long, caught the eye of one of them.

"Do not break the child's doll-trunk. It has nothing in it but doll-clothes," one of her sisters said, when the key could not be found.

"It is big enough to hold a pistol," he said, as he burst the top of the toy off.

A broken-open desk revealed the love-letters of one of the girls, and the perusal of these seemed amusing work.

They found the wine-cellar, and drank until they

were intoxicated. Then they called to the negroes to come up into the porch to join them, as they struck the necks off the bottles of wine. The negroes stood around the porch, but only one accepted the invitation. The others looked on silently while a loud-voiced drunken fellow, who seemed to be the leader, announced that he had come to hang the old gray-haired scoundrel to whom all this belonged.

"I will hang your father on the nearest tree, under your eyes," he said to the daughters. "He is well known. I have long known him as an aider and abettor in this rebellion. I mean to get him yet. I hear that he is coming home in a few days." And then he cursed and swore dreadful oaths.

One of them shook a whip over Emmy's head because she said, "Sister, do not be frightened. Only cowards try to scare women and children."

"You had better not exasperate me," he cried, shaking a whip passionately over her. He was drunk enough to go any lengths. In the midst of all they called up Tom and ordered him to produce the large quantity of powder that he had buried. He denied all knowledge of any buried powder, not recollecting at the moment that he had buried a powder-can. Being inflamed with drink, they became very angry at his supposed obstinacy and falsehood. Holding a pistol to his head, they commanded him to bring the powder or his brains should be shot out. They marched the boy across the yard and down the declivity of the hill in this way. We expected every minute to see the pistol go off, whether the man willed it or not. It came to Tom, or to somebody, that the men must refer to the powder-can, and he took them to the spot. They dug it up, and were disgusted to find it empty. Our little black boy, Peter, had told the soldiers of this powder-can. He was with Tom when he buried it.

We did not see Peter for many years after this occurrence. A few years ago an emaciated and prematurely aged negro man came to the kitchen door to beg. He was ill, he said, and starving for something good to eat,—would we give him some pickle?

It was our Peter. We could not see a trace of his former self in him. He spent the day by the kitchen fire, and said that he should come often to see us, but it was evident that his days were numbered, and we saw him no more. He died a few weeks after.

One of the soldiers said that Lelia was just the age of his girl, and asked for a kiss, much to her alarm, for the children looked on the Federal soldiers as little less than fiends. She escaped without the kiss, but Letty did not. Letty was Augustine's youngest child, just Lelia's age, and they were the dearest of friends and playfellows. One of the men on seeing the three little girls, Ida, Lelia, and Letty, said something about "putty little gals," and asked if "sissy" would not give him a kiss, puckering up his mouth with a smacking sound as he made the proposal. The three fled precipitately behind the bed. He pursued, and Letty being the hindermost of the little women, and with the face of a cherub, suffered the penalty of her position, and got the detested kiss. He must have been discouraged by her reception of it, for he did not attempt to kiss the other two. It so chanced that the father's valued sword had been thrown behind that bed, with the idea of getting it out of sight. The children in their haste rushed over it, and it fell with a clatter. But the men did not find it, though they looked under every bed in their search through the house.

"There's a heap o' pretty tricks in this house," one of them remarked, "not to be any silver."

They asked the servants about the silver, but none of them gave a satisfactory answer. Aunt Abby's girl, Hannah, had helped to pour peas over the plated-ware in a barrel in the cellar. She was alarmed at their questions, and told us that they said they were determined to get the family silver. "I tole 'em I thought you had sent it to Georgia or somewhyar a long time ago," she said. The silver and plate had been in Hannah's charge for years, and she did not wish to see it go out of the family. We had kept out a few forks and spoons for use, and had quite forgotten them, when all this searching was going on. But Hannah had them on her mind and took care to hide them, and they were not found by the soldiers.

One day they announced their intention of staying to dinner. When we went into the dining-room not a vestige of a silver spoon or fork was to be seen. Hannah had found a set of steel forks that had been stowed away somewhere, and she had got together an array of iron spoons,—one was at each plate, and a number were in the middle of the table.

The sight of these iron spoons, of all sizes and ages, created a revulsion, and we did not dare to look up at Hannah or at each other lest we should laugh outright.

Hannah walked around with such an air, as much as to say that she had not heard us talk and read the papers for nothing!

The cook, Maria Reeves, whom my father had bought at her own request, was always devoted to him. "Please, marster, buy me. You is so good to your people," she had said. She and Hannah must have got that dinner up between them. In our experience of Maria we never knew her to serve so wretched a dinner as she sent up on that day. A small dish of fried meat was at one end of the long table, and a plate of corn bread at the other, if I remember correctly, and a very insufficient quantity of either. Our guests ate very little, and did not again stay to a meal.

The cook, good, simple soul, thought they would want her pots and kettles. One day she secreted herself and all her cooking utensils in a gully, and she and we had no dinner that day. When she came to tell us about it that night, she looked woe-begone enough, and we told her that it was not necessary to take such precautions in future.

Papa had taken off his two fine imported rifles. He left a number of others of less value behind, the sporting guns of his sons. There were eleven of them in the hall. The Federals took them all out and broke them against two young water-oaks that had been set out that spring. It killed the two trees.

One day they got more angry than usual, and swore

with many oaths that they meant to shoot the overseer. They were drunk enough to do it. They gave him five minutes to prepare for death. The man was no coward. He said simply, "God will be merciful to my soul. He knows that I am taken suddenly in my sins. My poor wife and children!" He closed his eyes for a few minutes in prayer, and then said, "I am ready."

But we had called the two little girls up,—Letty and Lelia. We told them that they might save this man's life by their tears and prayers. We had argued and entreated in vain,—children might be listened to when grown people's prayers could avail nothing. The children burst out crying, wailing, as we knew they would, and threw their arms around Mr. Scarborough. Their innocent, childish grief made a scene that was more than the men had bargained for. One of the sisters threw herself between the pistol and Mr. Scarborough's body, saying that he had stayed there to protect us, and he should not be murdered.

Debased as the men were, they decided to release Mr. Scarborough and end this scene.

We then begged Mr. Scarborough to go home to his family. He had been cursed and dragged about the yard by his collar, and finally came near losing his life at the hands of a squad of irresponsible camp-followers, as we supposed they were. No one could protect us, and the sight of him seemed to exasperate the men. So Mr. Scarborough went home, and only women and children remained in the house, about twelve of us perhaps.

The men called up the negroes and asked if it were true that all the horses had been carried off the place by the Southern army, or ridden off by the owners. All knew that Gold Dust was hidden in the woods, under the charge of Uncle Harrison, and was fed and watered by him every morning and night. But not one answered.

One of the ladies became alarmed lest Uncle Harrison's fidelity to the family should be betrayed, which might get him into trouble with the men. She answered that a horse was hidden in the woods.

"Who can take me to him?" one of them said.

"Uncle Harrison," she replied.

The man ordered Uncle Harrison to show the way to the horse.

He did not move, but, instead, looked at his mistress.

"Go, Uncle Harrison," she said.

"Must I, missis?" and the old man moved off reluctantly. He had hidden him away off in the deep woods, where they could never have found him, he explained afterwards.

When the horse was brought up, one of these rough fellows leaped on his back and struck him with his great whip. The fine creature, that had been trained to go by the word and the reins, and did not know the meaning of a whip, reared and danced with pain.

The man Edmund who had drunk a glass of wine in the porch had always been a bad negro. He was set as a sentinel to prevent our leaving the house. We saw him standing on the quarters' hill about a quarter of a mile off watching the house.* Perhaps it was believed that we would attempt to carry off valuables. All night long the cavalry galloped around the house, sometimes under the very windows. We could not sleep for the noise of their horses' hoofs.

The servants were as respectful and kind as ever, more so indeed. Aunt Abby crept in the house and handed back the package containing watches and other trinkets. "I cyarn't keep it any longer," she sobbed, while the tears poured down her venerable face. "Dey tells me dey has a wand, and dat wand will pint to anything dey tell it. I gave up all I had. I had a tumbler glass full o' money, presents, an' things dat de ladies had give to me,—half-dollars an' things. I give 'em all up. But I couldn't give up your things. But de wand will pint an' dey will git 'em, an' I bring 'em back to you now."

---

* When the war was over, "Edmund Dabney," as he signed himself, wrote to his old master begging to be allowed to return to Burleigh. He sent messages of humble apology by all passing negroes. He was never allowed to return.

They had taken all the money from every negro on the plantation. Uncle Isaac had buried eighty dollars in gold,—the savings of years. This he was made to unearth. He had lately bought a new silver watch, for which he had paid forty dollars. This was taken from him. Uncle Isaac was not a special favorite with his master, but he had been his playfellow in babyhood and boyhood. Partly for this reason, and partly because he was the master's own age, sixty-three years, and had been for years afflicted with incurable lameness, Thomas Dabney made him a present of a pair of his old carriage horses. Uncle Isaac was a preacher, and the horses were intended to give him ease and comfort in going about and in ploughing his own little patch. These horses he sold to a stage-driver for fifty dollars. His master was disgusted, as he had not wished the horses to do hard work.

When Uncle Isaac was robbed he came to the house to pour out his full heart to us. He went over again his old story of being a child of the same year as master, and of his getting a share of the nourishment that nature had provided for the white baby "in your grandma's arms, an' I called her ma an' your pa brother till I knowed better myself. *She* never tole me to stop."

It will be remembered that my father was during this period about forty miles from home within our lines. Every morning when he woke up his body-servant, George Page, told him of the number of his servants who had slipped away, back to the plantation, in the darkness of the preceding night. They were homesick, and doubtless suspected that their master was as homesick as they were, and only half-hearted in keeping them in the swamp.

As the numbers of the servants diminished day by day, George Page, like Caleb Osbaldistone, tried to make up in himself for what he looked on as the lack of loyalty on the part of the other servants. They were field negroes; he belonged to the house, and his manner to his master, during these days in the swamp, was touching in its blending of affection with respect.

He had left his wife and a houseful of children of all ages, to whom he was tenderly attached, on the plantation. He let his master know in every way that he was ready to stay by his side as long as he wished him.

At Burleigh we heard every day of the arrival of the different negroes. We knew that our father yearned to follow them, and that he would do so soon. Each hour we trembled lest we should see him ride up.

It was at this time that we resolved to get to him before he could reach us. We had been living within the lines for a week, and we felt that we could no longer stay in our home under the increasing anxieties.

We packed a few necessary things in two trunks to be taken off by Uncle Isaac in a cart, and we prepared to get away on foot at daylight, before the soldiers came from the camp. They had said on leaving us the evening before that they were coming back in the morning for the silver and to send pickets in every direction to search for papa, and to burn up the house and us in it, too.

Heavy firing had been going on towards the north for some days. The Federal soldiers had told us with loud boasts that they were whipping our Southern soldiers from the battle-fields. Fortunately, we did not know that Edward was in these fights. We were as completely cut off from the outer world as if we had been ourselves in a state of siege, and knew nothing except what they told us. We tried not to believe their stories of our disasters. But they were true. We heard the battle of Raymond on the 12th, on the 14th the battle of Jackson, and on the morning of the 16th the heaviest firing that we had yet heard came from the battle-field of Baker's Creek,—Champion Hill General Grant called it. Fifteen thousand Union soldiers and twenty-three thousand Southern soldiers were present at that battle; but six thousand six hundred and sixty-six Southern muskets were not fired, owing to some disagreement between the commanders it was said.

When the sound of these guns reached our ears we were speeding away from home as fast as our feet could carry us. We were belated the morning of the 16th, and did not get off till near sunrise, and then so hurriedly that one was bareheaded.

We had not a moment to lose. In point of fact, we were pursued eight miles by two soldiers. They did not overtake us, but were themselves overtaken and hanged by Southern soldiers. They had about their persons the money and jewelry that they had taken from us and our neighbors. They had gone out too far from their lines in their eager chase.

They did not reach the house till we had been gone about two hours. They were angry that we had gotten off without giving up the silver and other valuables, which they felt sure we had secreted. They threatened to burn the house and then pursue us. Mrs. Allen, who was making her home at Burleigh, claimed her right to protection as a British subject, and they went off cursing, as they hurried after us.

Two miles from the house we met our father, with George Page riding close by his side, and the other negroes following. He was coming to us, as we knew that he would do. He hired a wagon and put us in it, and in this we travelled for a week across the country to the Mobile and Ohio Railroad. A little negro girl had accompanied us, running out of the woods to join us, just as we were turning out of sight of the Burleigh house.

"I want to go wid de white ladies," she said. "I didn't tell nobody, 'cus I was 'feared dey wouldn't lemme go. I was so 'feared de white ladies would git away 'fore I wake up."

So the plantation had known of our intention of leaving, and we had not been betrayed to the soldiers!

Papa had but twenty dollars in his pocket. We had run off without money; all that we had was buried within the enemy's lines. Everything was dear in the country through which we passed. We lived on a few square inches of corn bread and a few square inches of bacon a day during that week.

We could not see that little shiny-faced black child hungry after such trust in us. Each of the grown people cut off one-third of the allotted pittance of bread and of meat for Amy. The children seeing this did the same with their portions, and Amy was the only soul in that wagon who was not hungry during that week. She had no clothes, either, but the things that she had on. Her dress was of white cotton, clean and spotless during the first day only. We were wearing black for our dearest mother. Very soon we had to dress Amy up in one of our black dresses from the scant contents of the two trunks. She was the best and most useful of little maids, and happy to the end of her short life. She died of pneumonia a year from this time, mourned by all the family. She could never be made to admit that she was homesick or sorry for having cast her fortunes in with the "white ladies."

We spent a week in a wretched house near Enterprise, Mississippi. At the end of this time J. R. Eggleston, who had lately married Sarah Dabney, came up from Mobile with money to relieve present embarrassments and to take the family to Mobile.

Two of us were bareheaded as we travelled on the train and through the streets of Mobile. Three houses were thrown open to us,—Dr. Frank Ross's, Major William Ross's, and General Zachariah Deas's.

We rested for one week under the roof of Dr. Frank Ross and his dear wife, and then took possession, free of rent, of the house of General Zachariah Deas. The hospitable Mobile people said that they were happy to do anything in their power for soldiers or refugees. We lived for six months in the Deas house. But two months of wretched anxiety and suspense were ahead of us when we reached Mobile on that lovely day in May. We heard then for the first time that General Pemberton's command had fallen back into Vicksburg after the engagement at Baker's Creek. Edward was in this division, and we did not hear of his safety till two weeks after the surrender of Vicksburg. He rode to Mobile on horseback after his parole, and his appearance at the door was our first tidings of him. In the torn-up condition of the country it was often impossible to get letters through.

One of Thomas Dabney's friends, Adam Giffen, of New Orleans, himself a refugee in Mobile at this time, came to offer his purse to the family of his friend. Thomas was absent and his daughter refused to accept the money, fearing that she would not be able to repay it. "I do not care if I never see it again," Mr. Giffen said, as he thrust two thousand dollars into her hand. "Your father will pay me some day if he can, and if he cannot, I shall not consider it a debt."

She then tried to give to Mr. Giffen a receipt for the money, but he refused to receive it.

"A receipt from your father's daughter! No, indeed, and no thanks either." In a few weeks Thomas was able to return the two thousand dollars to his generous friend.

The cavalry company had withdrawn from their camp on the Tallahala Creek. Soon after the negroes were brought down to Mobile,—the one hundred who had not left the plantation. The money and silver and wearing apparel also of the family were brought down, and a good many books and a few other things that were valued as mementos. Then a sale was held at Burleigh, and not only were the furniture, etc., sold out of the house, but the stock and plantation implements of all sorts were disposed of. Our father was opposed to giving up the accumulations of years in this manner, but he yielded to his daughters, and the plantation and home were stripped bare. A handful of Confederate money was all that was brought by the sale.

CHAPTER XVIII.

REFUGEES.

At the end of the six months in Mobile, papa decided to take his family to Macon, Georgia. There he bought a little cottage with four diminutive rooms. As we drove up to it in the old family carriage, which we had been able still to keep, he handed us out, saying in his bright way, "Welcome to Burleigh No. 2."

He could not make his servants as comfortable as he wished, and this was a source of regret to him. Many of them were hired in good homes, near enough to come to him if they were in trouble; but some of them he preferred not to hire out, as they were not strong, and these, he said, were too much crowded for their health. They did not complain of this specially, and they seemed really to enjoy the novelty of town life.

Mammy Maria, who had left two husbands in Mississippi, came out in the new country as "Miss Dabney," and attracted, as she informed her "white children," as much admiration as any of the young girls, and had offers of marriage too. But she meant to enjoy her liberty, she said, and should not think of marrying any of them.

In that small cottage in Macon the rooms were little more than closets, and we were much thrown together. We were strangers too in Georgia, although we had some very good friends there; then the times were sad. We never felt the family ties stronger than we did in that year in Macon, in a house that was built for the humblest class of factory people. It was near the railroad station, and in the midst of the factories, and we had to stop talking at the train hours and when the factory whistles blew.

But the dear father had no plantation to attend to, and not much to feel interest in besides his little fireside and his absent children. So he sat with us, and he grew interested in everything that we said and did, and we talked to him as freely as if he had been another sister. At night he left the door of his sleeping cabinet open, and we left ours open. We had never been so intimate with him before. One cannot be in a large house, with rooms on different floors. He joined in all our talks, as we sisters lay in bed in our room and he in his room, and shared all our jokes. Ever since our mother's death he had been in the habit of singing in the middle of the night. We found out that it was because he was lonely, with no one to talk to.

In this cottage, when he sang his funny songs in the night, we laughed out, and he would be delighted to hear us. Then always a talk sprang up, and we talked till we were all sleepy. The calling from bed to bed of anything that was interesting or amusing, and many things that would hardly have seemed amusing at other times, brought out shouts of laughter and applause in our midnight gossipings. He enjoyed it like a boy on a lark, as the whole party did.

During our year in Macon he had the pleasure of meeting General Joseph E. Johnston, for whom he had a high admiration. An amusing incident occurred one day when General Johnston came to call on him. Lelia had wished much to see the hero of whom everybody was talking. Her nurse was fired with the same desire, and they planned a way of getting a sight of him through a transom over the parlor door. Accordingly chairs and boxes were piled up, and she and Lelia mounted to the top of the pile. But an unlucky movement caused the structure to totter, and it fell with a crash on the floor of the little back gallery. As a matter of course, the unusual noise made papa open the door to see what was the matter, and this revealed Lelia and poor Milly overcome with confusion and shame at having brought disgrace on the house at such a time. Papa was struck with the ridiculous aspect of the wreck and the culprits, and when General Johnston had heard the explanation he laughed heartily, and insisted on having the child brought in. He doubtless looked on the thing as a compliment to himself, as he had good right to do. But the child in her faded Confederate homespun frock, and Milly, the aider and abettor in the misdemeanor, were very uncomfortable as to their share in the adventure. Milly had a right to special indulgence, and the whole thing was laughed off.

Milly was in Raymond at the time the battle was fought two miles from that place, having been sent thither to learn dress-making. She was dreadfully frightened by the guns, and ran about crying, "Oh, I am 'feared dey will kill de ladies at Burleigh."

When General Stoneman made his raid on Macon, Thomas and his son were among the troops who went out to meet him. The following are Thomas Dabney, Jr's., recollections of this event:

"In the latter part of July, 1864, General Stoneman was sent by General Sherman to capture Macon, Georgia, to liberate the United States prisoners there confined, and to destroy the arsenal and ordnance department of the Confederate States of America.

"General Stoneman, accompanied by several brigades of picked men, eluded General Hood's army, and reached Macon about an hour before daybreak. But, unfortunately for him, a severe freshet, which occurred a day or two previous to his arrival, had washed the bridge over the Ocmulgee River away. The railroad bridge, about a mile lower down, was still intact, but before General Stoneman could recover from his surprise the market gardeners and butchers on their way to the city discovered his presence, hurried across the railroad bridge and gave the alarm. Soon the streets rang with the cry of heralds from the mayor calling upon every one who could shoulder a gun to run to the railroad bridge to defend it at all hazards.

"Father and I ran to the arsenal and got forty rounds of ammunition apiece, and then ran all the way to the bridge, over a mile distant. We were among the first to arrive, but soon old men and boys began to pour in from all quarters. A considerable number of convalescents from the numerous hospitals located in Macon joined us. We were none too soon, for already could be seen the long lines of the enemy not over a half-mile from the bridge, and every few moments shot and shell whistled over the heads of the defenders of that bridge.

"Father's company was Company A, Findley's battalion, but it generally went by the name of the 'Silver Grays,' from the color of the hair of the members. I was the only member in it without a gray head.

"Finally the enemy moved his position farther down the river, and General Johnston ordered most of his men across the river, leaving Company A to defend the bridge.

"A furious cannonade was opened upon this point, but as we, according to orders, were lying behind the railroad embankment, none of the Silver Grays were touched until Major Taliaferro placed two cannon on our side of the river and proposed returning the enemy's fire. Volunteers to man the guns were called for. In an instant father and many other old gentlemen were busy loading the two twenty-pounders that were to commit such havoc in those serried blue lines just on the crest of yonder hill. Our shot flew wide of the mark and the blue lines wavered not. Suddenly the enemy ceased firing, and horsemen were seen galloping up and down the long line. We were beginning to feel much encouraged, when suddenly an old soldier cried out, 'Look, the enemy is *massing his batteries!*' It was only too true. Cannon seemed to come from everywhere, and a perfect storm of shot and shell burst upon our devoted heads. In a few minutes our guns were silenced, but not until several of the Silver Grays lay dead beside the little brazen guns which brought us nothing but death.

"We were ordered to lie down again. The battle scene shifted, and finally General Stoneman and most of his men were outwitted and captured. A small brigade of Texans under the gallant General Gregg, I think, coming up in the enemy's rear decided the day in our favor.

"Father and I did not fire a gun during the entire day."

One night while we were in Macon papa was taking us to the theatre, and we happened to meet Mammy Maria on the way. Hearing where we were going, she said, "Why don't you take me too, marster? I never been to the theatre in my life." So he told her to come along. When we got there, mammy was quite disgusted at being told by the door-keeper that she was to sit in the gallery, instead of with her white people. When the play was over—it was "Taming the Shrew"—

and mammy rejoined us at the door, she was in a state of excitement. She had been dreadfully scared by the fighting on the stage, and feared that Petruchio might go up in the gallery and fight there too.

After the battle of Resaca and New Hope Church, the wounded were sent to Macon, and they were laid out on the floor of the railroad station in long rows. Their wounds had been dressed on the field two days before, but not since, and they had had no food during those days. Thomas Dabney took every available thing in the house to nourish them, and his daughters, under his direction, made lint and tore up linen into long strips. They accompanied him, and helped to minister to the suffering men, binding up wounds, giving them hot tea, milk, and other refreshment.

The surgeons soon discovered that he understood dressing wounds, as he went from one soldier to another, putting on fresh bandages and helping his daughters in cases that they could not manage.

Years after, as he was getting on a railroad train, a man seized his hand, and said, "I can never forget you, sir. You dressed my wound at Macon." Thomas could not recall the man's face, he had dressed the wounds of so many. But the man was not satisfied till he made him recollect which one he was.

"I asked your daughter to dress my wound, and she said that she could not, but she brought you to do it for me." And this recalled the circumstance to his memory.

The only groans heard from those wounded men came from two sweet-faced young boys. They were shot through the head, and were delirious, and both were dying. One of them said, "Kiss me, mother."

As they left this scene, Thomas's daughter said to him, "I could not get to the boy. I begged the lady standing near him to kiss him."

"Yes, I heard you," Thomas replied, in a husky voice.

The lady had passed her hand over the lips of the dying lad, and said, "That seems to satisfy him."

TO HIS DAUGHTER EMMY.

"MACON, GEORGIA, 16th August, 1864.

... "Tommy and I belong to an organization composed of citizens exempt by age,—a fine looking body of gentlemen. Tommy, I think, is the only member under fifty years of age."*

TO HIS DAUGHTER EMMY.

"MACON, GEORGIA, 18th September, 1864.

... "I write now to say, as you may well imagine, that our troubles are not ended, the Yankees still struggling to reach our abode, poor as it now is. We cannot now pretend to know the immediate objects of Sherman, but think it prudent to suppose that, either immediately or ultimately, Macon will become an object of interest with him. Under this view of the subject I have concluded to leave here on Wednesday, the 21st inst. I will take the family and the establishment of servants to Burleigh. ... Nothing could be more injudicious than an attempt on your part to reach us. The trains are all in the hands of the government, private travel excluded, except by freight boxes, on freight trains. Occasionally a few beg themselves into the express car, a close box, and this was the manner of my getting Mrs. Governor Brown off. We will have to go by the freight train, if at all, and I believe I shall succeed in this."

From the day that General Johnston was relieved from the command of the Army of Northern Georgia Thomas had no hope for the Confederacy, and he now wished to take his family back to Burleigh while it could yet be done.

He had never liked Jefferson Davis, and now he was confirmed in his view of his character, that he would brook no rival to his face. Thomas Dabney had never been introduced to Mr. Davis, although he had been several times in his company. When friends proposed

---

* He was fourteen.

to introduce him he refused. It was a great blow to him when Mr. Davis was made the President of the Confederacy. Sometimes, in the heat of discussion, he would amuse his friends by his prompt reply to the question, "Well, who would have done better?" "Why, you would." He tried to overcome his prejudice and to hope for the best, but still adhered to his resolution of not meeting Mr. Davis. He allowed his daughters to attend the receptions given to him at Mobile and Macon, in his progress through the Confederate States, and laughed when he heard from them, after each reception, that Mr. Davis had said in shaking hands, "Ah, Colonel Dabney's daughters; I am very happy to meet you."

He admired the gallant soldier who was put in General Johnston's place, but felt, with most other people, that General Hood's love of fighting would lead him to take too great risks.

By paying several thousand dollars in Confederate money Thomas was able to charter two cars, and in these he took his family from Macon, Georgia, to Jackson, Mississippi; the white family in one and the servants in the other. We were two weeks on the journey, and so well had everything been planned that we found it the most comfortable long journey that we had ever undertaken. The furniture was placed in our car, the beds made up, a table or two, with books and writing materials, set about, and the chairs placed as if we had been at home in our own house. Even the pet cat, whose mother and brothers and sisters had been on board the "Gaines" in the naval engagement in Mobile Bay, was in that car with us. She had been taken to Macon from Mobile, and on her arrival had promptly run away. A reward of twenty dollars, offered through the morning paper, had brought her back. When somebody laughed at the advertisement and thought it a joke, papa answered, "It is no joke. I offer it in earnest. My daughter is a refugee and has little enough to amuse her, and shall not lose the kitten if I can help it."

On our long journey we did not travel at night.

The servants cooked a hot supper and breakfast for us and for themselves every day, getting out and making a fire by the side of the car-track. Sometimes, most of the time indeed, they held big religious meetings in their car. We could hear the preaching and the hymns above the sound of the running cars. As we ran very slowly and irregularly, this was not strange. At several towns we spent a whole day, and on such occasions we got off and called on friends and shopped a little.

Our father's sister, Mrs. Chamberlayne, had joined him in Georgia, and accompanied us to our Mississippi home. A more delightful companion could not be imagined. Her rare mental gifts, disciplined and brightened by a lifetime of steady and judicious reading, inspired the most profound admiration in the circle of young people who gathered around her. She was practical, too, and made many happy suggestions to promote the comfort of the party.

Papa was singularly simple and unobservant in some of his ways. This peculiarity led him into an amusing *contretemps* on this journey.

A sudden shower had caught several of us as we were out walking while laying up for the night at Columbus, Georgia. One of the daughters was drenched to the skin, and had no dress to make a change. Our good neat Hannah had a blue homespun, which she had just washed and ironed in the nicest fashion, and it was decided to borrow her dress rather than run the risk of getting a cold. It was late in September and chilly. We had a family laugh over the ridiculous appearance of Hannah's long-waisted, ill-fitting dress. It was novel and very amusing until a visitor's vo'ce was heard at the car door.

At the first note the blue homespun whisked under one of the tables. The gentleman was ushered in by papa and introduced, and he was so well entertained that he sat there during the greater part of the evening. By and by he remarked that he had had the pleasure of meeting one of the young ladies some time before. But she did not seem to be present, as he remembered that she had very black eyes, while those whom he now saw had blue eyes.

"Where is your sister?" papa asked at once. It was in vain to hint to him that she preferred not making her appearance, that she had been caught in the shower, etc. "Mr. —— wishes to see her," he said. "Sue must be the one. She has black eyes, you know. My dear, where are you? Mr. —— is inquiring for you."

There was no getting out of it. Papa never could understand a hint or a wink in his life. So the head was thrust from under the table.

"Ah, there she is," said papa, not seeing the ridiculous aspect of the thing. And he performed the introduction formally, as he always did such courtesies, ending with, "She is the one. You see her eyes are black."

"Yes," said the visitor, as the two exchanged bows. "But there must be another. This is not the one whom I met."

"Ah, you mean my daughter Emmy, then. Yes, her eyes are black too. She is in Virginia, on a visit to some of her schoolmates."

And papa was so dignified throughout that there seemed no occasion to be amused. Perhaps the visitor concluded that as his host saw nothing peculiar in that under-the-table introduction, it was an every-day occurrence. The dark-eyed one drew her head back under the table, and was not again interrupted in her seclusion.

CHAPTER XIX.

OLD MASTER.

It was a great happiness to get back home, and to be welcomed by the dear Augustine Dabneys. They had lived at Burleigh during the year and a half that the family had spent as refugees. The home in Raymond had been rented out, and the two families spent several happy months together at Burleigh. We frequently numbered twenty-five or even more at the table during this time, and a gayer, merrier circle could not well be imagined. Flour was almost unknown in that part of the Confederacy, coffee and sugar were about as scarce as flour. We had coffee made of peanuts or potatoes, black tea made of blackberry-leaves, and green tea made of holly-leaves. We gave "war" names to all the varieties of corn-bread that appeared on the table. We had rebel bread, Beauregard cakes, etc. It was so delightful to be in the old home again, that the younger members of the family almost threw off the depressing feeling of the war for a time. Privations had almost ceased to be felt. We had scarcely any clothes. A percale apiece at fifteen dollars a yard had been bought as a great bargain; three hundred and fifty dollars had been given for a purple calico dress for Sophy, a pair of coarse shoes cost forty dollars, a pound of tea twenty-five dollars, and it rose to fifty dollars in two days. Our roasts of beef in Macon cost fifty dollars apiece. The only bridal present bought for one of our brides during the war was a pair of green kid gloves,—white could not be bought,—they cost fifty dollars, and were both for the left hand! Our shoes were made of the skins of oxen, roughly tanned by the plantation shoemaker, and manufactured into coverings for the feet by him. Some idea of the appearance and fit of his handiwork may be formed when it is known that his boast was that it was unnecessary for him to take measurements of the feet of the ladies. "I jes' have to glarnce at your foot, missis, an' I ken fit it."

It may be said of these prices that they were only Confederate money, but it must be borne in mind that each Confederate dollar represented to this family what had been a dollar in specie. The income in Confederate money was no larger than the income had been in gold. But people tried not to think of these things, and laughed as they saw the amusing substitutes contrived out of unsuitable and incongruous material.

The young people got up amusements in the house. The longest to be remembered with pride and pleasure was the acting of two plays,—"She Stoops to Conquer" and "Taming the Shrew." We had fourteen actors in our plays. The Raymond Dabneys had a natural taste for acting, and, though the cousins had less, the plays passed off to the satisfaction of all. Thomas Dabney said in his enthusiastic way that the star companies that he had seen in New York did not entertain him better.

But he could not stay at home with us. He had hired out some of his servants in Montgomery, and he felt it a duty to stay there. It was a great trial to him, at his age, to undertake this desolate life away from his family. The following letters were written at this period:

TO HIS CHILDREN.

"EXCHANGE HOTEL, MONTGOMERY, ALABAMA,
"22d October, 1864.

"MY BELOVED CHILDREN,— ... You must not trouble yourselves about my discomforts, for they are not to be avoided. They are doubtless sufficient, but how many others have to endure more! Just think of Sheridan's proceedings in the Valley of Virginia, burning every house, barn, mill, and every stack of hay, and killing or driving off every negro, horse, mule, ox, cow, and every other animated thing, leaving the entire white population without shelter or food."

TO HIS CHILDREN.

"MONTGOMERY, 4th November, 1864.

"MY BELOVED CHILDREN,—My last was addressed to Sophy, although under the above caption. This, in rotation, will be to Emmy, but all and each will be considered as addressed, as I have nothing to say that may not interest all equally. I have heard from none of you since Sophy's letter, but, out of sheer loneliness, have to write to you and imagine that I am talking with you. I wrote to Sarah several days ago, and have been inquiring at the post-office for letters, without getting any, until I begin to feel ashamed to trouble the clerk so much for nothing. In some respects this place

p

is better than Macon, but in others not so good, and especially to me. It is much better for the negroes, as they are all fed to the extent of their desires, both at the government establishments and by private individuals who hire them. And yet, meat is as high here as in Macon. I have to pay three dollars and fifty cents per pound for bacon, and two dollars to two dollars and fifty cents per pound for beef. Meal is not so high, nor are potatoes. For the latter I give six dollars per bushel, instead of twelve dollars to fifteen dollars as in Macon. Wood is dearer here, being fifty dollars per cord. The hotels here have raised their rates to thirty dollars a day, but that does not affect me, as I am keeping house, or rather rooms, and having my own cooking done. It is a poor thing, however, and monotonous, as I have fried beefsteak for each meal, with a pone of corn-bread and a potato or two. When I become tired of that I will vary it to pork or mutton. The fish here are out of the question, nothing but buffalo, catfish, and jumpers. Such as these I cannot eat, unless reduced to extremity, of which there is no fear. This place, to me, is not so good as Macon, because I have not as yet made the right sort of acquaintances, or not many of them. I find living here a Dr. Semple, a son of Judge Semple, of Williamsburg. . . . I also dined the other day with Mr. Woodleaf, refugee from New Orleans, whom some of you may remember having seen at Cooper's Well. . . . They gave me a fine dinner, good for any time, and some extra fine music afterwards, according to the Italian, Spanish, and French books, for we had some of each sort, done up in true operatic fashion, I suppose. It was a *leetle* too foreign for my ear, but that was my fault, and not the fault of the music.

"If I fail to get a letter from some of you within a day or two I shall go crazy, to use a favorite expression of Sarah's."

TO HIS CHILDREN.

"Montgomery, 5th November, 1864.

"My beloved Children,— . . . I really believe that I wrote to you on yesterday, and dumpsily at that, for

I was in the dumps and feeling badly,—lonely. But I have recovered of that and feel very well, and not lonely at all, especially now that I am writing to you all. I feel finely, in fact, and do not expect to feel otherwise again."

He was reproaching himself for that approach to a murmur!

The condition of the country during the war interrupted my father's life-long correspondence. His correspondence was very large for a private gentleman. His business letters were necessarily many, and his friendly letters occupied him during a part of every day. Unfortunately, scarcely any letters written by him previous to the war were preserved. It is especially unfortunate that his letters to his brother should have been destroyed. During nearly his whole life he wrote to him several times a week, at times he wrote to him every day, and even several times a day. He consulted Augustine on nearly all subjects, and wrote to him unreservedly of all that interested him, not only with regard to family matters, but his views and opinions on politics and all the questions of the day. These letters would give the best life of the two brothers that could be written.

At this time of his life he was often said to resemble General Lee in appearance. The Mississippi soldiers, coming home on furlough, often spoke of it. When General Lee reviewed the Eighteenth Mississippi Regiment, many of whom went from our part of the State, the men threw up their hats and shouted, "Three cheers for Colonel Dabney!"

In January, 1865, much to the regret of both households, the Raymond Dabneys left Burleigh. They moved to a house in the neighborhood, and almost daily intercourse was kept up during this year. Then they returned to the home in Raymond.

From this time the intercourse between the two families became less frequent. The ties seemed as binding as ever, but circumstances were changed. Many of the younger members of both households began to leave the home-nests.

The war ended in April. The news of Lincoln's assassination came a short time after this, and was received with deep regret by Thomas. "He was the best friend that we had," he said, "and his death was the greatest calamity that could have befallen the South."

It was no longer Thomas's duty to spend a part of his time in Montgomery, Alabama. He was at Burleigh when he heard of General Lee's surrender. On the day that the news reached him, he called his son Thomas to him, and they rode together to the field where the negroes were at work. He informed them of the news that had reached him, and that they were now free. His advice was that they should continue to work the crop as they had been doing. At the end of the year they should receive such compensation for their labor as he thought just.

From this time till January 1, 1866, no apparent change took place among the Burleigh negroes. Those who worked in the fields went out as usual, and cultivated and gathered in the crops. In the house, they went about their customary duties. We expected them to go away, or to demand wages, or at least to give some sign that they knew they were free. But, except that they were very quiet and serious, and more obedient and kind than they had ever been known to be for more than a few weeks, at a time of sickness or other affliction, we saw no change in them.

At Christmas such compensation was made them for their services as seemed just. Afterwards fixed wages were offered and accepted. Thomas called them up now and told them that as they no longer belonged to him they must discontinue calling him "master."

"Yes, marster," "yes, marster," was the answer to this. "They seem to bring in 'master' and say it oftener than they ever did," was his comment, as he related the occurrence to his children. This was true. The name seemed to grow into a term of endearment. As time went on, and under the changed order of things, negroes whom he had never known became tenants on his plantation; these new people called him master also.

This was unprecedented in the South, I think. They were proud of living on his place, on account of the good name that he had won for himself as a master. Not infrequently they were heard to express a regret that they had not belonged to him when they saw the feeling that existed between himself and his former slaves. Sometimes he came to us with a puzzled look to ask who those negroes were who had just called him old master and shaken hands with him.

"I cannot recall their faces," he would say; "surely, I never owned them?"

Finally the negroes on the neighboring plantations, and wherever he went, came to call him old master. They seemed to take pride in thus claiming a relationship with him, as it were; and he grew accustomed to the voluntary homage.

He had come home to a house denuded of nearly every article of furniture, and to a plantation stripped of the means of cultivating any but a small proportion of it. A few mules and one cow comprised the stock. We had brought a few pieces of common furniture from Georgia, and a very few necessary articles were bought. In the course of time some home-made contrivances and comforts relieved the desolate appearance of the rooms, but no attempt was ever made to refurnish the house.

He owned nothing that could be turned into money without great sacrifice but five bales of cotton. There were yet two sons and two daughters to be educated. He decided to get a tutor for them, and to receive several other pupils in his house in order to make up the salary. The household was put on an economical footing. The plantation negroes were hired to work in the fields, and things seemed to promise more prosperous days. So the first year was passed.

Of this time Mammy Harriet says, "When he come from Georgia he say, 'Harriet, I cannot do as I used to do. You know I used to send whiskey to you all the time. But I cannot do that now.'

"'Yes, marster, I understan'. I don't expec' it.'

"Ah, you don't know de good dat did me! We was

down de cellar, an' he had call me to ask ef I didn't want a piece o' de veal dat was hangin' up dyar. An' he cut it for me himself."

Here mammy's thoughts went back to the war-times, and she went on:

"Dat big man Edmund come to me an' he say, 'Ole 'oman, do you want me to box up your things? I have packed up a heap o' things for de udder people.' He had he saw an' hammer in he hand. I said, 'No, I don't want anything boxed up. I am not goin' anywhere.' He said I was foolish,—that all de people were goin' because dere was a ship-load o' money at Grand Gulf for 'em. I tole him dat it could stay there then. I would not leave. He was very mad and say, 'Yes, you an' ole sis Kitty are jes' alike. You are 'feared o' losin' some o' your plunder here.' I tole him to go out o' my door, an' he went out, an' I hab never seen him since. He come to a bad end after all. He was shot.

"After marster come from Georgia, he come to me one day an' say,—

"'Harriet, what made Becky leave me?'

"I tole him that Becky was forced off.*

"He say, 'Why did Major leave me?'

"I say, 'Marster, I will tell you de truth. You yourself did wrong. You leff your people. Two white men, Mr. —— and Mr. ——, tole us dat you leff dem to take us to Leaf River. *We would have died before we would have followed dem!*' Marster hadn't nebber tole dem! He was 'stonished. 'Yes,' I said, ' an' dey went in de field an' shot guns at our people to skeer 'em.' They wanted to force 'em to go wid 'em.

"Dey shot at my gal Mary as she was comin' home to her baby at night, an' she run an' fall in a gully,

---

* Becky was one of his greatest favorites. She was subject to violent illnesses, and at such times he bathed her head with his own hands, and he and his wife and children held her head and sat by her till the crisis was passed. Cakes that she specially fancied were made by the ladies themselves for her. A few days after her husband, Edmund, forced her off, she was dying, where many of the Hinds County negroes died, on the banks of the Big Black. As she lay dying, she cried out, "If I could only get back to my marster! If I could only get back to my marster!"

an' stayed out all night, away from her chile. An' I had to hold dat chile all night an' to feed it. When Mary got home she could hardly walk, an' she is lame in dat ankle to dis day in cloudy weather. Mary tole me dat dese men were goin' to whip her de nex' day, an' she say, 'Mammy, dey shall not whip me. I will run away before dey do dat.'

"Then God did something. I know that he did it.

"Young Mars Edward heard dat pistol go off dat was aimed at Mary, an' he an' his body-servant, William, come back home. An' dey stayed in de house dat night. I say, 'Mary, de young marster is here. He will protect us. Go straight to him; to no one else. Tell him all about it.' She went to him, an' de nex' day Mr. —— was sent off. God did it, I know.

"I always shall believe dat Mr. —— was one sent to 'seek out.'* He was not fightin' wid our people, who was so kind to him."†

My father had been troubled by the conflicting duties to his children and to his servants.

When he heard that mammy's last good boy, Major, had run away to escape being killed by these men, he said, "Harriet, I ought to have died ten years ago."

His faithful servant burst into tears at these words of her master.

CHAPTER XX.

THE CROWN OF POVERTY.

And now a great blow fell on Thomas Dabney. Shortly before the war he had been asked by a trusted friend to put his name as security on some papers for a good many thousand dollars. At the time he was assured that his name would only be wanted to tide over a crisis of two weeks, and that he would never hear of the papers again. It was a trap set, and his unsuspi-

---

* A spy.   † His entertainers at Burleigh.

cious nature saw no danger, and he put his name to the papers. Loving this man, and confiding in his honor as in a son's, he thought no more of the transaction.

It was now the autumn of 1866. One night he walked up-stairs to the room where his children were sitting with a paper in his hand. "My children," he said, "I am a ruined man. The sheriff is down-stairs. He has served this writ on me. It is for a security debt. I do not even know how many more such papers have my name to them." His face was white as he said these words. He was sixty-eight years of age, with a large and helpless family on his hands, and the country in such a condition that young men scarcely knew how to make a livelihood.

The sheriff came with more writs. Thomas roused himself to meet them all. He determined to pay every dollar.

But to do this he must have time. The sale of everything that he owned would not pay all these claims. He put the business in the hands of his lawyer, Mr. John Shelton, of Raymond, who was also his intimate friend. Mr. Shelton contested the claims, and this delayed things till Thomas could decide on some way of paying the debts.

A gentleman to whom he owed personally several thousand dollars courteously forbore to send in his claim. Thomas was determined that he should not on this account fail to get his money, and wrote urging him to bring a friendly suit, that, if the worst came, he should at least get his proportion. Thus urged, the friendly suit was brought, the man deprecating the proceeding, as looking like pressing a gentleman.

And now the judgments, as he knew they would, went against him one by one. On the 27th of November, 1866, the Burleigh plantation was put up at auction and sold, but the privilege of buying it in a certain time reserved to Thomas. At this time incendiary fires were common. There was not much law in the land. We heard of the gin-houses and cotton-houses that were burned in all directions. One day as Thomas came back from a business journey the smouldering ruins of his gin-house met his eye. The building was itself valuable and necessary. All the cotton that he owned was consumed in it. He had not a dollar. He had to borrow the money to buy a postage stamp, not only during this year, but during many years to come. It was a time of deepest gloom. Thomas had been wounded to the bottom of his affectionate heart by the perfidy of the man who had brought this on his house. In the midst of the grinding poverty that now fell in full force on him, he heard of the reckless extravagance of this man on the money that should have been used to meet these debts.

Many honorable men in the South were taking the benefit of the bankrupt law. Thomas's relations and friends urged him to take the law. It was madness, they said, for a man of his age, in the condition the country was then in, to talk of settling the immense debts that were against him. He refused with scorn to listen to such proposals. But his heart was well-nigh broken. He called his children around him, as he lay in bed, not eating and scarcely sleeping.

"My children," he said, "I shall have nothing to leave you but a fair name. But you may depend that I shall leave you that. I shall, if I live, pay every dollar that I owe. If I die, I leave these debts to you to discharge. Do not let my name be dishonored. Some men would kill themselves for this. I shall not do that. But I shall die."

The grief of betrayed trust was the bitterest drop in his cup of suffering. But he soon roused himself from this depression and set about arranging to raise the money needed to buy in the plantation. It could only be done by giving up all the money brought in by the cotton crop for many years. This meant rigid self-denial for himself and his children. He could not bear the thought of seeing his daughters deprived of comforts. He was ready to stand unflinchingly any fate that might be in store for him. But his tenderest feelings were stirred for them. His chivalrous nature had always revolted from the sight of a woman doing hard work. He determined to spare his daughters all such labor as he could perform. General Sherman had said that he would like to bring every Southern woman to the wash-tub.* "He shall never bring my daughters to the wash-tub," Thomas Dabney said. "I will do the washing myself." And he did it for two years. He was in his seventieth year when he began to do it.†

This may give some idea of the labors, the privations, the hardships, of those terrible years. The most intimate friends of Thomas, nay, his own children, who were not in the daily life at Burleigh, have never known the unprecedented self-denial, carried to the extent of acutest bodily sufferings, which he practised during this time. A curtain must be drawn over this part of the life of my lion-hearted father!

When he grew white and thin, and his frightened daughters prepared a special dish for him, he refused to eat the delicacy. It would choke him, he said, to eat better food than they had, and he yielded only to their earnest solicitations. He would have died rather than ask for it. When the living was so coarse and so ill-prepared that he could scarcely eat it, he never failed, on rising from the table, to say earnestly and reverently, as he stood by his chair, "Thank the Lord for this much."

During a period of eighteen months no light in summer, and none but a fire in winter, except in some case of necessity, was seen in the house. He was fourteen years in paying these debts that fell on him in his sixty-ninth year. He lived but three years after the last dollar was paid.

When he was seventy years of age he determined to learn to cultivate a garden. He had never performed manual labor, but he now applied himself to learn to hoe as a means of supplying his family with vegetables. With the labor of those aged hands he made a garden that was the best ordered that we had ever seen at Burleigh. He made his garden, as he did everything

---

* Thomas had read this in one of the papers published during the famous march to the sea. Whether General Sherman was correctly reported I know not.—S. D. S.

† His daughters did all the menial work of the house except the washing. An attempt to do this resulted in serious illness, and was henceforth sternly forbidden by the father.

that he undertook, in the most painstaking manner, neglecting nothing that could insure success. The beds and rows and walks in that garden were models of exactness and neatness. It was a quarter of a mile from the house and from water, on the top of a long, high hill, and three-quarters of an acre in extent. In a time of drought, or if he had set out anything that needed watering, he toiled up that long precipitous hill with bucket after bucket of water. "I never look at the clouds" had been a saying of his in cultivating his plantation, and he carried it out now. That garden supplied the daily food of his family nearly all the year round. He planted vegetables in such quantities that it was impossible to consume all on the table, and he sold barrels of vegetables of different kinds in New Orleans.

Oftentimes he was so exhausted when he came in to dinner that he could not eat for a while. He had his old bright way of making every one take an interest in his pursuits,—sympathy was as necessary and sweet to him as to a child,—and he showed with pride what he had done by his personal labor in gardening and in washing. He placed the clothes on the line as carefully as if they were meant to hang there always, and they must be admired, too! He said, and truly, that he had never seen snowier ones.

Oh, thou heroic old man! Thou hast a right to thy pride in those exact strokes of the hoe and in those superb potatoes, "the best ever seen in the New Orleans market," and in those long lines of snowy drapery! But those to whom thou art showing these things are looking beyond them, at the man! They are gazing reverently, and with scarce suppressed tears, on the hands that have been in this world for three-score and ten years, and are beginning to-day to support a houseful of children!

At the end of the hard day's work he would say, sometimes, "General Sherman has not brought my daughters to the wash-tub. I could not stand that."

General Sherman's words were as a cruel spur in the side of a noble steed that needed no spur, and was already running beyond his strength.

He urged some of his old friends to follow his example, and was quite disgusted at the answer of one, that he had no "turn" for working in a garden. "No turn!" he repeated, indignantly, in speaking of it to his children. "I hear that he allows the ladies to do all this work. I wonder what *turn* for it they have! I have no toleration for such big Indian talk."

His hands were much bent with age and gout. No glove could be drawn over them. They had been so soft that a bridle-rein, unless he had his gloves on, chafed them unpleasantly. He expressed thankfulness that the bent fingers and palms did not interfere with his holding either his hoe-handle or his pen. He wrote as many letters as ever, and an article for a State newspaper or a Virginia or New Orleans paper occasionally, if interested in anything that was going on. But he said that politics were getting to the state that only disgusted him, and he took no active part or interest even in State government till he saw a hope of throwing off "carpet-bag" rule. When he spoke of the expense of the postage on his correspondence, he said that he could not maintain himself in his station if he wrote fewer letters.

He tried hard to learn to plough, but he could not do it. It was a real disappointment. He tried to learn to cut wood, but complained that he could not strike twice in the same spot. It was with great labor that he got a stick cut in two. His failure in this filled him with a dogged determination to succeed, and he persisted in cutting wood in the most painful manner, often till he was exhausted. Some one told him of a handsaw for sawing wood, and he was delighted and felt independent when he got one. He enjoyed it like a new toy, it was so much better in his hands than the axe. He sawed wood by the hour in the cold and in the heat. It seemed to be his rule never to stop any work till he was exhausted.

His son Edward lived with him during these years. He tried to lessen his father's labors. But Thomas Dabney was not a man to sit down while his children worked. Besides, there was work enough for these two men, and more than enough. The arrangement of both house and plantation had been planned to employ many servants, as was the custom in the South. Everything was at a long distance from everything else. As time went on, an effort was made to concentrate things. But, without money, it was impossible to arrange the place like a Northern farm, with every convenience near at hand.

One fall, in putting down the dining-room carpet, Thomas heard his daughter say that she meant to turn the carpet, because it looked new on the other side.

"Do not turn it, then," he said. "I do not wish any one to suppose that I would buy a new carpet, owing money as I do."

In these years he was preparing once for a business visit to New Orleans. His daughter asked him to buy a new suit, as he spoke of calling on his friends in the city.

"No," he answered; "I should be ashamed to wear new clothes. What hope would my creditors have of ever getting their money if they saw me in New Orleans in new clothes? No; I am going in this suit that you say looks so shabby and faded. I shall call on all my creditors in this suit. I have not a dollar to take to them, but I shall let them see that I am not shunning them for that. I shall show myself to them, and tell them that I am doing my very best to pay them, and that they shall have every dollar if they will have patience. You see, my child, this is the only assurance I can give them that I mean to pay them. Now, could I expect to be believed if I were handsomely dressed?"

His merchants, Giquel & Jamison, were among the creditors whom he saw during this visit. They informed him that all their books had been burned during the war, and that they had no bill against him. They said also that they had accounts amounting to one hundred and fifty thousand dollars set down in those books, and that he was the only man who had come forward to pay them. He was not to be turned from paying his debt.

An humble neighbor had said years ago that he hated

Colonel Dabney because he acted as if he considered himself a prince. In these later days he admired Thomas as much as he had before disliked him. " I thought him a haughty man because he was rich; now I see that he is the same man poor that he was rich. Now I know that he is a prince."

One of his daughters had occasion to offer a draft of his to an ignorant man in a distant county of Mississippi. She felt a natural diffidence, as she was not sure that it would be accepted in payment of her indebtedness. She asked the man if he had ever heard of Thomas Dabney.

"Heard of him?" he said. "Every letter in his name is pure gold. I would as soon have that draft as the gold in my hand."

Seeing one of his daughters look sad and quiet, Thomas said to her, "My child, it seems to me that you look coldly on me. I cannot bear that. You are the very core of my heart. If I have done anything that you do not like, tell me."

Oh, what heart would not bound out to the father who could say that to his own child!

And the tender, satisfied look when he was embraced and kissed, and the real trouble confided to his sympathizing bosom!

His cousins in New York, Augustine and Mary Smith, the children of his uncle, endeavored to help Thomas at this time, and sent a large check to him. This he promptly returned, but when their kindness was offered to his children he could not wish to see it refused; and the first gleam of light and hope came to the family when these generous kinspeople gave them substantial aid.

The following letter is from one who visited Burleigh many times, our friend, Miss Marianne P. Eggleston:

"NEW ORLEANS.

"My first recollection is of a figure firmly knit and erect, with white hair and smooth-shaven chin, always clad in a suit of dark blue cloth, with brass buttons on the dress-coat. Riding back and forth twice a day over the sawdust-covered road, and both horse and rider thrown out in bold relief by a background of dancing blue water. The dress has a suspicion of the military about it, while the 'speech' as plainly 'bewrayeth' the Virginian. As a child, I was rather awed by the decided manner and tones, and the eyes flashing so brightly under the bushy brows. He seemed a man full of chivalry and action, to whom one, especially a woman, might turn for protection always, and for help in a real trouble, sooner than for sympathy in a small one. I wonder if the tenderness of after-years was latent there then, or if it only came with the need for it! Surely it was deep enough.

"The old house on the lake-shore seems to come back before my eyes again as it was, and I stand once more among the people who filled it thirty-five years ago. Many have fallen asleep, and those whose forms are still with us are as utterly changed to our eyes as if the grave had closed over those we then knew. There were but vague impressions of character made then; they are mostly recollections of form and color, and prominent among these is the dear old red silk handkerchief.

"Later on come recollections of Burleigh, and much better defined impressions of its master. How well I remember the day I saw it for the first time!

"After dinner we walked (or stood) in that little garden of pinks you had in the front yard, near the 'big gate.' There your father joined us, and standing outside, leaning on the low fence, he told us of an article he had read on the 'Genius of Shakespeare.' The author regarded the 'Tempest' as Shakespeare's greatest work, and Caliban as his most perfect creation of fancy. 'I cannot agree with him about the "Tempest,"' he said, 'but he may be right about Caliban.' As we returned to the house, we all stopped under the mimosa-tree, where a table was placed, and your father presided over an immense waiter of cantaloupes. I remember how he put back his cuffs and flourished his knife. I so often recall the Burleigh of those days,—the ready and apparently boundless hospitality, the abundant supply of all the necessaries of life (and much of what we call the luxuries now), the fruit in summer, the roaring fires and the 'hog-killings' in winter, and those delicious sweet potatoes!

"I remember how often we danced in the hall in summer, but I have no recollection of any music. We must have needed some. Your father was always ready to take his place with us, and I can see him now as he walked around the card-table, looking into the hand of each one, drawing his red silk handkerchief through his fingers as a bad play was made, regarding it as a serious business, and being by far too honorable to 'tell.' He never seemed to think we were doing it for fun, and enjoyed a bad play as much as a good one.*

"The first time I saw the white beard was on the day of the memorable barbecue at Terry. I recall so well your father's appearance that day, as he took his place on the stand among the Democrats. His bearing was a compromise between the respect he felt for 'these gentlemen' individually, and a protest against that vile thing known as Democracy. The red silk handkerchief was often brought into requisition that day, like a Whig banner flaunted in the face of Democracy,—as if to say, 'We two old Whigs are as stanch and true as ever, although we allow you Democrats to approach us to-day on terms of familiarity. We make no concession, nor do we propose to make any.'

"You remember the introductions we had to pass through? A group of us (myself included) would be presented as 'my daughters;' then, out would spring the old 'bandanna,' and after a clearing of his throat, he would give a little sketch of each, as we were

---

* "I should not have said that everybody laughed, for my grandfather did not even smile. . . . He was totally absorbed in contemplation of the enormity of playing out one's ace of trumps second in hand. And that Charley,—Charley, whom he had trained from a boy to the rigor of the game according to Hoyle,—that *he* should seem to defend such—so—so horrible a solecism! It was too much. He was a picture to look at, as he stood erect, the nostrils of his patrician nose dilated with a noble indignation, his snowy hair contrasting with his dark and glowing eyes, that swept from group to group of mirthful faces, and back again, sternly wondering at their untimely merriment."—*Don Miff*, page 239.

brought to the front in rotation. It was as good as a tooth-drawing!

"I can recall so many movements and gestures,—that way he had of throwing his leg out,—I often try to do that, but have never succeeded to my satisfaction. I think it must be some 'Old-Line Whig' sign, and no one but one of them can achieve it.

"This is the bright side of the picture, and I turn with reluctance to the other, the one which looks like a dark one, but is far more beautiful than the former, and is bright with an inner radiance which is not seen in the earlier time.

"My first visit to Burleigh after the war seemed like an evil dream. The old nursery, where the long line of 'knitters' were ranged on rainy days, is a kitchen now with all the necessary appointments; the well-furnished apartments look almost bare now; not a servant appears about the premises. I find the same warm greeting, but the hands extended to welcome me are no longer the soft ones of a gentleman. Instead of them I seem to grasp the toil-hardened ones of a laboring man, and such they are. The man born and bred in all the comfort of a Virginia home, in manhood saying to his servant 'do this, and he doeth it,' has in advancing years found himself bereft of the faithful wife who for so many years shared his life, and deprived of nearly all his possessions. How does he bear himself now? The time formerly devoted to the care of his estate, to the exercise of hospitality, to enjoyment, is now given to manual labor. A few faithful servants still linger around the old home and cling to 'ole marster;' but times are changed with them too, and they must toil for their daily bread, formerly dealt out to them without stint from 'ole marster's' table. So I see that dear 'ole marster' cutting with his own hands the wood for the fires, toiling with it up the long flight of stairs, making fires, doing the family washing, and after a hard day's work, seeing you make the starch over the dining-room fire he said, so regretfully, 'I wish I could make the starch too.' I recall how he insisted on washing my clothes also, and how I let him believe he was doing it.

"Not a word of complaint was heard, no matter how coarse the fare was; if he *could* eat it, he did so. I remember once he handed his cup for tea the second time, saying to me as I passed it, 'With some people it is an evidence that the tea is good when they take a second cup, but with me it is the reverse. I must have a certain quantity of tea, no matter how much water I drink to get it.' Late one cold evening we heard a tramping of many feet as we sat around the dining-room fire. Soon the door to the kitchen opened wide, and your father ushered in as many as five forlorn-looking females in thin calico dresses and long sun-bonnets, some with babies in their arms. I can see him now, seating them as if they had been the greatest ladies in the land, and telling them to stay there until the fires were made in the cabins he had given them permission to occupy for the night. I suspect each one had a beating from her husband that night because she did not make a fire for him.

"When the old place was deserted, and your father came down here for the winter, I took the same train at Brookhaven. He was quite sick all day and seemed pleased to have me near him. I saw him frequently during the winter at Tom's and at Emmy's rooms; and no matter where I was, he never thought it too much trouble to find me. It is very gratifying that one you love and revere should feel confidence in your affection and value it. So, I am confident, he felt towards me. When I went to bid him good-by I found him out and waited for him. I can see now the smile on his face when he came in. He insisted on seeing me down-stairs, but I succeeded in effecting a compromise, and we parted at the landing. He said good-by and kissed me as if he thought it was for the last time, then took my hand again and said, earnestly, 'God bless you.' I love to remember that when his voice fell on my ear for the last time, it was to call down a blessing on my head."

In the changed circumstances of the family it was impossible to attend the services at the Raymond church. The deprivation of a parish church was much felt, and it was resolved by Emmy Dabney to try to build a church nearer to Burleigh. She begged her father to allow her to go out as a governess that she might use the money made in this way to build a simple wooden church. He gave a reluctant consent, as he disliked to see women work. The year's salary was insufficient for the purpose, and very little was contributed in the neighborhood. There was but one communicant outside of the Burleigh house,—the country people who cared for religion belonged to other religious bodies. All the sisters and a family of cousins went to work with their needles to make up the deficiency in funds. Although they made a great deal in this way the desired end seemed a long way off, and they set to work to make appeals to the church people of the North, asking for one dollar from each one. A generous response came at once; money came by dollars and hundreds of dollars. In a short time, instead of the one thousand dollars that was asked for, about five thousand had been received. The letters that came were as much prized as the money. Of the many hundreds received but one was unkind in its tone, and a few months later the writer of that letter sent a large sum of money, accompanied by words of Christian sympathy. Our father had never felt other than kindly towards the North. His long residence in New York as a child, and his broad sympathies with them as a part of the nation, had made him, as already stated, a stanch Union man as long as there seemed to be any hope of keeping the Union unbroken. He enjoyed these overflowing Christian letters with his children. Warm friendships were formed with some of the writers, and were among the most lasting and prized of our lives. The large amount of money received enabled us not only to complete the little church, but to purchase a glebe and rectory. The work connected with this church and Sunday-school became a part of the life at Burleigh.

CHAPTER XXI.

THE CROWNING BLESSING.

The crowning blessing of our lives came in these days of poverty and toil. The beloved head of the house took his baptismal vows on himself, and became a regular communicant in the church. His daughters had come to him one night as he sat on the porch, talking with Edward, and had urged him to be confirmed. They told him that they were unworthy of the name of Christians, and felt especially in approaching him how unworthy they were. But the Saviour's command was explicit. He called the sinners and not the righteous. He ought to obey that loving call and not wait to feel worthy. The day would never come when he would feel so. "Oh, papa, how can one go to heaven who does not obey Him? Even earthly parents require obedience. And what would heaven be without you! Oh, let us all try to go there together!"

With tears and kisses and every endearing epithet, and with arms around his neck, they hung about him. He was completely overcome. He seemed scarcely able to control his voice as he said, "My children, you are right. I see the justice of what you say. I will be confirmed when the bishop comes. But you came near killing your father. I thought that you had killed me. My heart stopped beating when you said all those sweet things to me. I do not deserve all those good things that you believe of me."

His son Thomas knelt by his side and was confirmed with him in St. Mark's Church, Raymond, when the bishop came. Bishop Greer was a child of the same year as our father, and but four months younger than himself. As he placed his hands on the venerable head bent before him, and bent his own snowy one over it, he was visibly affected, and many tears fell in the church. It was said that there was not a dry eye that night that looked upon that scene. The class that went up for confirmation was larger than had been expected. It was said that when Thomas Dabney walked up the aisle several persons who before had been undecided now rose and went forward as candidates for confirmation.

"I don't believe in all the people who call themselves Christians," a plain neighbor said, in talking of this step of Thomas, "but I believe in Colonel Dabney's Christianity. *He* is no hypocrite."

Awhile after this he began to ask a blessing at his own table, and gradually he grew into asking a blessing at the tables of his friends, unless a clergyman was present. But he never led the family prayers. "I want you to do that," he said to a daughter. Among the letters that he valued I find one received about this time from a young girl, one of his servants whom he had placed in Montgomery.

"MONTGOMERY, February 10, 1867.

"MY DEAR OLD MASTER,—I am anxious to see you and my young masters and mistresses. I often think of you, and remember with pleasure how kind you all ever were to me. Though freedom has been given to the colored race, I often sigh for the good old days of slave-times, when we were all so happy and contented. . . . I am tolerably pleasantly situated. I am hired to a Mr. Sanderson, who treats me very well. I am very well, and hope I may have an opportunity of coming to see you all next Christmas. I am still single and don't think much about beaux. I don't think the men in these days of freedom are of much account. If I could find one whom I think a real good man, and who would take good care of me, I would get married. Please, dear old master, ask some of my young mistresses to write to me.

"My kind and respectful remembrances to all.

"Your former servant and friend,

"ALICE DABNEY."

This letter was written with Alice's own hand.

His former servants showed affectionate attentions to him, and they were deeply appreciated. George Page sent all his best fruits and vegetables to his master's table, especially those that were rare and difficult to cultivate. When George's girl brought over a bucket of strawberries one year, the daughter who received them asked casually if she had been enjoying the strawberries that spring.

"No, marm, I ain't tase one," the child answered. "Daddy say dat we sharn't tase one 'twell ole marster hab de fust dish, an' dese is de fust."

Sometimes a fat gobbler, the finest of the flock, would be sent over for the master's Christmas dinner by Mammy Harriet. George's wife or children, who were sent with his offerings, had strict orders from him, which they did not dare disobey, to receive nothing in return. "Law, missis," his wife would say, "I 'feared to take anything back. George would run me out in de woods. Yes, marm, to be sho' I want de things, but I darsen't take 'em."

Finally we hit upon the plan of sending an express-messenger to George's house with such things as we had to bestow. He was by no means pleased at this turn of affairs, but saw no way of evading it. He had to be consoled with the assurance that our presents were for Susan, and not for him.

When George himself brought his gifts, he would try to drop them in the kitchen without being seen, and when discovered, his manner was as deprecatory as though he were serving an Eastern despot. As a slave his bearing was independent. He often thought his opinions worth more than any one's whom he knew, and he constantly gave advice to his owners, not being discouraged by their neither asking nor adopting it. But, from the day that he saw them reduced to poverty, he strove to throw into his carriage all the deference that could be expressed in one human body. As soon as his bag of melons, peaches, and roasting ears was found, he would be seized with regret at having brought them.

"Don't look at dem things," he would cry, snatching the bag, that we might not see the contents. "I dunno what I bring 'em for. Dey ain't fitten' for marster an' my young ladies. Here, lemme throw 'em 'way. Dey ain't fitten' for nothin'. I know you got plenty of them."

He always brought things that he knew we did not have, but this feigned belief that his master was as well off as ever was soothing to George's pride.

In proportion as he reverenced his master he felt himself superior to the white people of the plainer sort. This was in right of his having been brought up by "one o' de big bloods," as George and others of this aristocracy-loving race expressed it.

One day papa sent a note by George to one of the neighbors. The man could not read it, and said something about the handwriting being hard to read. George's ire was fired by this implied imputation on his master's penmanship.

"My marster's handwritin' hard, sir?" he asked. "My marster has de educationey, sir. It is you who do not know how to read, sir."

It is needless to say that George became unpopular with those who could not see beyond the surface, and recognize the proud, loyal heart under this bluster. In these days of poverty our Caleb Osbaldistone felt himself called on to maintain the family honor and dignity. He delighted in relating to strangers, who had not visited Burleigh in former years, marvellous stories of the champagne that he used to have from the dinner-table every day, throwing in such other adjuncts as seemed to him in keeping with this style from that inexhaustible storehouse, his fancy.

One Christmas, one of the white family sent a little money to George and his wife. "What de debble do I want wid money?" he cried, as he threw it on a shelf away from him.

Susan kissed hers and shed tears over it.

They had been free for twenty years, and after their crop was sold but twenty cents had come to them.

Thomas exercised a protecting care over the negro tenants, his own old servants and others, long after

they were free. It seemed instinctive with him. One
dark night one of the tenants came over and begged
him to go to the quarters to drive off some men, who
were, he said, frightening the negroes. As our father
was upwards of seventy years of age, and as we were
not sure that in these lawless times personal harm was
not meant to him in this affair, we entreated him not
to go. The quarters were from a quarter- to a half-
mile off, and half the way was up a precipitous hill.
But he seemed scarcely to hear our remonstrances,
and went in all haste to find out what was the matter.
Everything was quiet when he got there, and he received no connected account of the disturbance.

In the spring of 1868 Thomas had the great pleasure
of a visit from Dr. Thomas Cooke, who had been his
ward in early Gloucester days. Dr. Cooke's eldest son,
Thomas Dabney Cooke, had spent a year at Burleigh
in boyhood, and his father had long intended to bring
some of his daughters to see his old friend. But time
had slipped away, and still he had never felt that he
could afford the journey. This spring he resolved to
delay no longer. He was afraid, he said, that he might
die without having brought his family to see the dearest friend of his life, and he came with three of his
daughters. This visit was made at a time of the
greatest poverty in the Burleigh house. A beautiful
little incident that took place will show the courtly
polish of this gentleman. One of Thomas's daughters
was about to go to the wood-pile to get some chips for
the fire. Dr. Cooke offered her his arm, and the two
proceeded and collected the chips together in the basket,
and came back in the same formal style. He felt intuitively that the young lady would not allow a venerable guest to go alone to perform this office, and his
fine breeding showed him this way out of the difficulty.

In the fall of 1869 Thomas met with a serious pecu-
niary loss. A negro riot took place in the height of
the cotton-picking season, and among other unhappy
consequences the negroes abandoned the fields until
the cotton had been spoiled by the wind and rain.
Nearly the whole crop was lost. The seat of the

trouble was eighteen miles from Burleigh, but it was chosen by the negroes as their rendezvous. We knew nothing of the trouble. But the white men of the neighborhood heard that they were preparing for a fight, and about fifty of them marched to the plantation to meet the negroes. Wild rumors were afloat, among others, that not a "white face" was to be spared. Our first intimation of the riot was to hear about one hundred rifles go off in the park, followed by loud cries and yells and battle orders. And presently a riderless horse or two, one shot through the body and dying, rushed past the gate. This was all. After that one volley the negroes fled. The carpet-bagger who had urged them to this riot had gotten to a place of safety before the fight came off. Four negroes were killed and two white men wounded. About fifty negroes had been in the engagement.

Our cook clung to me as I went in the kitchen. "Oh, they have killed Robert! Oh, he say all de time dat he warn't goin' to hurt his white people! He say all de time dat he b'long to you."

The negro men on the plantation disappeared, as has been said, and did not come back for weeks. The women came to the house; the hall was quite full of them, and we could not persuade them to go home all that day. Mammy Maria got under the chair on which one of "her white children" sat, and embraces and pattings on the back and all the affectionate words that could be thought of were needed to get her up from the floor, where she was crying bitterly. All this had taken place just as we were about to go in to breakfast, on a lovely morning in October. In a short time a body of one hundred and fifty men from Crystal Springs rode up. They had ridden from there, a distance of sixteen miles, under whip and spur, and were so covered with dust as to be almost unrecognizable.

Our cook had gone to her dying husband, and these men had had no breakfast. Thomas opened the storeroom to them; several of the more experienced were soon engaged in cooking for the company. For a week the country was in a state of apprehension, and patrols were out and guards set day and night. The younger men were needed for patrol service, and only our father and a delicate young visitor were left to guard the Burleigh house. Papa called us all up, and asked if we were willing to shoot if there were need. He found but one coward among his daughters, the writer of these memorials. The others were willing to receive the pistols and guns which he handed them. There were not enough for all. Sarah kept a pot of water boiling as her means of defence. But the negroes were scattered in every direction and not thinking of another outbreak.

Papa went to see Robert, and was disarmed by the poor fellow's sufferings and affectionate greeting. He assured "marster" that he had not meant to hurt him or his family. He only wanted to kill the "poor white trash" who insulted his race. "I had to be true to my color, marster." His old master gave him such comfort as he could, telling his wife how to allay his sufferings, and promising protection. He died in a few days. Robert's wife related an incident that took place on the preceding night, at the drill, before the battle. A negro from a distance proposed that the work of destruction should begin by burning the Burleigh house. Two brothers, old family servants, stepped from the ranks and said that would have to be done over their dead bodies, if at all.

On the night before the fight a strange negro had begged to be allowed to stay all night, and offered to work Lelia's flowers if she would let him stay. He seemed nervous and miserable, and Edward, to whom she had appealed for advice, felt sorry for the man and gave the desired consent. When the Crystal Springs troops arrived, they informed the family that the chief agitator among the negroes had been harbored by them. He was running from a riot that he had gotten up under the direction of the carpet-baggers, and in which the negroes had been worsted, of course, when he took refuge with us. He wished to be found among us when the impending fight in the park should take place. The Crystal Springs men were for making an example of him. But Edward and Lelia, to whom the poor misguided fellow clung, saw that he was quite conquered. They interceded for him and he was not molested. We were thankful when that wretched week was over.

In November we had a visit from the saintly Bishop Wilmer, of Louisiana. When he went away several of the ladies of the house accompanied him a part of the way in the carriage. One of them, in the hurry of getting off, had left her handkerchief behind, and Aunt Abby, who discovered it, ran out to the carriage and handed it in. Bishop Wilmer held his hand out to her and said, "Let me shake hands with you, mammy. I want to shake hands with a faithful servant." Then, as he held the small, withered black hand in his, he went on: "You thought that you were not doing much when you ran out with that handkerchief. You were doing more than you thought. You were doing a faithful part by your young mistress. There shall a day come to you in which your ears shall hear a voice saying, 'Well done, thou good and faithful servant. Thou hast been faithful over a few things. I will make thee lord over many.'"

As he spoke the last words, he had the manner of one of God's prophets delivering a message. Every one in the carriage was weeping. His rare and boundless sympathy had enabled him to read her character. Some one asked him what had moved him to say such words to a stranger. He replied that he had seen what she was as soon as he looked at her. She spoke of him after that as the "good gentleman." Those who knew Bishop Wilmer and his incomparable powers of conversation, will not be surprised to hear that we were laughing or crying, or doing both together, all the way during that drive of two and a half miles.

Seeing us draw on our gloves, he said, "Girls, I ought to have brought gloves to each of you. There were three reasons why I did not. In the first place, I did not know the numbers that you wore; in the second, I had no money; and, in the third, I did not think of it."

Thomas had been patient and forbearing with his

servants when he owned them, but he had small patience for the shiftless, lazy ways of the negro race after they were set free. Very few of his own remained on the plantation. Many had gone off when he was absent with his family in Mobile and Macon, and a large number had been left in Montgomery when the war ended. Tenants were brought in from other plantations, but they were more fond of barbecues and big meetings and hunting and fishing than of keeping the grass out of the fields. It became so onerous to Thomas to look after plantation affairs conducted in such a manner, that he decided to turn over the management to his son Edward.

He longed to visit a tide-water country, and it was arranged that he should spend a part of nearly every summer at Pass Christian with his kind friends down there. He was now too old to hunt. Some of the following letters show his keen enjoyment of fishing.

T. S. D. TO HIS DAUGHTER EMMY.

"PASS CHRISTIAN, 4th August, 1870.

. . . "Mr. —— enacted a droll scene, or one that would have been droll had it not been so discreditable. He was very drunk, but he managed to get into his little wagon and started for home. Meeting two ladies on the way to whom he wished to pay distinguished attention, he *uncovered* with the 'grand flourish,' and bowed so profoundly that he bowed himself clean out of the wagon, head down, and had it not been for the prompt seizure of the horse by the head by one of the ladies, whilst the other was engaged in disentangling and disengaging Mr. ——'s legs from the reins, Mr. —— would probably have been gathered to his fathers!

"I do not allow plantation affairs to obtrude themselves upon my thoughts. This I intend as a period of rest, mentally as well as physically. I expect to hear from Tom to-morrow, and hope to hear that Sophy and Fify and Lelia reached home on the 28th, as expected.

"This is no very good place to write letters at, as I cannot very well do it in the morning, on account of fishing and getting back from fishing, and then bathing, and then dressing, and then dining, and then people are coming to see me, and then I am going to see people, and then—and then—I feel lazy and *very* comfortable!"

T. S. D. TO HIS DAUGHTER EMMY.

"PASS CHRISTIAN, 7th August, 1870.

. . . "I will move to Mr. Harrison's to-morrow, for the purpose of waging regular war on the trout nationality. . . . It may be a difficult thing to determine which is the most delightful, the catching or the eating. For myself, greatly as I enjoy the eating, I would forego that, and take the middling and greens, rather than to have my rod and line taken from me. I have actually been so nervous as to fancy, after going to bed, that I had a large trout on my line, and would give my arm a twitch in order to hook him good!"

T. S. D. TO HIS DAUGHTER EMMY.

"MR. J. P. HARRISON'S, PASS CHRISTIAN, August 12, 1870.

. . . "Mr. Harrison's horse being very lame to-day, I lose my fishing, which is a sore disappointment, but I ought to be thankful that nothing has kept me from the bayou until to-day. I have fished eleven days, starting at about half an hour after sunrise and returning about eleven o'clock. In these eleven days I have caught one hundred and thirty-eight of these splendid trout, one sheepshead, besides various brim, goggle-eyes, perch, etc., which are never counted here. I hope to resume operations to-morrow, as Mr. John Harrison intends hiring a horse for the campaign, if possible, and he thinks he knows where he can get him. On the whole, I am satisfied with my performance, as I put the best of them up to all they know to keep tally with me. When I am beaten (which is seldom, and a very small beat at that) the cause is obviously some disadvantages that I had to encounter. With a fair show, there is not a disciple of old Izaak that can allow me an inch of margin."

T. S. D. TO HIS DAUGHTER EMMY.

"BURLEIGH, 11th September, 1870.

"MY BELOVED DAUGHTER,—I have not for seventy-two years, eight months, and seven days perpetrated so stupid an action as when I sent your trunk to New Orleans, by express, instead of to Baton Rouge. It never occurred to me that the express could take a package on any other than a straight line; and I never knew better until Ida asked me, on yesterday, how I had directed the trunk. I was near not replying, but did reply, with some impatience, 'To New Orleans, care of office, etc., etc., *of course!*' But she took me from my high horse with a jerk by asking me if your costly clothes would not be ruined by the rotting pears in consequence of the delay of the trunk, which would have been avoided had it gone right along by express. Now, I want to hear from you, and I don't; but, as I must hear, sooner or later, I hope somebody will report on the damage, as soon as it is ascertained. It was a stupid thing to put pears in that trunk; but I thought myself smart in my manner of putting them up. You found that each pear was wrapped up separately in strong brown paper (except two, that could not be gotten in with the wrappings), packed without pressure in a pasteboard box, and the box duly secured at the very bottom of the trunk. All this was done with a proud consciousness that it had been 'done up brown.' Brown? Very brown! your fine silks reeking with rotten pear-juice. But I don't *know* how the thing stands, as the people at the New Orleans office may have sent the trunk right ahead on Saturday. But I fear they did not, and actually believe the chances against their having done so.

"Now, the fact is, I thought of nothing hardly but that I had not only some fine pears, but also an opportunity to send you some. Had I not sent them I know they would choke me if I attempted to eat them. I always feel choky when eating good things beyond the reach of my children. But I must master this feeling, as it impairs the judgment sometimes,—as in the pres-

ent case, most deplorably. But—bah! This does no
good; so let me hear from you. This pear-silk-dress-
bottom-of-the-trunk-express business is quite too interesting to admit of the introduction of any other topic
in this missive, and so I will conclude."

T. S. D. TO AUGUSTINE DABNEY.

"BURLEIGH, 19th October, 1871.

"I reached the Pass on the night of Monday. I got
there in a storm, and when I awoke on Tuesday morning the equinox was upon us. The wind howled and
the rain came down—just as it can when it chooses—
through that day and most of the night. On Wednesday morning it was not raining, but there had been no
abatement of the wind. It came from the east, piling
the water up in Lake Ponchartrain at such a rate that
on Wednesday morning it was found surrounding the
Clay statue in New Orleans. But I had two enthusiastic friends at the Pass, who, like myself, had gone there
to fish, and would not be balked. They called for me in
their carriage, and I jumped in, as a matter of course,
being but a boy myself, as you know. As we knew
the woods were flooded and the bayous out of their
banks, the only chance was the railroad bridge over
the bay of St. Louis; and so we struck out for that,
but, on our arrival at the bridge, neither of my friends
would venture on it, for fear of being blown off. We
should then have gone home, but did not. We went
to one of the bayous, and found it exactly as we
expected. We threw in, though (having plenty of
shrimp), but 'nary' bite had we. We determined to
try it lower down, where the bayou was wider, and
could hold more water. But that cost me a walk
through a marsh of a mile, the grass from waist- to
shoulder-high, and very stubborn and thick, and the
water shoe-deep every step, except when I trod in a
hole, and then I did not measure it. Meanwhile I had
a three-gallon bucket of water to carry (with my
shrimp) in one hand, and my angle in the other.
'Nary' fish again! I have a faint recollection of
getting out of that marsh, and of drinking some excellent brandy in commemoration of the auspicious

event; and I remember, too, that I went to bed (sick) the next day, but I have no recollection of wetting a line since. The fishing was wonderfully fine afterwards, but I was unable to go, although I remained a week, being too unwell to undertake the journey, and I have ventured to my garden but twice since my return, and was doubtful about getting back to the house the last time I went."

T. S. D. TO HIS DAUGHTER EMMY.

"BURLEIGH, December 14, 1873.

... "We are having a hard road to weed just now, but, with a stout heart and honest intentions, we will wade through."

T. S. D. TO HIS DAUGHTER EMMY.

"BURLEIGH, 17th December, 1873.

... "The almost cheerful tone of your letter of the day before yesterday gives me more pleasure than I can well describe. I understand the thing now entirely. It was hope deferred. 'Hope deferred maketh the heart sick.' Yes, sick unto death very often. ...

"The reality now stares us in the face, and I am happy to learn from you that your husband will meet it like a man. This I never doubted, however, and I am not at all surprised at his tardiness in taking hold. It is a tight thing to take a subordinate position on a road where he had ruled for a long time as head of the scientific department; but it is manly and honorable to take it, and, if this be strictly true, as I think it is, it would not be manly or honorable to decline it. So, cheer up, you and your glorious husband, and utilize such opportunities as offer, without fear of compromising yourselves by doing so. There is but one position on the railroad that I would have objected to his taking, and that is brakeman on a freight-train; not on account of the humbleness of it, but on account of the danger."

T. S. D. TO HIS DAUGHTER EMMY.

"CRYSTAL SPRINGS, 7th February, 1874.

"MY DEAR, DEAR CHILD,—I cannot defer until I get home writing to you to ask your forgiveness for having hurt your feelings, as I know I did. Forgive me, my good child, for I was so much excited as to be incapable of acting right."

T. S. D. TO HIS DAUGHTER EMMY.

"BURLEIGH, 1st May, 1874.

"My last letter to you has miscarried. As I gave you particular instructions how to plant cotton, I will repeat; and, as you will want every seed to come up and to do its best, my object will be to show you how to do that. I once planted forty seed with this object in view, and I had every one to come up finely, but one was cut down by a worm the first day. Thirty-nine lived to do their best. The seed from those thirty-nine I planted again as at first, and the third year I had three hundred acres in cotton from those thirty-nine plants."

T. S. D. TO HIS SON THOMAS.

"BURLEIGH, 17th May, 1874.

... "Last Wednesday the bishop, assisted by Mr. Douglas and Heber Crane, ordained a Mr. Jackson, a negro as black as any on this land, a deacon in the church. The ceremony was very interesting, and Jackson preached in the afternoon to as enlightened an audience as ever goes to our church. His sermon was admirable and admirably delivered. I have heard but few who read so well, and fewer who had so good a manner. He is a well-educated man, having a considerable knowledge of Latin, Greek, and Hebrew. He has been living in one of the rectory houses for two years, is a hard student under Mr. Douglas, and is without reproach. My family has had him by the hand during the whole time, and now every one of our respectable people show him kindness. I will send you the paper containing the proceedings."

During a period of thirty years Thomas had the pleasure of an annual or semi-annual visit from the venerable Bishop Green, of Mississippi, as he went on his round of visitations. He was a close friend of Thomas Dabney's, and was beloved in that house, as he was in every one in his diocese. After these aged friends had attained fourscore years they fell into a way of exchanging birthday letters. On Bishop Green's departure, after his last visit to Burleigh, Thomas accompanied him as far as Dry Grove, two and a half miles, where he bade him good-by and returned home on foot, the bishop proceeding in the carriage.

T. S. D. TO HIS DAUGHTER EMMY.

"BURLEIGH, 8th July, 1875.

. . . "You must not take so much note of my looking sad, my dear child, as it is contrary to my philosophy to cultivate unhappiness. That I cannot always be merry, or even cheerful, should be expected; as there are shades as well as sunshine with all humanity, as I suppose. But God has been wonderfully kind to me in giving me such children. . . . And now let me say, my love, that you give way too much to despondency. Restrain yourself in giving expression to sad thoughts, unhappy thoughts, and they will become mollified after a time for want of aliment to feed on. The indulgence in gloomy thoughts, not to say gloomy expressions, can be made instruments of self-torture like any other vice, for I class such a disposition, or the giving way to it, among the vices. God gave you three children and has taken one away. The other two He has spared to you so far, but, if displeased, He may take the others. Look at your husband and your father. Is it nothing to have such a husband and such a father? Does not their affectionate appreciation of you (it is in this sense that I am introduced) count for nothing? If for anything, think of them, and the countless blessings by which you are surrounded, and then humble yourself, my lonely child, and seek forgiveness for your forgetfulness.

"Lelia has a juvenile party to-day, consisting of the shavers of both sexes from the rectory,—twelve in all, —and they are making noise enough. But I am out of the *mêlée*, having resigned my room to Sophy, taking roost right over her. It does me good to see Sophy charging about, helping on the housekeeping in all manner of ways and fattening apace. Her recovery may be set down among the marvels. God bless you, my dear child."

CHAPTER XXII.

LIFE AT BURLEIGH.

T. S. D. TO HIS SON-IN-LAW B. H. GREENE.

"BURLEIGH, 29th August, 1875.

... "WE are having lively times in the political way. I have seen nothing like it since 1840,—those days of 'hard cider,' 'log cabins,' ''coon skins,' and what-not, by means of which the Whigs gave Van Buren and the Democrats so signal an overthrow. I believe the impulse under which the outraged white race of the South are now being urged on will be equally irresistible. At a mass-meeting held in Raymond on the 18th instant, falling in with T. J. Wharton, I remarked to him that such an uprising was wonderful! 'Uprising?' replied he. 'It is no uprising. It is an insurrection!' To give you some notion of the enthusiasm of the people, I only have to say that they do not straggle in to such meetings, but go in clubs, each club with its band of music, flags, and regalia, and a cannon in many instances, and these cannon they make roar from every hill-top on the road. The procession of cavalry from Edwards Dépôt (some other clubs having joined the Edwards Club) reached from the court-house far beyond John Shelton's house,—the length of the column being two miles, as one of the number told me. That from Utica, taking in my club and one other, was a great deal longer. The thing to be appreciated had to be seen. The 'carpet-baggers' and negroes are evidently staggered. We have been carrying on this thing for a month without their having moved a peg. They do not know where to begin. I suppose something will be hat' 'ed up in Washington after a while, and the cue be given to the faithful, and then 'we shall see what we shall see.'

"Among the anomalies of the canvass upon which we have just entered, not the least significant is that *we have not a single candidate in the field who, for himself, sought office*; whereas every 'carpet-bagger' and a large percentage of the negroes are clamorous for some place or other. All of our candidates have been brought out by nominating conventions; many of these against their wish,—for these conventions pick out our best men. For example, we are running John Shelton for supervisor, A. R. Johnston for the State senate, Daniel Williams for magistrate at Dry Grove, etc. None of these desire the positions proposed for them, but it would be considered in very bad taste in either to refuse.

"The upshot of the whole is that I am kept on the 'pad,'—being president of the Dry Grove Club, that has to march, or *be marched to*, at every whip-stitch. We held two club meetings last week, and I have ordered one for this week. Next week, on the 11th of September, we go in a body to Edwards Dépôt, where preparations will be made for ten thousand people. I suppose Jackson will respond, as I know other places will, and so many barbecues will be given by the clubs, to each of which the others must march in a body, and in military order, that I will esteem myself lucky if I get through alive. But I expect to be lucky to that extent, as my whole soul is in it."

It was early in 1875 that the citizens of Mississippi, believing that it was unmanly and stupid to submit longer without protest against ruinous misrule of "carpet-baggers," backed by negro voters, determined to lay aside all minor interests and make an organized effort to throw off the incubus which was rapidly involving the whole State in financial bankruptcy and social degradation and misery. Hence the formation of Democratic clubs.

From 1865 to 1875,—ten long, weary years,—tenfold harder to endure than the four years immediately preceding 1865, the State had been under military rule, our last governor from Washington being Adelbert Ames (a man honest and brave, but narrow and puritanical), who seems to have hated the Aryan race of the South. In proof of this I merely cite the fact that he was impeached by the State Legislature for fomenting race strife, but, by advice of counsel, he wisely or unwisely evaded the issue of trial, and fled away to his own.

During the years 1870–74 the taxes, imposed by aliens and the misguided African element, in many cases exceeded the incomes derived from the plantations; and it was then that men, nerved with a courage born of despair, cast about them for suitable leaders (men of unquestioned integrity, cool judgment, and dauntless resolution) under whose guidance relief might be attempted. Intuitively all eyes were turned to Thomas Dabney, and he was chosen president of the Democratic club of his neighborhood.*

T. S. D. TO HIS SON THOMAS.

"BURLEIGH, 15th October, 1875.

... "I will have my house as full as it can hold tomorrow night, as Utica, Raymond, Clinton, Boltons, Edwards, etc., will send their clubs here in force. You will perceive that a great many will have come long distances. I must take as many as I can accommodate reasonably, having already invited a number. It will put your sisters to much trouble, but as it is unavoidable, they undertake it with great cheerfulness."

The daughters worked by day and night on the uniforms for Thomas and his friends. Some of the negroes joined the club, and uniforms must be made for them too, and it was the patriotic thing for the ladies in the house to make these also. Besides, an immense United States flag was called for by the club, and was made by us in those hot July days and nights.

Thomas was as ready to extend the simple hospitality

---

* Written y Edward.

of his house in helping on this movement as he had been in former times to render more extensive aid. His life-long friend, Mr. John Shelton, in writing of this side of his character, says,—

"We were both Henry Clay men while he lived, and Whigs of the straitest and strictest type. . . . A most zealous Whig before the civil war, the leaders and candidates of that party were often the recipients of his unbounded and princely hospitality, and, as a zealous party man, he took a great interest in whatever elections were pending, and shared his means with an unsparing and free hand for the advancement of party ends."

T. S. D. TO HIS DAUGHTER EMMY.

"BURLEIGH, 20th October, 1875.

. . . "We are in a very hot political contest just now, and with a good prospect of turning out the carpet-bag thieves by whom we have been robbed for the past six to ten years. They commenced at Clinton on their old game of getting up riots and then calling on Grant for troops to suppress them,—these troops to be used afterwards to control elections. They succeeded in getting up their riot, which was put down by our own people after so sanguinary a fashion as to strike them with a terror not easily described."

T. S. D. TO HIS DAUGHTER EMMY.

"BURLEIGH, 24th November, 1875.

. . . "I am in a laughing humor to-day, as I have just sent E—— to pay my taxes, and I had to fork over only three hundred and seventy-five dollars for that purpose,—a very different affair from the operations of many years back. Last year it took over eight hundred dollars, and the year before more than that."

In 1873 the taxes on the plantation (Burleigh) amounted to over nine hundred dollars, and the income was less than eight hundred dollars. This state of affairs was the result of carpet-bag rule,—a rule more harassing, humiliating, and destructive than people beyond our borders can conceive.

In one of these years a lawsuit was brought against Thomas about one of his line fences. He had kept up his own fences dividing his plantation from his neighbors,* not sharing the expense and labor with them, as was the custom in the country. The negroes were summoned by his counsel as witnesses. They must have talked the case over with indignation among themselves, for their testimony given, one after another, sounded in the court-room as if they had been trained for the occasion. They used the same words: " Course I know all 'bout it. 'Twas when Mr. M—— was de oberseer. Hi! I help to split dem rails. Dey's marster's rails. Didn't brer Gilbert lay de worm o' dat fence? All marster people know dat. Dey all 'members dat dey split and tote dem rails, and brer Gilbert lay de worm."

A good many, fifty perhaps, had been summoned, but after five or six had said these words, Thomas's counsel decided at once that the case would probably go against him if the whole band should be allowed to go through with this formula, and, greatly to the disappointment of the negroes, no more were allowed to give their evidence. Their pride in their old owner had risen to its height, and their indignation against the neighbor was proportionally great. The case lasted for three days, and, during this time, one of the daughters was alone at Burleigh. The negroes showed much sympathy for her. Every evening about dusk Mammy Maria's husband came to the steps where she was sitting. He was a shy man, and had scarcely ever before spoken a dozen words to her. He appeared with his hat in his hand and the graceful bows and salutes of the negro race.

" Good-evenin', missis. 'Ria, marm, say dat I must tell you 'bout my garden. She 'bleeged to go home to 'tend to things now. She say dat I ken tell you how my garden was gittin' on. I plant potatoes, marm,

---

* With one exception, which was in the case of a connection.

an' I wucked 'em. Oh, yes, I'se wucked 'em. An' peas an' greens, marm, an' I wucked 'em. An' I git sprouts to eat out o' my garden, marm. I wucked 'em all, marm. 'Ria say dat I mus'n't let you be lonely. She tole me to tell you 'bout dem things. An' she say dat you mus'n't feel no ways oneasy 'bout dat law business. She say dat some o' de people is come down from Raymond and dey say dat she must tell you 'bout how things is goin' on, an' dat eberything is goin' for marster. An' you ought to hear how he people talk up for him. Hi! dem lawyers stop Ellis 'cus he talk up so. Dey sent some o' de people back an' wouldn't let 'em talk. But dey was all ready to say de same thing 'bout dat fence. Dey was ready to stan' up for marster, but dey wasn't 'llowed to do it."

"John say he couldn't talk to you," mammy explained afterwards. "But I tole him to tell you all 'bout he garden; I know he could talk 'bout dat."

Great was the rejoicing on the plantation when the case was decided for the master, and he and his witnesses came home together. A good many came to the house to say how glad they were that he had gained the case, and to explain how much they had done in bringing about the result.

When Thomas Dabney's fortunes were at their lowest ebb he heard that a widow living a few miles from him was in need of the necessaries of life. The case was represented to him very strongly that she and her children were in danger of starvation. He turned visibly white, and said afterwards that he thought his heart had stopped beating for a moment when he heard of such a thing so near him. He hurried out and sent a wagon-load of corn and a supply of meat to her, and he went himself and put ten dollars in her hand. "My daughter is also a woman" were the words with which he accompanied the money. "She knows that you may need money to buy some little things as well as food." He was so poor at the time that the lack of the corn and meat would be seriously felt in his own larder, and it is doubtful if anything were left in his pocket after he gave away the ten dollars. It seems almost needless to say that his daughter, knowing the family at Burleigh was living almost without the use of money, did not suggest to him to give that. But what woman could have devised a more compassionate and gracious way of bestowing a gift?

A poor woman in Mississippi has said of him, "The time that my son fell in the well and he was there,— oh! I could have hugged him in my arms. My son told me that the first thing that he saw was that white head bending over him."

T. S. D. TO HIS DAUGHTER EMMY.

"BURLEIGH, 21st February, 1876.

"The mail of to-day brought me your sweet and truly dutiful letter of the 16th instant. You only want my 'orders,' my dear child, to obey them. God forbid that I should ever give 'orders' to one who is ever ready to anticipate my wishes by the time that I know them myself. I had to write that letter to you, painful as it was to me. All that you say of —— I already knew but too well; but the knowledge came too late to be of any benefit to us, and it can now do no good to grieve over it. What we now have to do is to look the thing in the face as it stands, and I will tell Coker that he may look to me for that one hundred dollars next winter. I cannot pay it any sooner, as I find, after my last pound of cotton has been sold, that I have thirty-three dollars and some cents left."

T. S. D. TO HIS DAUGHTER EMMY.

"BURLEIGH, 14th July, 1876.

... "When I fish in the bayous back of the Pass (which I generally do, in preference to fishing in the gulf), I start at sunrise and get back at half-past twelve to one o'clock, and the distance, eight miles, is nearly the same as from Alexandria to Trout Creek. With a buggy and a good horse I never thought anything of the distance; and, besides, I always wanted the family with whom I stayed to enjoy the fruit of my rod. I have caught thirty-two trout (we never counted the perch, goggle-eyes, etc.) in the three hours that we had for fishing. But that is the largest number that I ever caught in any one day. We always caught more than the family wanted, however; and Mrs. Harrison and Mrs. Smith were in the habit of supplying their neighbors with many a fine dish, for two to three of us would bring in a goodly pile of them."

He was at this time planning a trip to Pass Christian.

T. S. D. TO HIS DAUGHTER EMMY.

"BURLEIGH, 3d May, 1877.

"MY BELOVED CHILD,—I wrote to your brother last Sunday, but without mentioning your children. When such a letter comes from me, it may be considered as clean a 'bill of health' as can possibly be written. But I would have noticed them had I not expected Ida to stick in something. In all letters from me to any member of my family, if anything is the matter with another member, I always write the *worst*, not exaggerated, not extenuated, but precisely as the thing stands, leaning, if leaning at all, to the bad, but avoiding all leaning, if that be possible. But you know all this, and yet I find you as wretched as you can make yourself over imaginary sufferings of Emmeline. The child has not grunted once since my telegram to you, nor for four days previously to the date of that telegram. There is no need of studying what she likes or dislikes, whether sweet milk or sour, bread or crackers, for she eats right and left four to five times during the day. The day before yesterday (1st May) the rectory children were all here, a May-party having been gotten up for them. They had various 'goodies' spread on a large table in the yard, the entertainment coming off late in the evening. After the children had satisfied themselves the grown folks partook. No long time afterwards, the company having left and Sue very tired, she said to Emmeline, 'Well, come along now and we will go to bed.' Whereupon Emmeline, with all the naïveté imaginable, inquired if they were not going to have supper

"So make yourself easy. I will never leave anything to your imagination about these dear little fellows; so, 'go 'long' and get yourself well as soon as you please."

T. S. D. TO MRS. H. CAMPBELL SMITH.

"BURLEIGH, 6th July, 1877.

"MY MUCH BELOVED NIECE,—You can't know how much pleasure your eminently characteristic letter of the 20th ultimo gave me—gave all of us. It is so like you to remember a promise that I did *not* make, but which you chose to believe I *did* make because you wished to have it so. I was too fearful of being unable to visit you this summer to promise such a thing, and yet could not give expression to that doubt; and hence you were left to draw your own inference, and you only know one way of solving such problems as these. I now know that it is impossible for me to enjoy the hospitality of Cam and yourself this summer, as we are expecting my brother's family,—the whole tribe, consisting of himself and wife, Nanny, Mary Ware and her son Toby, and perhaps Martha, to spend the month of August with us. They are all together on Honey Island (except Martha), but they know that they can't stay there through the summer, and so they propose to divide about three months between Aggy, Colonel Porter, and myself. So you see, my dear, that I am nailed hard and fast right here for this summer, at least. But I don't relinquish the hope of seeing the inside of your new home some time or other, and will do it as soon as I can, for I wish to see you all very much. As you say nothing about gnats in your letter to me, I hope those vile pests left you quickly after your letter was written to Mrs. Douglas. They are a great deal worse than mosquitoes, I think, as they light on you in clouds—in your eyes, nose, and ears,—are not to be frightened off, bite like ——, and pass right through ordinary mosquito-bars. I fear your region is subject to them at certain seasons of the year.

"I don't know whether to congratulate Cam on his

elegant leisure or not. If he had much professional employment, you would probably have to burn the lamp o' nights.

"If your neighbors wish to see your old uncle, he is indebted to the kind words of his niece for that wish. But what is the use of having friends if they fail to show it on proper occasions!

"I am glad that you have *some* garden. I have had a scuffle to have even that, as it rained eternally during the spring, and then dropped off to no rain at all, and we are having the hottest summer I ever witnessed in Mississippi. I have to take the garden in broken doses, homœopathic at that, as I came near a sunstroke, or something worse, the other day, frightening the girls nearly out of their wits.

"Lelia, poor child, is very far from being well. I was in hopes of getting her off to the North, but could not make it out, and so she has gone to her kind friends in Brandon for a change of air and scene. If she is not improved by it, I must send her to New York when her brother returns to that place after his summer vacation terminates. Emmy has been in New York three to four months, but is expected to arrive at Terry to-morrow night. Her children have been with us during her absence, but she will have no fault to find when she sees them, as they are as hearty a trio as ever discussed bread and butter and *sich*.

"Charlie and Kate are as loving as ever, I believe, which is saying a good deal for this hot weather. The girls send any amount of love to you and Cam and the children. My love all round."

T. S. D. TO MRS. H. CAMPBELL SMITH.

"BURLEIGH, 19th December, 1877.

"MY POOR AFFLICTED CHILD,—I received, yesterday, a letter from Dr. Baird, giving the particulars of the dreadful calamity that has befallen you. I was waiting for that, or for something of the kind from some member of your family, being more than willing to postpone so mournful and difficult a task as writing a letter to you that could be satisfactory to me or in any way a comfort to you. To lose one's husband or wife I take to be the greatest calamity that can befall any one who may be happily married, and that you had that comfort in Cam I have every reason to be absolutely certain of. But, my dear child, it is among the inevitable laws of nature that these unions must be broken up at some time or other, and one or the other be left to mourn. It is therefore seemly that we should be grateful for such measure of happiness as we have been permitted to enjoy, and to bow our heads reverently and without a rebellious spirit when the All-Wise sees fit to checker our path. I trust you may succeed, after a time, in schooling your mind to this necessity.

"Dr. Baird's letter to me shows him to be a very sincere friend of yours. He discusses your situation with a great deal of feeling, and exhorts me to go to see you, if possible, and, if not possible, to send some one on whose friendship you may be supposed to rely.

. . For myself, you may remember that I returned from the Pass a month or two ago (or were told that I did) so entirely indisposed as to make it doubtful whether or no I should ever get over it. I am unable now to undergo any extra exertion, and get to my garden with some difficulty, but force myself to go, as better than continuous inactivity. I never even go to Dry Grove if it can be avoided. It was therefore impossible for me to accede to Dr. Baird's suggestion by going to your house."

T. S. D. TO HIS DAUGHTER EMMY.

"BURLEIGH, 6th January, 1878.

"God bless my child and her children and her husband! And you thought of me in connection with the 4th, and your husband thought of me in connection with Christmas and oysters, and you *forgot* to write to me about it! But all is well that ends well, as you say; and I now know more about oysters than I ever did. I thought they *must be* lost, but I told Edward to bring them out unless they would knock a buzzard over. There were but two spoiled ones. The mouths of a good many were a little open, but, as I had to open all of them, I found they were *not* spoiled, and in they all went to the dish. I even ate some of them raw. I took them all out of the barrel on Tuesday morning, placed them on the ground in the north cellar, with the *deep shell* down, sprinkled them with salt and meal, and then with just enough water to make the salt run a little. They were a little too fresh at first, but on the second day after their removal from the barrel they were as salt as could be desired, and perfectly delicious. I could have kept them— well, I don't know how long,—a week, perhaps; perhaps a month. They improved every day (I mean those with their shells closed), the last being the best. You need never mind the temperature hereafter; and, as New Orleans oysters are generally too fresh, you can, in one day, season them to your taste and make them equal to York River oysters,—perhaps! . . .

"Letters from Virginius and Ben remind me of the 4th. Good boys! Neither did Tom fail. Good boy, too! These things, and such thoughts as they suggest, make me happy. . . .

"THOS. S. DABNEY."

Several of Augustine's children had moved to California, and in January, 1878, he and Mrs. Augustine Dabney went there to make their home among their children. It was the first separation of the brothers.

T. S. D. TO AUGUSTINE DABNEY.

"BURLEIGH, 20th January, 1878.

"Although you have been throwing off suggestions from time to time of the likelihood of your going to California, I was still taken by surprise when I read your card of the 12th, informing me that you were packing up and expecting to be off in two hours. I hope Mary stood the trip reasonably. Unless some accident befell, I have no good reason for hoping that you and sister E—— had a good time, as you both like travelling, she especially. No amount of 'hoping' would do any good under such circumstances; as of all modes of getting about, the only *intolerable* mode to me is by rail. There is no walking about on a railroad car; the only change possible is to change from one seat to another,—from an erect to a recumbent or a prostrate position. When on one of these luxurious vehicles I am reminded within an hour or two of the man of leisure who would escape, if he knew how, from the 'rack of a too easy chair.' I suppose to be stretched on a hot gridiron, or on a bed of fleas, with my hands tied would be worse, and that is about the best I can say for such luxuries as palace cars. And yet I take them, of course, when I have to go, but on the principle that a nauseous dose of physic cuts short disease. I think Mary extremely fortunate in having made her escape from cotton-planting; as, indeed, from every interest now known to this side of the Sierra Nevada. From my stand-point I can discover nothing but an early crash and a universal bankruptcy. Corn is selling in Kansas at fifteen cents per bushel, and is worth but little more at Bonham, Texas, where Ben lives. Molasses can now be had in New Orleans at six dollars per barrel and sugar at six cents per pound. Edward sold cotton at Terry a few days ago at six and a half cents. It was inferior cotton, but a large portion of my crop is no better, as we had four overflows of the creek in three weeks, when much of the crop was open, and necessarily was washed out, and what remained was badly damaged. Ten to eleven cents in New Orleans is now about the price of what little tolerably good cotton we have. Under such figures the whole country must sink, except the few who are free of debt, and this class goes about as far towards making this Southern country as one swallow does towards making a summer. Tom has taken the alarm promptly by entering the medical college as a student, but without giving up his school, attending lectures and the dissecting-room out of school hours. It will be too much for him, I feel certain, although he is very strong. But I will watch him closely, you may judge. His school hours are from nine A.M. to three P.M. Lectures from half-past three P.M. to five P.M., and dissecting from seven to eleven and twelve at night. You will perceive that he has but thirty minutes to pass from his school to the lecture-room, and but one hour and a half for dinner, recreation, and travelling, from nine in the morning till eleven or twelve at night. No man can stand this, I think; or, if at all, but for a short time. But Tom is a fellow of pluck and will stand as much of it as any man. I will keep a sharp eye on him, however.

"We had a very humdrum Christmas,—none but my own family, and many of them away, as you know. I had a fine beef for the occasion, but had to let him enjoy a reprieve, as the weather was quite too warm to kill him at that time. But we are enjoying him now, and each day as I look upon a part of him smoking on the table I think of ante-bellum times, in a small way."

T. S. D. TO AUGUSTINE DABNEY.

"BURLEIGH, 3d March, 1878.

"Yours of the 1st February reached me 'on time,' as I suppose, and went through the family, interesting each one of us very much, as it abounds in incidents of travel and California affairs. One incident, however, was far from agreeable, but when a man tumbles down a strange and dark staircase, he may congratulate himself upon finding no bones broken. I hope your hand has recovered. I did not intend deferring this reply so long, and did not know that it was *so* long until I referred to the date just now. I truly hope that Mary finds the climate agreeable to her, and I hope that Toby is doing as well as Mary can desire. As to yourself and sister E——, I have no apprehension but that everything in that great country will suit you both perfectly, and prolong your lives. . . . You will be seventy-eight to-morrow, dating this reminds me of it. . . . I was interrupted and lost the mail, and have read over your letter again, with renewed interest. It is very full, and strictly conforms to the description of Mark Twain, in his last book, 'Roughing It,' which I have just read; which is remarkable, as you were rushing along by rail, whereas he took it by stage, horseback, and footback. The Desert and the sage bushes, the sharp air and snow of the Sierra and the sudden transition to perpetual spring on reaching the Valley of Sacramento. All this is more like enchantment than like anything to be looked for in real life. . . .

"Although I have, for the past ten or fifteen years, only given myself three to five years of furlough at a time, I yet live, and with a breathing apparatus and casing as perfect as ever, to all appearance; but yet the vigilant old fellow 'Time' has not slept, but has increased day by day my repugnance to locomotion, making it more agreeable to me to read or talk in an arm-chair than to trundle a wheelbarrow up a steep hill; and it requires so much engineering to pull on my socks, that Sue comes into my room every morning before I am up and shoves them on for me. Some one has to tie my shoes; not that it is impossible to me, but vastly disagreeable. Now, although I have not mentioned either of old Dodson's (or Dobson's) infirmities in the Table, you will recognize this as a kindred picture. . . .

"The people here, with few exceptions, are becoming poorer and poorer, and without the least prospect of amendment, as the prime cause is to be found in the worthlessness of the negro. As I am now physically unable to take charge (active) of the plantation, I am utterly at a loss as to what is best to be done. If I could sell this place, the problem would be solved, but nothing can be sold here now." . . .

Thomas's own words will best show how he felt the loss of his brother, that occurred in April of this year.

T. S. D. TO MRS. AUGUSTINE DABNEY.

"BURLEIGH, 28th April, 1878.

"MY DEAR SISTER,—A note from Marye, received this morning, informs me that I have lost my only brother. If there was a rule in such cases he would have been the survivor, but there is no rule that I know of. I have no consolation to offer beyond the expression of my sincere sympathy,—an oblation that I need nearly as much as you do. It will doubtless occur to you, without your being reminded of it, that you have been wonderfully passed by the hand of fate during the whole course of your married life, amounting to about forty-five years, I think. When you think of the few, the very few, who have carried their cup of happiness over the rough paths of life for such a time with so little loss, you may be surprised into self-gratulation rather than be weighed down by this calamity, great as I feel it to be on you and on myself. You are wonderfully blessed in your children. Do you know any one with whom you would exchange, maternal ties being severed, and you free to choose? Take me from the list, and do you know another? Verily, no! It becomes you, then, to accept this visitation of Providence without a murmur, or the appearance of one. Mourn we must, and may, and be forgiven.

"For myself, I feel like some hoary obelisk, with a circle of desolation steadily widening, but few, if any, of the contemporaries of my early manhood surviving. Not one remains, I think. . . .

"You have no plans at present, I suppose. Should you elect, at any future time, to return to this State, you will remember that my door, equally with that of your children, will be open to you." . . .

T. S. D. TO HIS DAUGHTER EMMY.

"BURLEIGH, 13th August, 1878.

"That you and Ida are quite able to take care of yourselves I entertain no doubt, but still it does me good to find you asserting the fact with so much boldness. Of all the principles developed by the late war, I think the capability of our Southern women to take care of themselves by no means the least important. With ten to twelve years of nominal peace, however, the necessity for exemplifying that principle might be supposed to be at an end; but so long as such men as Governor —— have it in their power to control and set at defiance the decrees of the judiciary, just so long you will have to take care of yourselves, and lucky to be able to do it. The responsibility that he is assuming is fearful; and to make it as bad as possible, there was no necessity for it, no matter what his opinions might be, for a governor has no right to an opinion on a law after it has been acted upon by the Supreme Court. He still has the *power*, as an engineer has to blow up his passengers, but he does not blow them up for all that, except by accident. I suppose the bread of two thousand people has been denied them by the folly or wickedness of this one wrong-headed man."

After the death of Augustine several of his children made arrangements to come to Burleigh with their families to board during the summer months. This was not only a source of material aid to their uncle, but it brought back the old delightful intercourse between the two families. This had been interrupted, as well by other unavoidable circumstances of life as by Thomas's poverty. Four happy summers were spent in this manner at Burleigh. But the latter part of the first summer (1878) was a sad time all over the South. The yellow fever was raging in many of the cities and towns. Late in August a suspicious sickness appeared at Dry Grove. As this little village was situated in a healthful part of the country, and as there was a theory that the fever could not reach it, the people felt no alarm. The following letters were written by Thomas at this period.

T. S. D. TO HUGH STEWART, ESQ.

"BURLEIGH, 31st August, 1878.

"DEAR SIR,—In view of the pestilence that has broken out at Dry Grove, I wish you to bring your wife and Nellie here immediately. You have not a moment to lose. . . .

"My carriage will be moving the rectory family this morning, and when it completes that job will bring yours.

"Don't hesitate, as the loss of a day may cost you

your life. I will tell you how you can manage the post-office.

"Most truly your friend,
"THOMAS S. DABNEY."

T. S. D. TO HIS DAUGHTER EMMY.

"BURLEIGH, 7th September, 1878.

"Mrs. Governor Brown's servant-girl, Eliza, as you will remember, went to Canton a year or so ago. She returned to her old home about two weeks ago, and died of yellow fever or some kindred disease in the course of four to six days. Four days after her death the governor was taken ill. Three or four days after that Edward went to Terry, and, hearing of the governor's illness, went directly to see him. He found him very ill, and announced to Mrs. Brown his intention to remain with him. But she positively refused to allow this, and he came home and told us of it, and added that he would immediately return. This Mrs. Brown probably expected, but would not allow him to wait on the governor without first obtaining my sanction. She raised no objection to his remaining after his return. He was to have written to us by every mail, but five days passed without a line from him or from any one there. Mr. Douglas then went to see after them, and found Edward with the highest fever on and the reddest face he had ever seen. . . . We had a terrible scare about the Dry Grove people a week ago. It seems that two of the men there, in order to deepen the pond on which the little mill at Dry Grove depends for water, cut the dam and drew off the little water that was in it, and then turned in to drag out the mud. The stench was described by Dr. West as terrific. In three days half of the inhabitants were flat on their backs, some of them ill. Nearly all of Mr. Douglas's family were sick. In this exigency I wrote to Mrs. Douglas (Mr. Douglas having left home that morning, but to return in the evening) to lose no time about it, but to send one of the Castons immediately for my carriage and to bring her whole flock here. I said they could take possession of the two rooms in the library building, where they might keep house according to their own taste; for they would have to bring their own bedding, cooking utensils, and provisions, and do regular 'camping out' except for the tents. Mr. Douglas returned home in time to bring Mrs. Douglas and provisions, etc., that afternoon, Miss Carrie and the children having preceded them in my carriage. All of the children, or nearly all, were pouring down quinine at three to four hours' intervals, and Miss Carrie had to be taken up bodily and placed in the carriage, and two of the children got up from sick-beds. The change in their condition is remarkable. They all appeared to be as well as possible on the morning after their arrival here, and Miss Carrie appears to be as well as I ever saw her. I have suggested to Mr. Douglas that all hands had best remain here through September and get a good stock of health, as they are not in my way in the least. I think they will stay, although he made no reply. I also invited Hugh Stewart to bring (I to send for them) his wife and Nelly, as we would squeeze them in somewhere, but they declined, feeling, as we suppose, too poor to leave their property—fowls, etc.—to be stolen in their absence. You cannot imagine how grateful they are. Nelly stayed here the night before last and thanked me in tears. . . . I neglected saying in its proper place that Mr. Douglas left here yesterday morning with instructions from me to telegraph to Tom to come immediately to the assistance of his brother and the governor, if, after seeing them and consulting Edward and Mrs. Brown, that step should be deemed necessary. The first thing I wished to know from Mr. Douglas last night was, had he telegraphed for Tom, and I never heard the word no with so much delight."

A part of the following letter also bears on this time:
"If I undertake to say much of my dear and honored uncle, it will necessarily be a repetition of what others can say much more ably than I, so I will endeavor to confine myself to a few lines.

"I knew him well only after he grew old. His old age, like the sunset, was more beautiful, if less useful, than the mid-day. Age softened without weakening his character. I was much struck, in reading one of the last letters he wrote, with this expression, 'We must have sympathy even with the imaginary troubles of others.' This was hardly in accordance with my previous knowledge of him. Of a healthy nature, with strong self-control, he thought (and rightly) that people should control their imaginations; that there was enough real trouble in the world without any indulgence in morbidness. But, without relaxing his hold over himself, he grew more tender towards the weaknesses of others. He was the most thoroughly natural man I ever knew, without one particle of affectation. Of course he often refrained from uttering his sentiments or opinions, for fear of giving pain; but never, in his whole life, I imagine, did he say anything he did not entirely feel with the motive of pleasing. Of whom beside can we say the same? Praise from him might be justly valued, since he sounded his mind and weighed his words before speaking. He was not irritable or prone to take offence, because he took but little heed of trivialities, yet his was no easy-going amiability that includes all men and all ways in its indolent charity. Meanness, cruelty, and lies were so utterly abhorrent to him that he needs must speak and feel strongly against their perpetrators.

"Not all the heavenly host sing eternal praises. His guardian spirit must have been Michael, the strong, the terrible, warning all powers of evil! That lightning glance, those words so weighty in truth, so keen in insight, have made many an evil-doer quail before him.

"To see my uncle, in his old age, performing the homely duties of the farm with the same care and exactness he formerly bestowed on matters of great moment; to see him doing the honors of his plain board with the same courtly dignity as when it groaned in luxury; to see him turn to books with the same judgment and interest he formerly bestowed on men, was a lesson never to be forgotten. Circumstances might change, the man did not; loss of wealth, political weight, youth, even wife and children, left him unshaken. In that healthy mind and strong soul wounds healed, leaving scars, it is true, but no sores.

"We were there during the dreadful plague of '78, and I was struck almost with awe by my uncle's wonderful foresight as to the fever coming to so apparently an unlikely spot, his wise advice and generous offers of aid to others, which, if acted on, would have saved many valuable lives and prevented his own family from being exposed to infection. His sagacity was almost superhuman; but what shall I call the feeling which prompted him to send his beloved daughters from their place of safety to nurse the very people who had rejected his aid while it was yet time, and even to bring the plague-stricken sufferers into his own home?

"I feel how poorly I have expressed in these lines the love and admiration I felt for my dear uncle. I pray that his qualities may flow in every drop of his blood forever; so shall he live and not die, even on this earth!

"LETITIA DABNEY MILLER."

The yellow fever broke out in all its virulence at Dry Grove in a week from the date of Thomas's invitation to his neighbors to take refuge at Burleigh. Of the first twenty-nine cases, twenty-eight died. There were not enough well people to nurse the sick. Thomas refused to allow his daughters to go to see their sick neighbors merely to call, but when they signified their willingness to nurse them, he took them to Dry Grove himself. He threw the doors of Burleigh open, and it was made headquarters for the Howard Society. There he entertained the Spanish physician sent by the Howards from New Orleans, as well as the trained yellow-fever nurses whom he brought with him. All the rooms in the house, not excepting the dining-room and kitchen, were turned into sleeping-chambers. Even the gin-house had its occupant, and three children were quartered in the little honey-house among the bee-hives. They were in quarantine there, as both the Burleigh house and the cottage in the yard had its fever patient. In addition to the people in the house who had fled there for safety from the fever, one or two convalescents came to recuperate, and the nurses came to rest after their patients had either died or gotten well. There were white nurses and negro nurses, and they were of both sexes. Augustine's son Thomas had come on a little visit just before this time, and seeing the trouble in which his uncle was involved, resolved, in spite of earnest remonstrance, to stay to render any assistance in his power. Augustine's daughters, Nannie and Letty and her husband and young children, were with difficulty induced to leave us. They became at length convinced that their presence would only add to the anxiety and horror of the time.

My father was told that he could not see his ill daughter. His presence seemed to excite her too much. One day as Sophy opened the door of the sick-room she found him standing there. "My child," he said, "when Sue falls asleep let me know. I must see her. I shall not disturb her." Accordingly he was summoned, and he got down on his hands and knees and crawled from the door across the large room till he reached the bedside. In this humble posture he remained many minutes, occasionally touching her hand, which lay outside the cover, lightly with his lips. When she awoke, he said, "My child, if I excite you, say one word, *go*, and I will go. If I may stay, say *stay*." That word was spoken, and he took her hand in both of his and covered it with his tears and kisses.

Thomas's friend, John Shelton, and his son were ready to come to nurse the sick at Burleigh, but were informed that they were not needed, as trained nurses had arrived from the New Orleans hospitals. Supplies of provisions, medicines, and wines sent by the North and the South were received and distributed at the Burleigh door.

For miles people sent for provisions, for the quarantine regulations made it impossible to get supplies from the neighboring towns. A barrel of vinegar that had been made as the year's supply by the family was exhausted in a week. It required all the time of one person to attend to this part of the business. Wagons, buggies, and horses stood waiting at the gate for the doctor or nurses or provisions, or for all three. Supplies were exhausted so rapidly that sometimes no meat was to be had for the immense household except the squirrels killed by my cousin Thomas. And sometimes there was no food in the house of any kind. As long as it held out it was distributed. But the larder was never empty more than a few hours. The "shot-gun" quarantines at times made it a matter of peril to bring us this relief. One gentleman, a prosperous citizen of Jackson, himself drove a wagon filled with provisions to our door, because he could not hire a driver to do it. He travelled all night, and arrived just in time to avert serious want. Another man was shot at by his own nephew because he persisted in passing the picket-line which divided the infected district from the rest of the country. Over one thousand dollars were sent by the Howard associations in different cities and by friends to the family at Burleigh. Three of them had the fever, but all recovered.

It was found necessary during these days of horror to keep up our spirits, by avoiding as far as possible all reference to the pestilence and its ravages. At the table, especially, such allusions were forbidden. The list of deaths occurring the night before was not to be spoken of at breakfast. Afterwards the names of friends who had just died passed quietly and without comment from mouth to mouth. There was no giving way to emotions. A man who had lost his wife and two children, a woman whose husband, mother, brother, and child had died, a young girl who saw eight members of her family borne from the house, these, like the rest, gave no sign.

It seemed so easy to die. Why should we weep? We will soon follow them. Besides, there is no time for tears. The suffering and the dying are calling us. And the dead lie unburied, wrapped in blankets just as they died, across the church pews, waiting for a tardy coffin and a shallow grave. At last the coffins do not come fast enough, and many are buried in goods boxes without a prayer save the silent one breathed by the two men who give all their time to these last offices.*

Thomas was in his eighty-first year, and the strain and anxiety and the labor he performed came near killing him. One day he drove forty miles in passing back and forth between his house and Dry Grove, carrying food and fresh nurses to relieve exhausted ones. He said afterwards many, many times that he could never forgive himself for placing his children in such a position of danger. His daughters had obtained his consent before going into the fever-stricken village to nurse their friends. He seemed to think he had failed in his duty, and never ceased to express the deepest self-condemnation at having yielded his judgment to their wishes.

The neighborhood was desolated by the fever. During preceding years family connections and friends had died or moved away, and the circle of congenial friends, always small, had grown smaller as time went on. Under these circumstances, and as there appeared to be no hope of improvement in their surroundings, the Burleigh family resolved on leaving the old home forever, as soon as the last of the debts were paid. A sum of money sent by Frederick Dabney as a gift to his uncle he sent at once to his creditors. Still, three years were to elapse before the final payments were made. Our dearest father had been so shaken by the scenes that he and his children had passed through during the fever, that we thought it best to persuade him to take a change every winter by going to visit one or other of his married children. The summers were made pleasant at Burleigh by the society of his affectionate nieces and nephews and their families, but the winters were lonely and depressing. We were the more earnest in this, as during the years 1879 and '80 he

---

* As in time of war the favorite sport of children is playing soldier, so in the last days of the pestilence the forlorn little orphans made mimic graves, decking them with wild flowers and grasses and marking head and foot with broken bits of china.

lost three old and valued friends,—Mrs. Mary Roy Cox, of Louisiana, Dr. Thomas A. Cooke, of Louisiana, and Governor A. G. Brown, of Mississippi. The first two were life-long friends whom he had first known in Gloucester, and Dr. Cooke was the dearest friend of his life.

T. S. D. TO HIS DAUGHTER EMMY.

"BURLEIGH, 14th June, 1879.

... "As you have not seen that article of mine and can't get it, I enclose it to you; not so much on account of any supposed merit that may attach to it (except historically) as to keep you and the major *up* with whatever I may be about. The paper contains enough of Buena Vista for one time, I suppose; but, as I know a good deal more about it (from General Taylor's own lips to me at Pass Christian), I may give you more incidents from time to time.... Three days ago Sue asked me to pour some boiling water from the big teakettle, which I proceeded to do, and more than was desired, as I turned the spout on myself, and poured a tablespoonful or two in my shoe. As it was impossible to get the shoe, and particularly the sock, off until the water had cooled of itself, I have a burn that will annoy me for some time. My foot is considerably swollen and hurts me badly, and, as I cannot wear a shoe, I am confined to the house, and pretty much to my chair, with my foot cocked up on a pillow in another chair. This gives me leisure to think over my sins. Mr. Root, the great bee man of the North, offers through his paper one dollar a quart for bees, to which Sophy has responded by driving about a peck into a box and sending it to him....

"A sad accident happened to George Page's daughter Puss and her husband two days ago. They had some powder in a trunk, which they attempted to take out, in the night, torch in hand. The powder ignited and burned them both terribly." ...

Thomas happened to have a few pounds of ice in the house and some ice-cream, which he sent to the burnt woman. She had not slept since the accident occurred, thirty-six hours before, and was in much agony. The ice-cream and ice acted like a charm, and she slept many hours, awaking quite refreshed late in the next day.

"I ain't goin' to no Kansas," Puss said, when we went to see her. "I would have been dead now ef I had been in Kansas, away from marster."*

It was characteristic of George Page that, when some of "his young ladies" went to his house on hearing of the accident, he met them at his gate and made demonstrations of not allowing them to enter. He and his house were not fit for us, he expressed in his earnest manner. But Susan came out with the tears running down her face to take us in and to explain that we must not mind George. "Heish, George," she exclaimed. "Didn't I sen' fur de ladies? an' here you tell 'em not to come in! Don't mind George, missis. He dunno what he talkin' 'bout. Go 'long, George, you talk so foolish."

Thomas enjoyed much a visit from Bishop Quintard, of Tennessee, this fall. The bishop preached a Thanksgiving sermon in the little church at Dry Grove. Before the sermon he said a few very earnest words on the subject of the kneeling posture in prayer. He had observed that many of the congregation kept their seats during the prayers. The country people belonging to the denominations in that part of the world do not, as a rule, kneel in church. Thomas was much impressed by what the bishop said, and he resolved never again to fail to kneel at church or in his private devotions. At the next prayer nearly the whole congregation knelt, but the man sitting next to Thomas, an old neighbor, maintained his sitting posture. Colonel Dabney gave him a thrust in the side, and said, "Why do you not kneel down?" On which the man promptly knelt.

T. S. D. TO HIS GRANDDAUGHTER, SOPHIA THURMOND.

"BURLEIGH, December 3, 1879.

"MY DEAR GRANDCHILD,—. . . And I am proud of your standing in your other classes. Do not be satisfied

---

* There was quite an excitement among the negroes at this time in our part of the State on the subject of moving to Kansas.

until you reach the head of all of them. As some one must be at the head, I wish you to be the one. Of course, I see your letters to your mother, and think very highly of them and of your progress at school. Continue, my dear, as you have begun, and you will never cease to rejoice over your attainments when you have become a woman."

T. S. D. TO HIS SON BENJAMIN.
"BURLEIGH, 27th December, 1879.

... "Many thanks, my dear, good boy, for your thoughtful presents, which are appreciated with a full knowledge of the toil they cost you, and the many uses you had for the money. But you rather overdid it, as one barrel of oysters and half a barrel of oranges would have been ample. Should I live to afford you the opportunity to repeat this thing, please be more moderate. Major Greene performed his duty in executing your orders, as he selected himself the oysters, splendid single ones, and he had the oranges gathered from the trees on Monday, only two days before they came into my hands; and they are the finest I ever saw, their excellent quality being due to their freshness and to the fact that our summer ran into our winter down to the 24th of December; the temperature on that day, in my passage, being up to 78°. John Dabney is expected to visit his Vicksburg relations within a week or so to spend a week, and then some of them will come out here for a week on a big partridge and squirrel hunt. Marshall Miller says he will *certainly* come, but the work on the Vicksburg jetties may prevent Edward and Tom Greg from accompanying him. I hope John may be able to come. He is a noble specimen of a man, and so is Miller." ...

T. S. D. TO HIS DAUGHTER EMMY.
"BURLEIGH, 28th December, 1879.

"MY BELOVED CHILD,—Your anxiety to have Ben's presents here in time for Christmas made you underrate, or disregard, all other considerations. As it happened that Dr. Douglas opened the mail on Tuesday and found a card for his son Taylor and a letter for me, both from you, he immediately brought them to me, so that I received the earliest possible information of your intention to send perishable things up to me on that very day. Had he not been at the post-office I should have remained in ignorance of these facts, as it was not convenient to us to communicate with the office on that day; and, expecting nothing particularly, a messenger would not have been sent, and this goes to show that I should have had more notice. But I got the notice, sent to Terry that night, and had the oysters in the cellar and spread out before I went to bed. But I never saw oysters in such a condition, as they were actually hot, as in a state of fermentation. Ida and I turned in upon them and separated the dead from the living (there being but few of the latter) and spread these few on the cellar floor, and covered them with salt and meal and sprinkled them afterwards with water. These few gave us soup for two days. We were so keen for oysters that I opened some of the best-looking fellows *with open countenances*, and had them for our breakfast next morning. We all escaped death; Ida's escape being due, perhaps, to her getting clear, in a hurry, of oysters, breakfast and all, by throwing them up. The balance of us managed to hold on by a tight squeeze.

"Please observe, my child, that oysters are good at other times than on Christmas day, and had the shipment been deferred but three days they would have done us great service. And *sufficient* notice should *never* be dispensed with; the notice, in case of oysters, to run as follows, viz.: 'A barrel of oysters will be sent to Terry for you on —— next if the weather be suitable, and if not, when it becomes so, of which due notice will be given.' I am not finding fault with you, my dear child, and if you think my words imply fault-finding, you must forgive me, for I know the misfortune had its origin in overzeal on your part to promote my happiness and that of your sisters. The oranges are the very best I ever saw, due to the care in their selection, and to the fact that our summer ran into our winter down to the 24th of December.

"P. S.—Don't let Ben know that any accident happened to the oysters."

T. S. D. TO HIS DAUGHTER EMMY.

"BURLEIGH, 15th June, 1880.

"Sophy and I returned from Governor Brown's yesterday, our admirable friend having died the previous night of apoplexy, or something of that nature. Mrs. Brown was quite sick, and the governor went to Terry in the afternoon (Saturday) for a doctor and some ice, taking his carriage-driver along. The doctor left immediately, the governor following soon after. Arriving at the gate opening upon his lawn, he dismounted to open it, and leading through, he again mounted the horse and proceeded to the pond to water him. In about ten minutes afterwards the cook observed the horse loose, and gave the alarm. The carriage-driver went to the pond immediately, saw the hat floating and the governor's shoulders and the back of his head protruding above the water, which was two feet deep at that place. He was in a crouching posture, his arms thrust forward and downward, embracing his legs, and his face submerged. Neither his shoulders nor the back of his head had been in the water. How the equilibrium was maintained is a mystery. A doctor was there, who pronounced him dead. He was in the water not exceeding fifteen minutes, perhaps ten. His lungs could not have acted since the moment of the submergence of his face, as not a drop of water issued either from his mouth or nose. He therefore did *not* drown, neither did he fall from his horse. Had he fallen, he must have gone clear under. It is supposed, as the only tenable conjecture, that he lost his hat, and in attempting its recovery by means of his cane, he lost his balance, and, finding he must go, he clung to the horse's neck and mane until he got his feet into the water, and then sunk down dead. He had been complaining for some days of an undue determination of blood to the head, which Mrs. Brown had attempted to subdue by wet cloths, etc. . . . As he was not wet all over, he did *not* fall, and, as not a drop of water was in his stomach or lungs, he did *not* drown. After satisfying myself fully on these points, I told Mrs. Brown that the governor must have been dead by the time he struck the water, to which she said yes. . . . She had decided on nothing further than that she would go to Washington. We urged her to make Burleigh her home in the mean time, and at her pleasure, Sophy adding that either she or Sue would go to Chicama and stay with her, if she preferred it to coming here. She made no reply by words."

The summer of 1880 was a very happy one, the house being full of his brother's children and grandchildren and his own. We had many merry dances, in which our dear father joined us when we represented to him that he was needed as a partner. He never danced after this summer. In the latter part of August he met with an accident that confined him to his bed for five months, and produced a stiffness of the legs that lasted as long as he lived. Happening to be engaged in conversation as he was about to take his seat, he moved backward to his chair and sat by the side of it, instead of in the seat. His fall was heavy, and he struck his head with force against the sharp edge of a door as he went down. He fainted four times in quick succession from pain, and then fell into a five hours' sleep, from which it was impossible to rouse him. We tried everything before the doctor got there, among other remedies putting mustard-plasters on the legs. In our hurry and grief the plasters were forgotten till they had burned deeply. At the end of the sleep he awoke perfectly in his senses, and would have been as well as ever in two days but for the mustard-burns. His patience and brightness during this confinement were the surprise of all who visited him, for he had led an active life, and had not had the discipline of bodily suffering. Not a complaint escaped his lips, although at times the pain was almost unbearable, and it was more than once thought that amputation only could give him a chance for his life. He was quite helpless, of course, and could not be left alone during the day or night. His old servants took care of him at night for weeks, coming in turn to sleep on the floor by the side of his bed when their day's work was over. Some whom he had thought ill of, and had sent off the plantation, came now and nursed him. On Sundays they came in large numbers to visit him. He was extremely gratified by these spontaneous attentions. Books and letters from his children and friends filled up the days.

In the prime of his busy life he had quite given up reading everything but newspapers, but after he no longer had the cares of a plantation he turned to books with almost the love of a bookworm. History was his preference, and he went through the excellent and rather large collection in his library. Some of them he read many times. After they were exhausted he grew omnivorous in his tastes, and read every book that came in his way, frequently reading from morning till night, and, unless his eyes were too tired, until late at night. His wonderful power of adapting himself to changed circumstances and surroundings was in no way more conspicuously shown than in this turning to books for entertainment when he was over sixty years of age.

T. S. D. TO HIS DAUGHTER EMMY.

"BURLEIGH, 22d December, 1880.

"MY BELOVED CHILD,—I am confined to the house almost entirely, walking out in the yard two to three times in a week, which I can just do by the help of a cane, and very slowly at that. But this is a great improvement on confinement to one's bed, or the incapacity to walk at all. These sores on my feet have proved more obstinate than either Dr. West or Tom anticipated, although they both knew that a burn by mustard was the worst of all. They are tantalizing to the last degree, assuming a convalescent form for a week or two and then falling back to their old tricks."

T. S. D. TO HIS DAUGHTER EMMY.

"BURLEIGH, 16th September, 1881.

... "We have had a lively time here, with the biggest crowd that was ever in the house. In addition to Letty's family, who are here yet, we had the Rev. Dr. Tucker's, from Jackson (wife and three children), Mrs. Sidway and three children and nurse, Nanny, my brother's wife, Martha, Kate Nelson, a Miss Coffey (a friend of Tom's, from New Orleans), and callers constantly coming in. The tables had to be set diagonally, and sometimes three to four had to sit at a side-table."

In the fall of 1881 Thomas was in New Orleans when the great-grandsons of General Lafayette were received by the city. They were informed that he wished to be presented to them, and they gave him an audience of an hour before the opening of the ball which was given in their honor by the people of New Orleans. He knew no French, and these young gentlemen knew no English. Two of Colonel Dabney's daughters acted as interpreters. The French gentlemen said to him on this occasion that he was the only person whom they had met in their tour through the United States who had seen their great-grandfather, the marquis, when he was in this country. Thomas gave them an account of the dinner at Yorktown given to General Lafayette, which he had attended. He amused them very much by saying that the champagne drunk on that day laid many an American on the floor, but the French guests were not affected by it, though they drank quite as much as their entertainers.

In December he went to Bonham, Texas, to spend a few months with his son Benjamin and his family.

T. S. D. TO HIS DAUGHTER IDA.

"BONHAM, TEXAS, 5th January, 1882.

... "I have seen a rabbit-hunt, and found it to be very exciting, even under the disadvantage of being in a buggy, and therefore incapable of joining in the chase. But we (Ben and I) kept pretty well along, as the scene was an open prairie, without obstruction to the vision for many miles. There were fourteen huntsmen and eight greyhounds, who run by sight alone, as you probably know. When the quarry gets out of their sight they relinquish the chase, as they have no sense of smell, or too little to be available on such occasions. The huntsmen 'breast' it across the prairie and rouse the rabbits themselves, the dogs taking no part in that portion of the programme. A rabbit being roused by one of them, he claps spurs to his horse with a yell, and puts right at him at full speed, the dogs and the other huntsmen rushing to that point without loss of time, and away they go. Four of them were caught; one of them kept ahead of dogs and huntsmen for two miles or more, but the others were taken at less distance. One was not taken, and remains for another day. On the whole, I think fox-hunting better, but this is the natural sport of the prairies."

It was in February of this year that my father heard with profound sorrow of the death of his nephew, John Hampden Chamberlayne. This rarely-gifted young man had already made his influence felt throughout the State of Virginia, and he was regarded as her ablest citizen among the rising generation. The briefest notice of Hampden Chamberlayne would be incomplete without some mention of his incomparable powers as a conversationalist. Persons familiar with the most brilliant society of the Old World have declared that he would have shone pre-eminent and almost without a peer in London or in Paris. In heart and character he was as richly endowed as in mind, and his big-hearted, loving ways won the enduring affection of all his Southern kinsfolk. He had already sent loving messages of welcome to his uncle's family in anticipation of seeing them settled in a home so near his own, and had promised to come to Baltimore as soon as he heard of my father's arrival there.

T. S. D. TO HIS NIECE, MARTHA C. DABNEY.

"NEW ORLEANS, 24th February, 1882.

"MY BELOVED NIECE,—Sophy sent me your sweet letter, and as every member of my household is always hungry for anything that comes from you, I placed the letter immediately on its travels again, sending it to

Bonham, Texas, where Sue now is, and where she will be until about the 1st of April, when she and those still at Burleigh will pull up stakes for their final and permanent removal to Baltimore. I will remain here until warm weather, as I find that my capacity to generate heat has become much enfeebled within the last two to three years, or ever since the epidemic at Dry Grove. I was with the dead and dying there many days before Sue was stricken, and then, although she recovered, the strain on my whole system was so intense as to leave me pretty much a child, physically, when it relaxed. I have never recovered from it, and was ten to fifteen years older within a week or two; but they are taking good care of me, and affect to expect to tide me over several sand-bars yet. They are good children, these of mine, and the same may be said of my nieces and nephews, for I cannot discover the difference in affection between the two sets. I am here with Emmy. The profession of Major Greene allows him very little time for his family. Emmy is delightfully situated within the French district, but within easy walking distance of Canal Street, and in a French boarding-house, where her children are restricted to the French language."

CHAPTER XXIII.

QUIET DAYS.

In April the Burleigh family moved to Baltimore. Our dear father was with his daughter Emmy, and did not come to join us in the simple home till November.

By this time we had made it as comfortable and home-like as his limited means would allow.

T. S. D. TO HIS DAUGHTER EMMY.

"BALTIMORE, 8th December, 1882. 93 JOHN STREET.

"Thanksgiving-Day gave Virginius a good chance to close the doors of his school for four days. He devoted those four days to me, coming down on Wednesday night and remaining until Sunday night, when he returned home. Those were four happy days to all of us. He brought his son Noland to show him to me, as I used to take one of my children every other year to Virginia to show to their grandmother. My grandson Noland is a very fine boy, indeed. As the Christmas holidays in the schools in New York last two weeks, Virginius will come here then for some days. . . . Our cousin, Mary Smith, wrote to Sue a few days ago that she would send her a teapot with a broken spout, some cracked glass, and some chipped china. A hogshead and a box arrived yesterday, and was found to contain the teapot, sure enough, and some splendid glass (cracked, to be sure, but we had to hunt for the cracks), with a good deal that is not cracked. The china consists of a full set of dinner dishes and plates (four dozen plates, I suppose), and dishes for all purposes,—for the largest fish and sirloin and round of beef and vegetables. There are some exquisite glass pitchers and peculiar tumblers and other things in the glass line, not cracked at all. Of *chipped china*, I suppose there may be half a dozen plates, with little specks chipped off the edges, that you must look for to see. Well, those things only filled the hogshead two-thirds full, and that *little crack* was filled with table-cloths, napkins, and other things that I do not know the name of. The box contained the most exquisite parlor-chair I ever saw. Mary writes that she will make another consignment shortly! She is a good girl, decidedly.

"Last night, cold as it was, Lelia (you know she never allows anything to turn her) went three-quarters of a mile or more to attend some society of which she is a member, and was half frozen when she got back.

She said the wind—a keen northwester—blew her dress up above her knees in spite of her efforts to the contrary. An old gentleman running near them (there were three girls with Lelia) had his hat blown off in spite of his efforts to keep it on, and it gave the four girls some trouble to recover the hat, but they persevered until they captured it.

"I look out of the window at the ice and snow and at the car-drivers and others in the street, all muffled up to the chin and nose, and I, meantime, in a temperature of seventy degrees, unconscious, personally, of winter, except for the glowing fires in the stoves, that keep the whole house at about seventy degrees throughout the day and most of the night. So you see the *climate* of Baltimore is a matter of no consequence to me at all. I have about arrived at the conclusion that should I ever be able to divide my time between the North and South, I would make Baltimore my winter and Pass Christian my summer home. But this can never be, of course. . . . The people here suit me entirely. The neighbors met me for the first time as if they had known me always. The city is full of poor Virginians, made poor by the war, and being poor and well bred, all ostentation is tabooed, and they give you what they have without apology."

T. S. D. TO HIS DAUGHTER EMMY.

"BALTIMORE, 98 JOHN STREET, 1883.

. . . "As my acquaintance extends I find that the girls made no mistake when they elected Baltimore as their future home. I say *their*, because I cannot expect to enjoy it with them very long; but it is my wish to have a good place whilst I am with them, and with the hope of seeing you and your dear little ones sometimes."

T. S. D. TO HIS DAUGHTER EMMY.

"BALTIMORE, 5th January, 1883. 98 JOHN STREET.

"MY BELOVED CHILD,—My birthday dinner wound up with a snow-storm last night, and the wind this

morning is pretty sharp, but it does not affect me in
this house. Virginius came on the 3d to be in time,
and we had the pastor of this parish and his wife (Mr.
and Mrs. Dame) to join our family. The girls gave us
a very fine dinner,—a turkey that the dealer in the
market could not sell, because it was too large, Sophy
bought; and a noble gobbler he was, and elegantly
cooked. A ham of bacon and vegetables constituted
the first course after soup. The best plum-pudding I
ever tasted, with other things, then came in, to be succeeded by oranges, apples, etc., to wind up with coffee.
We were at the table two and one-half hours, and well
employed all the time. Mrs. M., aunt of Virginius's
wife, and a splendid woman she is, dropped in while we
were discussing the pudding, and was induced to take
a seat at our table. I had called on her on the 1st of
January in conformity to the custom in these cities. I
had previously called at S. T.'s, and wound up at two
other houses, when I broke down, and could not call
on other ladies with whom I have become acquainted,
but all of them most kindly excuse me on such occasions on account of my age, and come to see me in the
most kind and polite way. I receive such attentions
constantly. . . . It does me more good than I can well
describe to see Virginius. He comes in with open
arms, with which he encloses me, and then kisses me
with the fervor of a lover when first accepted. He
kisses me and lets me go, and then kisses me again. It
makes my old heart quiver. But I kiss him in turn!"

T. S. D. TO HIS DAUGHTER EMMY.

"BALTIMORE, 8th January, 1883, 6 P.M.

"MY BELOVED CHILD,—We are enjoying winter in all
its loveliness, as I am still boy enough to enjoy snow.
If I had to attend market before day with a few vegetables, on the sale of which the daily bread of a wife
and half-dozen children depended, it is more than probable that my taste would be different. But, as it is,
the sight of falling snow exhilarates and elevates my
spirits."

T. S. D. TO HIS DAUGHTER EMMY.

"BALTIMORE, 21st January, 1883. 98 JOHN STREET.

... "Snow has lain on the ground for two weeks, and the Baltimoreans have been using sleighs for that length of time, with a prospect of continuance, as it is very cold now, with a prospect of heavy snow to-night. But these things do not concern me, as I am not obliged to go out, and so I keep my shins warm, read and write, and feed the sparrows from the dining-room window. . . . I am more and more pleased with Baltimore and the Baltimoreans."

T. S. D. TO HIS DAUGHTER EMMY.

"BALTIMORE, 98 John Street, February 20, 1885.

"MY DARLING CHILD,—Something, I do not know what, turned my attention to the condition of these four single daughters of mine on yesterday, and made me shudder. With all of Ida's energy, Burleigh has proved inadequate to their support, as she has been forced to spend most of the rents in building houses, digging wells or cisterns or ditches, and clearing up the creeks and bayous, and this work is far from being completed yet. I pictured to myself what would become of these daughters if I died, with my old will of fifteen to twenty years ago left in my desk as my last will and testament. Under that will the Burleigh estate would have to be divided into nine equal parts, as near as might be, each of my children taking one part, except Virginius, who, I thought, had had his share. If the whole estate has proved inadequate to the support of four, how could these four support themselves on four-ninths, and these chopped up into detached pieces? I saw at once that something had to be done, and that quickly, and I did it this morning without the slightest suggestion from any one. I now wonder why it took me so long to see it. What fearful risks I have gone through during the last few years, and yet have lived to do it! As all of my children (and I devoutly thank God for it), except these four, are now able to take care of themselves, and are taking care of themselves, I made a new will this morning, leaving the Burleigh plantation and all that is on it, and the furniture that is here, to these four daughters of mine and Sophy's daughter Sophia. The silver is to be divided equally among my ten children, after taking out the large urn, which I give to you, and this is the only earthly thing that I have to bestow on my dear children, and that could not be divided. To avoid mistakes, I will state that the urn must be considered as your share of the silver, the rest to be divided among the other nine, so that each one will have something with my initials cut on it. This is the best I could do, and I have no doubt about the others being satisfied at your having the lion's share, as some one had to get it, and none more worthy than you, whom I picked out to have it, having the undoubted right to do so.

"I hope, my darling, that you will approve the whole will, and I am sure you will do so after thinking over the matter a little."

T. S. D. TO HIS DAUGHTER EMMY.

"BALTIMORE, 22d March, 1883. 98 JOHN STREET.

"MY DARLING CHILD,—I cannot thank you sufficiently for your sweet, loving letter of the 18th, just received from your quiet, delicious home at McComb. Those two arm-chairs, called mine by you, remaining still in the front porch and awaiting my occupancy, must remain without my corporeal occupancy yet a little longer, perhaps indefinitely; but my heart hovers over them and every crack and cranny of that establishment without ceasing; not that I lack loving hearts here, for they hover round me and anticipate every imaginable want of mine, as though I was an infant,— as I am indeed in too many respects. They have to undress and dress me partially every night and morning. I am getting old, old, old, faster and faster, having been broken down again by a very severe attack of cold when in New York. I went too early, and was caught by the three worst weeks of the winter. When I said I had to return home Virginius considered it necessary for him to accompany me, and he accordingly delivered me into my arm-chair that now stands before me before he let me go.

"My first two weeks in New York were most royally spent. I dined at No. 4 twice, and they had another dinner on the tapis for the day before my departure, but I had to decline on account of serious indisposition. Virginius, Anna, and my grandchildren hovered over me as a hen would over a sick chicken, and left me nothing to ask for or to wish for, so that I was not reminded while there that I had lived too long."

The stiffness of our dearest father's limbs made it so painful for him to kneel that we begged him not to attempt it at family prayers. Soon it grew to be impossible. One Sunday, as one of his daughters sitting next him in church asked him to go to the communion with her, he said that he could not, because he would not be able to get up if he knelt at the altar-rail. She answered that he could receive it standing, and she would stand with him. He feared that the rector would not approve, and asked her not to fail to explain to him as soon as they reached the chancel. This she did, although the rector's look showed that he understood, and no explanation was needed. As he turned to walk to his seat, there were some moist eyes in the city church, where he was comparatively a stranger. During the last two years of his life he might be seen on communion Sundays standing to receive the sacred elements, the snowy head bent in prayer. A bishop said that the venerable standing figure preached many sermons.

The following account of one of his Scott County hunts was written by Thomas at the request of a friend:

"BALTIMORE, MD., April 17, 1883.

"MY DEAR SIR,—In conformity to your request, I subjoin an account of some of my camping experiences in Scott County. . . . I procured a tent large enough to accommodate twelve persons, took a small four-horse wagon, to which I attached four fine mules, and took a man along besides the wagoner, to take charge of the first deer that I might kill, and save me from packing any until I had killed two. I had a box made, into which my gun and rifle fitted perfectly, so that, no matter how rough the road might be, they were secured against chafing. From the time that I left Scott until a year later the cover never came off that gun, so that the first deer that I might kill the next fall fell by a load that had been in the gun twelve months. I had always thought such rounds more effective than those more recently put in.

"But you want to hear about that remarkable hunt. It was the last, or next to the last, of my series of eight years in Scott.

"Our 'regulars' were on hand, as usual, on the Friday after the first Monday in November. We pitched our tents on the east of Line Prairie, and stuck our pegs in the same holes that they had occupied for the first two or three previous years, as we could not hope to find a better location,—good water at hand and abundance of game. We would start out from camp 'in line' a quarter- to a half-mile long, breasting it round the prairie, and it would take us all day to make the circuit. I have many a time, after 'drawing a bead' on a fine doe that had jumped up within three feet of my horse's nose, replaced my gun across my lap upon finding that no horns were on the head of the quarry. This, perhaps, will give you a better idea of the number of deer to be found in that locality at that time than anything else that I could say. I did not do that every time, but only after I had killed a certain number, and was tired. I then went for the bucks alone.

"As I have said, we formed in line, thirty to fifty yards apart, and moved forward as the word reached us from the captain, who occupied the centre; but at the report of a gun every man suddenly stopped. If a deer was killed, one or two nearest to the shooter went to him to viscerate and help to throw the deer on his horse, when he, having reloaded and remounted, would shout out 'go ahead,' and the line again moved forward. It was a rule that no one should move until the word came; but this rule required no enforcing, as to be in advance of the line would be to occupy a very dangerous position.

"On one occasion a dozen harum-scarum fellows joined our party when we were but one day out. We had but little knowledge of some of them, and none of others. They set all rules at defiance, tearing through the woods in all directions, sometimes observing our line of march, and sometimes meeting us. How it happened that none of them were killed is a mystery. One of them shot the horse of another, and seemed to think it was part of the fun. As one of our party was passing within two or three feet of a large post-oak, the bark of the tree was thrown so violently against his face as to hurt him, and two buckshot were afterwards found in the horn of his saddle,—all the work of one of those fellows. We could stand it no longer, and upon our suggesting that we could do better in two parties they left us. But they had interfered with our hunt, almost consuming one of the three days of that memorable hunt. At the end of the third day, however, finding that we had killed and hung up ninety-three deer, a proposition was made that we should start next morning for the public road, six miles off (and so far on our way home), and it was agreed to. We accordingly gave the necessary instructions to our servants, and struck out by compass for a certain point on the public road, and missed it by very little.

"When about to start, some one remarked that we must get the other seven, to which another replied, 'We will do that and not half try.' We got thirteen. We had not proceeded more than one mile before I had killed three, and the hunt was closed. . . . I cannot close without giving you some account of one of our 'regulars.' His name was Mount, the most harebrained, crazy fellow in the woods I ever saw, and but for his good nature and willingness at all times to take hold of anything and everything heavy or dirty, and to make himself useful generally and particularly, he could not have been tolerated, as it was dangerous to hunt with him. Towards the last, and for some time, no one but myself would ride next to him, and I required him to ride at my left side. He would shoot at the flash of a deer's tail, without estimating the distance, and he was known to use up a bag of buckshot in every hunt of several days' duration, and often had to go to Hillsborough for a fresh supply. On one occasion, he and I being close together, he crippled a buck (for he killed one occasionally), and although a deer was already tied to his saddle, he raised the shout of an Indian, clapped spurs to his horse, and was off at full speed, I after him. He flushed a little deer that took the back track, but Mount saw him, and without drawing rein, or turning his head, threw his gun over his shoulder and let fly; but the muzzle of his gun was a little depressed below the perpendicular, and no harm was done either to the deer or to me. I could fill a dozen pages with Mount's pranks, but must let this suffice."

At this time my father got into a correspondence with a distant kinsman, Mr. William H. Dabney, of Boston, whom he had never met. He was now in his eighty-sixth year, but he enjoyed this correspondence, and kept it up with the freshness of youth. A few selected from his many letters to Mr. Dabney will show this.

T. S. D. TO WILLIAM H. DABNEY.

"BALTIMORE, 29th June, 1883.

"My son, Virginius Dabney, of New York, has forwarded to me your letter of the 25th inst., in which my name is mentioned as the oldest known member of the Dabney family, and I presume I will have to accept the patriarchal position, as I am in my eighty-sixth year, having been born on the 4th of January, 1798. I have read your letter with great interest and pleasure, although restraining with difficulty a blush at my utter inability to aid you in your labor of love. . . . But I do know something of my family.

"I know that my grandfather lived on the east bank of the Pamunkey River, in King William County; that he had a numerous family of sons and daughters, some of whom remained on the paternal acres, as they were divisible. Others went to Cumberland County with a Mr. Thornton, who married one of the daughters. My father, Benjamin, who was a lawyer, removed to York River, and afterwards to North River, in Gloucester County, where he died in 1806. His eldest brother, George, retained the mansion-house on the Pamunkey River, known during the war, as before and since, as Dabney's Ferry. Two other sons, Dr. James Dabney and Major Thomas Dabney, lived and died, the first on North River in Gloucester County, and the other near Aylett's in King William.

"Should any matter of business or pleasure draw you to Baltimore, you will please make my house your home for the time. . . . Have you read Dick Taylor's book (General Richard Taylor's), 'Destruction and Reconstruction'? If not, I advise you to get it, as the best and most readable book that the civil war has brought out,—better written, interesting, and fresh as a novel, with the impress of truth on every line.

"There is not a doubt in my mind but that Grant saved this country from some—God only knows how much—of the scenes of the French Revolution. Andy Johnson, with Morton and Stanton, backed by other hyenas of the Senate, were for blood. They were outspoken for making 'treason odious' by punishing the leaders of the 'rebellion.' Think of having R. E. Lee, Joseph E. Johnston, Stonewall Jackson hung! Could any Southern man or woman have stood by and looked on quietly? Could many Northern men have looked on with hands in their pockets? Did the twenty-two Girondins and Danton and Robespierre expect their turn to come, and so soon, when they saw the guillotine doing its work so glibly on Louis and Marie Antoinette? Does it not make the heart sick to think of what we have escaped, and so narrowly? When Andy Johnson announced his intention to make treason odious, Grant said NO, and the power behind the throne was greater than the throne itself. Lee was allowed to retire without even giving up his sword or even formally to acknowledge himself as on parole (that is my impression); but men of their style consider themselves as much bound by a tacit understanding as by a formal one under oath and bond. How grand and lovely is that idea, and how worthy of such men! But perhaps, my dear cousin (if I may take so great a liberty as to call you so), I am giving you more than you bargained for. It is quite certain that I have strayed very wide of the original object of this correspondence, and I will therefore return to it by the recital of a single anecdote in which my branch of the Dabney family is concerned, for I see plainly that this is not the last letter with which I shall have to trouble you.

"Mr. Philip Tabb, of Gloucester, of whom you may have heard, when on his way to the White Sulphur Springs, fell in with a great-uncle of mine, James Dabney, and they not only put up at the same inn, but were put into the same room. As they were undressing, Mr. Tabb did not fail to observe that he was in the company of a man of extraordinary physical power, and his curiosity prompted him to ask my uncle to be so good as to strip to his shirt, as he wished to see and feel his muscular development. This was done with a laugh, and then Mr. Tabb asked him if he had ever struck a man, thinking, obviously, that the man must have been killed. 'Yes,' was the reply; 'I struck one, and came near being whipped for my impudence.' Of course he had to tell the story. He had occasion to make a journey of eighty to ninety miles from home (on horseback, of course), and on the way he observed a very mean cornfield,—mean from neglect, obviously, —and having some negroes working in it (or affecting to do so). He inquired who was their overseer. Upon being told, he said to the negroes, 'Tell your overseer that I will return day after to-morrow, and will give him a whipping for not having his corn in better order.' 'Yes, master!' shouted the negroes in chorus, showing their teeth from ear to ear. He returned on time, and on approaching the place he observed a man sitting on the fence, facing the road. Remembering his message, he measured the man with his eyes, and saw that he was no baby. He had been observed, too, and recognized as the gentleman to whom he was indebted for the message. He accordingly slipped off the fence (the negroes coming to it at the same time), and with a bow asked my uncle if he was the gentleman who had left a message for him two days ago. He acknowledged it with a laugh, and tried to turn it off with a laugh, and as a joke, but the overseer was no joker, and told him that he had to make good his promise, taking hold on his bridle and inviting him to dismount, which he had to do. All the rules of chivalry were observed. The horse was tied to a limb of a tree, and both knights (!) went at it. My uncle told Mr. Tabb that he was fairly whipped twice, and on the point of giving up, but his pride came to his aid, and he held on until the overseer stopped battering him, and said he thought they had better quit, and he acknowledged the gentleman had redeemed his promise. The negroes in the mean time had mounted the fence, and shouted and laughed, as only negroes can laugh, throughout the fray. My uncle was laid up two weeks, with his face and eyes so swollen as to make him partially blind for one week or more. He never struck a man afterwards. I suppose Francisco was the most athletic man Virginia ever produced. He was doorkeeper to the House of Delegates for many years, and I have often seen him at his post."

T. S. D. TO WILLIAM H. DABNEY.

"July 31, 1883.

"I consider the conduct of your brother in opening his doors to Mr. Cover, who was sent to Fayal to supplant him, as one of the most remarkable acts of magnanimity I ever heard of, and Mr. Cover's acceptance of hospitality under such circumstances not less remarkable. His early death and abdication, if such a view were admissible, may be looked upon as acts of courtesy in requital of your brother's kindness. I have never mentioned to you that my wife died just on the eve of hostilities between the sections, leaving me ten children to care for,—four sons and six daughters,—all of whom are now living and doing fairly well. I fought against secession as long as there was any sense or patriotism in it; but when the war came, three of my boys shook hands with me and shouldered their rifles. It was my great good fortune to greet them on their return. My youngest, Benjamin, was but fourteen years old when I took leave of him; my eldest you have some knowledge of. He belonged to General Lee's army, and was with him at Appomattox, dividing the general's breakfast with him just before the meeting of the two generals took place; for neither had eaten anything up to that time. My son had nothing to eat, and the general only a few slices of ham and bread in one of his pockets. A part of this he *ordered* him to accept, for he had to put it in the form of an 'order' before it was accepted. And here again Grant acted the gentleman, as he apologized to General Lee for not having his sword on, giving as the reason that he had no time to go for it, taking care to forget that General Lee's sword might have supplied the deficiency.

"I got an item from your last letter of more than ordinary interest: nothing less than that a son of mine and a nephew of yours were at Appomattox. Their swords were in their scabbards then, but they had been naked, and might have been plunged in the bosoms of each other. Such a war! If the scoundrels who brought on that war could have been pushed to the front and kept there until the last one of them had been annihilated, it would have been well; but that was not in the Southern programme. The Whigs, who, to a man very nearly, opposed secession, did the fighting, *soft* places being provided for the Democrats, who did the shouting; but enough of that.

"I may have mentioned to you, but am not certain, that my father was married twice, and that I am the oldest of the second batch. He left two sons (George and Ben) by his first wife, and one daughter (Ann). George went into the navy, was present at the battle of Tripoli, and had the good fortune to save the life of Decatur in that memorable and desperate affair by running his bayonet through a gigantic pirate (Algerine), who had Decatur down, and was about to transfix him to the deck of the frigate ('Philadelphia,' I think, was her name), when my brother, who was near, took him on his bayonet and bore him over the side of the ship, the pirate taking the musket to the bottom in his death-grip. George was as strong a man as the pirate, and probably much stronger, as he killed a large dog with his fist at a single blow, and may have killed a man in this city in the same way, but this is not certainly known. My brother had come here with his wheat; had sold it and imprudently drawn the money, and, more imprudently still, had gone out on a 'spree' after dark; had pulled out his roll of money in a drinking establishment to pay for some drinks; was noticed by a ruffian, who followed him and attempted to stab him; but his dirk struck the knife that was in his waistcoat-pocket, splitting the buckhorn incasing it, only giving my brother a jar. He threw his left hand round behind, seized the fellow by the collar, and felled him to the pavement. He appeared to be dead. He had but one of two things to do,—to call the watch or to escape to his schooner that was to sail in the morning. He called the watch, showed him the broken-pointed dirk that lay on the pavement, his broken knife in the pocket of his waistcoat, and the gash that had been made in his waistcoat by the dirk. The watchman believed my brother's account of the affair and did not arrest him, but summoned him to attend the police court in the morning; but he was far down the bay at that hour, and heard nothing more of the ruffian. My brother Ben was a powerful man too, but not as strong as George, though more active. Feuds were in fashion at William and Mary College when Ben was a student there, between the students and the young men of the city. Ben was always the champion of the college, and would accept a challenge to fight any two of the citizens, and sometimes three at a time, and generally came off victor. My maternal grandfather was the Rev. Thomas Smith, of Westmoreland County, Virginia, of the Established Church of England, of course, and General Washington was one of his parishioners."

T. S. D. TO WILLIAM H. DABNEY.

"BALTIMORE, 29th September, 1883.

"Enclosed you will find the long-coveted letter from my erratic friend, as you call him, and I hope you may not find it as difficult to unravel as Dr. Slop found untying Obadiah's knots.

"I think it will amuse you for some time, and, not to be entirely idle myself, I will not take advantage of your kind permission to give myself no further trouble in the premises. I will still continue to dig about the tree that you are so faithfully endeavoring to decorate with fruit.

"I am much engaged just now in arranging my house for a 'new departure' in housekeeping, and must defer the interesting anecdotes that my daughters imagine they can extract from me for the edification of yourself and daughters."

The concluding words of this letter are full of pathos to those who know the gloomy circumstances under which the brave, gay lines were written.

One year's housekeeping in the new home in the city had taught the family that the expenditures were larger than the income. The simplest way—indeed, the only feasible way—of keeping an unbroken family circle around the father was to rent out all the rooms except those actually needed. By this arrangement he would be cut off from the greatest comfort and pleasure of his old age, the visits from his absent children. Virginius had made it his pious duty and pleasure to come four times a year to see him, spending several days each time. He never said good-by without mentioning the period of his next visit, and this broke the pang of parting to the affectionate heart. They were like two boys in the enjoyment of these occasions, the man of nearly fifty sitting close by the arm-chair of the aged father and going over college pranks and jokes and scrapes and war reminiscences, to the great amusement and delight of my father. The brilliant eyes glowed and flashed with the fire of youth at the recital of any brave deed, or moistened at the account of suffering, or almost closed with merriment as he heard of some youthful frolic. It was a picture not to be forgotten by those who saw them thus.

Edward had spent his two months' summer vacation with him, and much did he enjoy this and the hope of many more such summer holidays. The society of his sons was very delightful to him; no one could take their place.

Benjamin had promised to send on his wife and his little band of four boys the next summer. Thomas also had made his plans for coming on for a long visit.

All these delightful visions were swept away when a large part of the house was given up to strangers.

T. S. D. TO HIS DAUGHTER EMMY.

"BALTIMORE, 29th October, 1883.

"MY BELOVED CHILD,—To say that your long-looked-for letter of the 27th, from Augusta, was hailed with joy this morning would be putting it too mildly. It was simply devoured by many hungry minds. Yes, your daughter Emmeline is happy here, and it would be strange if she was not, although her aunts and grandpapa cannot spread as good a table now as she sees at home. But we try to make up deficiencies in the first courses by an elaborate dessert, consisting of unbounded affection for her and good humor in general. Scant fare, you might say, but my sweet grandchild appears to be as well satisfied as if she had started on canvas-back duck and wound up on ice-cream and what-nots. There is a great preference in favor of wealth over squalid poverty, but when you come to the intermediate grades, there is less choice for real happiness than is generally imagined. And yet, with this fact acknowledged, how prone we all are to reach up, up, up! and so would I if, by tipping-toe, I could reach the thing that is universally coveted. But good-by to that; and yet I am far from desolate, as I still have the hearts of ten loving children."

T. S. D. TO HIS DAUGHTER EMMY.

"BALTIMORE. 18th November, 1883. 98 JOHN STREET.

... "Last week Dr. Latimer stepped in with Mrs. Ann Foote Stewart, daughter of Governor Foote, and wife of the Nevada Senator, from Washington. She came expressly to see the Dabneys, accepting his escort. She had been to Burleigh, and my daughters had been in her father's house many a time. I had been her father's friend in Confederate times, when friends to him were not as thick as blackberries in August. She knew it, and had remembered it to us. Mrs. Stewart will do to tie to, as would her father, who was as true as steel to a friend. He was much misunderstood. She has the colloquial powers of her father, is never at a loss, and never talks nonsense. . . . We are getting along with our lodgers unexceptionably. We have to see them occasionally, but never obtrusively."

T. S. D. TO WILLIAM H. DABNEY.

... "I was in the civil war, too, but unfortunately have no wounds to show or brag on, although a man was shot uncomfortably near my position. My eldest son, Virginius Dabney, when acting as aide to General Gordon, of Georgia, caught a minie-ball on the handle of his pistol (it being strapped to his side in a holster) at the second battle of Manassas, bending one or two of his ribs, that have not yet straightened out, and are yet troublesome. I had two other sons in the army, although I despised the war, and those who brought it on, and do yet. And here ends the military career of these Dabneys, all of us perfectly satisfied with the record *as it stands*, and without the slightest wish to improve it.

"Note.—I thought I was through with military matters, but find myself mistaken, as my girls on hearing the foregoing read, remind me of another exploit to our credit. We were in Macon, Ga., when we found the city suddenly and unexpectedly raided upon by General Stoneman. He had planted his battery, unobserved, on an eminence within rifle-range of the city, and opened upon us at a lively rate. No organized force was there, but a good many large hospitals, and necessarily more or less convalescents, and others approaching convalescence. These, with the citizens, were in the streets in a few minutes, fully armed, and on their way to the battery, the location of which was revealed by the smoke and the whistling of the shells, that came tearing by us. My youngest son (twelve years old) and I ran to the arsenal for ammunition, and having obtained a supply, joined the throng that headed for the enemy, but as yet without seeing him. My son and I were ordered to defend the bridge to the last extremity, or till further orders. We stopped, and the others crossed over the bridge, as the enemy was on the opposite side; shells and bullets as lively as ever, the bullets a good deal more so, as our arrival gave him additional targets to practise at. Our men turned their attention to the infantry supports, and soon detached them from the guns. A running fight of ten to twelve miles ensued. Stoneman got confused and lost, and surrendered to a force not exceeding one-third his own, and without regular organization. But officers were among them, and their orders were promptly obeyed. General Johnston and Governor Cobb (Johnston had been 'relieved' by Jefferson Davis but a few days previously), with Stoneman between them, passed within twenty yards of me, to the prison, I suppose, for I never saw him afterwards. The artillery soon followed. Neither my son nor myself fired a gun on this Waterloo of a day!

"I have something for you in civil life more sad than the war. My then eldest son, Charles, after passing through William and Mary College and the literary course of the University of Virginia, and graduating at Harvard in 1853, contracted yellow fever and died within two months after leaving Cambridge. Will you do me the kindness to look into the records of that institution and judge for yourself of the measure of my loss?"

His son Thomas, and Augustine's youngest son, John, knowing that he was denying himself many things in the straitened circumstances of his family, made remittances to him at stated intervals, with the expressed desire that these sums should be used exclusively for his own small indulgences. But the greatest pleasure that this gave to him was to return to the old ways of many years back, and bring home presents to his children and to others to whom he thought little gifts would be acceptable.

"You used to like to find nice things in my pockets," he said, "and I treat you like little children now."

T. S. D. TO HIS EIGHT-YEAR-OLD GRANDDAUGHTER, SOPHY GREENE.

"BALTIMORE, 15th December, 1883.

"MY DEAR LITTLE PET,—. . . I am very glad that the poor bracelet that I sent you enables you to save your nickels for some other purpose than the purchase of one of them. It was a poor thing, but your grandpapa could do no better. I hope your mamma may bring you here some day, that I may hug and kiss you to make amends for the poor bracelet."

T. S. D. TO HIS DAUGHTER EMMY.

"BALTIMORE, 27th December, 1883.

. . . "Yeatman is from Gloucester, and his wife from Princess Anne County, Virginia. We gravitated to each other immediately, for I knew Yeatman's father and mother before he knew them. They are delightful people, both of them. He expects me to dine with him *every* Sunday. For decency's sake I sometimes fail to go, but I generally do, and get as fine a dinner as this market affords. . . .

"Mr. James R. Randall is the editor of the Augusta *Constitutionalist* newspaper, and the author of 'Maryland, my Maryland,' a song that the boys used to sing during the war. I fell in with him in the rooms of Mr. and Mrs. Yeatman at Barnum's Hotel." . . .

T. S. D. TO HIS GRANDCHILDREN, SOPHY GREENE AND THOMAS DABNEY GREENE.

"BALTIMORE, 16th January, 1884.

"MY LITTLE DARLINGS,—Your sweet letters, enclosed in one from your dear mother, came to hand two to three days ago, and were read by your aunts and myself with much pleasure. You must continue to write to me on all such occasions, and never allow your mother or father to write to grandpa without putting in letters yourselves. In this way writing will become very easy to you, and I will be kept up with your progress in education, in which I take very great interest. As I know nothing of French, you cannot practise on me in that language, but you will learn to write good English, which will be a high accomplishment."

T. S. D. TO HIS SON-IN-LAW, B. H. GREENE.

"BALTIMORE, 5th February, 1884.

... "In 1832, I think it was, the South Hampton insurrection occurred in Virginia, and stirred the State to its centre, although only a dozen to twenty whites were murdered, according to my recollection. But the attempt was so bold that the people took a serious view of it. The *Richmond Enquirer* took ground for the gradual emancipation of the negroes. The Bruces, among the largest slaveholders in the State, took the stump on the same side, and the largest slaveholder in my county of Gloucester made a speech (which I heard) in favor of the measure. The State was drifting rapidly into it when the Northern abolitionists undertook to advise and cheer us on in the good cause. Agitation in Virginia ceased. Those who had openly espoused the cause took back their word, the *Enquirer* ceased to advocate it, and the old State relapsed into her old views and remained there till her negroes were taken from her by violence. Mr. Clay's proposition to the same effect in Kentucky shared the same fate, but I forget by what agency, but the same, I suppose. We will not submit to foreign dictation or advice either."*

---

* "And there was a time when many Virginians now living began to see this; and had they been let alone not many years would have passed before we should have freed ourselves from the weight that oppressed us. . . .

"From that day all rational discussion of the question became impossible in Virginia, and a consummation for which many of the wisest heads were quietly laboring became odious even to hint at under dicta-

T. & D. TO WM. H. DABNEY.

"BALTIMORE, 14th April, 1884.

"Since my last to you I have inquired of some judicious friends if they had ever heard of a case of rudeness from a negro to his mistress or her children during the war, and the invariable answer was in the negative, with the emphatic addition, 'nor ever will.' Had such instances occurred but a few times the Confederate armies would have been broken up without the aid of Grant or Sherman, as the men—a large proportion gentlemen, you will understand—would have broken ranks, without regard to the shouts of their officers, who, by the bye, would have generally joined in the stampede, intent only on protecting their own families. The more the problem is studied the greater is the marvel. I have arrived at the conclusion that the universal quiescence of the negroes was due to their enlightenment, and not to their ignorance. You will remember that the San Domingo negroes were nearly all savages but recently imported, and very few to the manner born. These, when turned loose, were like howling wolves, intent only on blood. It was the common practice among Southern ladies to teach their servants to read, and as many of the out negroes as chose to attend. That amount of knowledge enabled them to separate the clothes when they came in from the laundry, and deposit each piece in its proper drawer. That might have been motive enough; but many were educated far above that. A negro man, living on a very fine plantation but a few miles below Vicksburg, rented the plantation, as it stood, from his

---

tion from outsiders; and on the day when the first abolition society was formed the fates registered a decree that slavery should go down, not in peace, but by war; not quietly and gradually extinguished, with the consent of all concerned, but with convulsive violence,—drowned in the blood of a million men and the tears of more than a million women."—*Don Miff*, p. 183.

Virginius Dabney, the author of the above lines, on reading his father's letter, said it was a curious coincidence that they should have expressed exactly the same views when they had never exchanged a word on the subject. My father passed through the events he recorded; my brother knew them as a matter of history.

former master, at the close of the war, and was soon known as the best planter in the county, and perhaps in the State. His cotton, at the Cincinnati Exposition, a few years ago, took *all* of the prizes! And large ones they were, too! These are curious things to think about; and the good behavior of the negroes was not due, as you suggest, to their ignorance. . . .

"The Spanish salaam to which you call my attention, although new to me, is very much admired. I hereby adopt, and request that you 'put me at the feet of your daughters.'"

T. S. D. TO HIS DAUGHTER EMMY.

"BALTIMORE, 26th April, 1884.

"I suppose that I will have both Tom and Ida with me in the course of a week or ten days; and I am glad to believe so, as I have hungered after Ida a long time, and Tom will always be acceptable, of course. James Dabney's wife and one of his daughters left the city a week ago to return home, after spending two weeks in Baltimore. It was a grievous mortification to us that we could not offer them a room during their sojourn here. The girls found it necessary to rent out every inch of room that we did not need for ourselves. I know it was unavoidable, but this new rôle sits very awkwardly on me yet, and always will, I suppose. Notwithstanding we could not entertain them, for want of room, they insisted, having room, on entertaining us, and we have agreed to visit and spend a week with them in 'strawberry times,'—some time in June. We are making desirable acquaintances every now and then, having made two within the past month,—Mr. Hairston and his wife, of North Carolina; the other, Colonel Mark Alexander, of this city. They are all three fine whist-players, Mrs. Hairston being equal to her husband, and equally fond of it. Before the war Mr. Hairston and his family were the largest slave-owners in this country, and perhaps in the world, as they owned five thousand negroes. Just think of that! Five millions of dollars in negroes! These three now belong to my whist club, and meet here twice a week certainly, and as often on off days as convenient."

T. S. D. TO HIS DAUGHTER EMMY.

"BALTIMORE, 29th April, 1884.

. . . "Sue says the mosquitoes at Key West are the most vicious and audacious she ever saw anywhere. Be sure, therefore, to have mosquito-bars to take along, so as to be prepared for them the first night and the first day, for that matter.

"I am very glad that mademoiselle is determined to stick to you, as it sounds well both ways. You took me by surprise when you stated that you are two years older than I was when I emigrated to Mississippi. Time glides by on greased wheels, it seems. I have never looked upon you otherwise than as one 'lill gal,' as Madame Delphine says of her daughter, adding that she is one 'hangel.' I think so of you, my child."

The marriage of his son Thomas, and a visit from this son and his wife, a few weeks afterwards, added much to our father's happiness this spring.

T. S. D. TO EMMELINE GREENE.

"BALTIMORE, 11th July, 1884. 98 JOHN STREET.

"MY DEAR GRANDDAUGHTER,—Had your excellent and sweet letter of the 8th been in my possession when I was about writing to your dear mother, I would not have written to her as I did. I wish you to understand, my dear, that when I read a letter from one of my children or grandchildren, it is not with a view to discover the excellencies of the composition, but the faults, and I have been in the habit of pointing out whatever faults I may find, and in that way to promote their education in the art of letter-writing. As this can hardly be attained to a high degree of excellence in any other way, I still adhere to the rule adopted when my children were young, and apply it now to my grandchildren. The thing is not pleasant to either of us, but must be endured if any good is to come of it, and your mother will tell you, I hope, that what I write is intended for your good, and not because I like to find fault, and especially with my dear grandchildren. I don't know why there is such a difference between this last letter of yours and its predecessor; but there is a difference, and with this I let the subject drop, with the remark that you must not let anything that I wrote to your mother check your disposition to write to your loving grandfather, but, on the contrary, you must 'fire away,' and put down whatever comes uppermost, for this is the natural way, is pleasanter to me, the most improving to you."

T. S. D. TO WILLIAM H. DABNEY.

"BALTIMORE, 17th July, 1884.

"I was very fond of politics from my youth, and took great interest in elections, until secession and war left my opinion at a discount; but since then I have never offered to vote. I will take a 'new departure' next November, and cast my vote with the party that may come in with clean hands, as it has had no opportunity to befoul them for many years."

T. S. D. TO HIS DAUGHTER EMMY.

"BALTIMORE, 19th July, 1884.

"MY DARLING CHILD,—Did I mortify my sweet granddaughter by my strictures on her letter? I think that hardly possible, and yet I have to guess at the meaning of your long silence, and I have guessed the first thing that occurs to me. I have not guessed it, I know, as none of your dear family *could* be mortified at anything I could write. Let one of them write, then, and if they prefer to think in French, and then turn their thoughts into English, let them do so, as I would prefer a translation to nothing. Emmeline's last was entirely free from that blemish, and was a beautiful letter throughout.

"I spent fifteen to twenty days with James Dabney's family and the friends of my youth and early manhood in Gloucester. Much remains as I left it forty-nine years ago; and, notably, the same open-handed hospitality that then prevailed, prevails still, as though it was inherent in the soil. The present owner of Toddsbury (the family nest of the Tabbs, comprising formerly three thousand acres, perhaps) is a gentleman from Long Island, and he finds one hundred and eighty acres as much as he needs. These he cultivates up to their full capacity, and better than ever before. The garden is innocent of a single weed or sprig of grass, and is made to yield all that one acre can yield of the choicest vegetables and fruits. The strawberry season was over when I got there, but I saw the immense vines, and was told that some of the berries measured nine inches in circumference. The raspberries were in full blast, and twice as large as any I ever saw. They had a full peck for dinner when I dined with them, and Mrs. Mott sent Emory about a peck for her dinner one day."

T. S. D. TO HIS DAUGHTER EMMY.

"BALTIMORE, 27th July, 1884.

"MY BELOVED CHILD,—Forgive me, my darling, for intimating that you might be angry with me. That is just as impossible as that I can be angry with you. I was at a loss to account for your long silence, and made the suggestion because it was convenient and close at hand. You had equal cause to complain of me, although I was not aware of it."

T. S. D. TO WILLIAM H. DABNEY.

"BALTIMORE, 15th August, 1884.

"I have taken very little interest in politics since the war, as a military government immediately succeeded it, with all the offices in the hands of negroes and carpet-baggers,—the profitable ones in possession of the latter, such as the sheriffalties, judgeships, clerkships, etc., and were not responsible to any power (you can well imagine how rapidly they feathered their nests under such circumstances), while the Legislature,

magistracy, seats in Congress, were freely bestowed
on negroes. The thing had to run its course, and I
gave myself no concern about it, and I have only voted
once since the war. But I had proposed to vote next
November, as I thought I saw an opportunity to give
an effective vote in the right direction; but if civil-
service reform means, as you think it does, the eviction
of a consul whose family has served without reproach
through three generations to make room for a brawling
newspaper editor, I am not in favor of civil-service reform, and I am now standing with my hands in my
pockets. The reputation of Cleveland *at the South* as
mayor and governor is without a blemish as a fearless
man of honor; that of Blaine a tricky politician, who
went into politics a pauper, and, without any other
profession but politics, has within a short time become
a millionaire.... I remember when young men of
talents, with a practice as lawyers worth five thousand
dollars, could not afford to take a seat in Congress at
eight dollars per diem. This was in Virginia. John
Randolph could go and give his per diem to his land-
lady at the end of the session, but Mr. Clay went in
debt every year, and was relieved *once*, to my certain
knowledge, by a check covering his indebtedness anony-
mously. You know that Mr. Webster had to be *prized*
out frequently by his friends. Mr. Monroe died a
pauper, after serving eight years as President, serving
as minister to France, and filling other high offices.
But it is useless to follow this theme further. Public
men can now do what they did not do then, and are
not condemned. I cannot vote for Blaine; if I vote at
all it must be for Cleveland, under the hope that his
civil-service reform will not be equivalent to Marcy's
'To the victors belong the spoils of victory,' the most
infamous sentiment that was ever uttered in the Senate
of the United States. I think your idea of a party
'that is to bind us North, South, East, and West,' if
you will forgive the word, is rather Utopian; and I
think it should be so, as no one party can remain
honest but for a short time. It has been always so.
Whenever a party has become strong enough to do

wrong they have not been slow to perpetrate outrages. It is only necessary in this connection to point to Jackson's reign, for it was nothing less. But enough of politics.

"I very much regret that I failed to see Mrs. C. H. Dabney when she was in the South. My daughters and I would have received her with open arms, and have greeted her as one having a supreme right to claim kin with us. Her correspondent (being one of my daughters) is my oldest, Sarah, wife of Lieutenant J. R. Eggleston, who commanded one of the hot-shot guns on the 'Merrimac' when she burned the 'Congress' frigate, as I have already informed you. They live in Carrollton, Mississippi. My next oldest is Susan D. Smedes, widow of Lyell Smedes, of Raleigh, North Carolina. My third is Sophy D. Thurmond, widow of William Thurmond, Kentucky. My fourth is Emmeline D. Greene, wife of Benj. H. Greene, civil engineer, McComb City, Mississippi. My two unmarried and youngest daughters are Ida and Lelia, both living with me, as do also their two widowed sisters. This information is furnished on your suggestion that you wished to know their names, and I give them in full and with great pleasure."

T. S. D. TO WILLIAM H. DABNEY.

"BALTIMORE, 17th September, 1884.

"The Benjamin Dabney of Gloucester, Virginia, whose death occurred in 1806, was my father, and, as we are bringing ourselves nearer and nearer together as our correspondence progresses, I will at once throw off all reserve and say that he was a lawyer of eminence, having few peers and no superiors in Virginia. Governor Littleton Walter Tazewell, of Norfolk, Virginia, himself almost without a peer, and possessing intimate relations with my father, gave me that estimate of his character. My father died prematurely, killed by the ignorance of his physicians, as was General Washington seven years before. There were two other Benjamin Dabneys, one of them a half-brother of mine, and the other a first cousin, he being a son of

Major George Dabney, of Dabney's Ferry, King William County, the birthplace of my father, and the same place, as I presume, at which Cornelius and John Dabney originally settled. The 'Thomas S. Dabney' whose marriage you call my attention to was myself, as you conjecture. I married Miss Mary A. Tyler, daughter of Samuel Tyler, of Williamsburg, Virginia, chancellor of the State (there was but one chancellor in Virginia at that time, and the position necessarily implied eminence as a lawyer and a reputation for integrity as a man, and both of these conditions were squarely met in him). The marriage took place in 1820, as represented in the Boston paper. Two sons were the issue of this marriage, but both died young, the mother in childbed with the second. My second wife was Miss Sophia Hill, daughter of Charles Hill, Esq., of King and Queen County, a lawyer of high respectability, but more remarkable as a member of a family remarkable then and yet for the inflexibility of their virtue. This union gave me sixteen children, of whom six daughters and four sons remain alive and grown. You already have an account of them. . . .

. . . "And yet the negroes are looked upon with more kindness (when in their places) here than at the North. My daughters still call the woman who nursed them in their infancy and waited upon them in their girlhood mammy; and these mammies are always privileged characters in the presence of their old masters, on whom they will call for anything without fear of a refusal."

T. S. D. TO WM. H. DABNEY.

"BALTIMORE, October 14, 1884.

. . . "About half a century ago I paid twenty cents postage on a single sheet of paper; now two cents will pay for a letter, and the postman (letter-carrier) calls at my door four times a day! Is the human race rendered happier by these improvements? Verily I doubt it. In my father's time, or in that of my grandfather, one ship a year would ascend the Pamunkey to the tobacco-warehouse, with the latest fashions from London, having on board magnificent dresses, gloves, shoes, etc.,

etc., for the 'quality' for fifty to one hundred miles around, and the whole province was made happy."

T. S. D. TO MARSHALL MILLER, ESQ.

"BALTIMORE, 13th December, 1884.

"Has it not occurred to you that you will soon have an opportunity to do something that you could not have done during the last twenty years, no matter how anxious you might have been to do it,—I mean, of course, to see a Democrat inaugurated as President? It will be *an event*, and a big one. It makes me shiver when I look back to see on what a narrow margin it was won. A leading New York Republican said, when the thing was decided, that that old fool, 'Rum, Romanism, and Rebellion Parson,' elected Cleveland. Just think of it! It required a fool to do what sagacious men could not have accomplished! Perhaps that thing has been done before without being observed. Unless you mean to come to Congress pretty soon, I hope you will elect to attend the inauguration, or it will be likely that we will never meet again in this world, as I will be eighty-seven on the 4th of next month. But I can play whist and backgammon yet; although I am aware of having fallen off at whist, but not at backgammon. . . . I can get no spectacles that will enable me to read by artificial light, although I write by it without glasses, as I am now doing at 8.30 P.M.

"As Sue and Ida are both at the South at present, I have only Sophy and Lelia to sit at the table and cheer me at other times. We have made as many desirable acquaintances as we can exchange visits with; but everybody here, except myself, has something to do during the day. I have no resource except newspapers, magazines, and books, so that if I am not up with current events, and some old ones, I must make bad selections."

T. S. D. TO HIS GRANDDAUGHTER, SOPHY GREENE.

"BALTIMORE, 21st December, 1884.

"GRANDPA'S DARLING,—And so you want me to write a long letter to you! I will have to write to

Dabney in a few days, and I suppose he will want a long letter, too; and how am I to write two long letters to the same house within two to three days of each other, and make them interesting? But I only have this one on hand at present, and it will be best to dispose of this before we begin to talk about the other. You would like to have me down there, to show me how nicely you can fix my collar and pull on my socks, and do all the other things that I would like to have done to dress me up comfortably. I know you would do it, and do some parts of it well; but you could not make me walk after I was dressed without assistance on rough places, or slippery ones, or other bad places in the road or woods, for if you attempted such a thing we would both come to grief together. I am too helpless, my dear little pet, to wander far from home now, and must hope that your mamma may find it convenient to bring you to Baltimore some time or other before I have finally to leave you all.

"I am very glad that your dear mamma allows you to write to me without dictation, as I enjoy your style, knowing it to be yours.

"Your grandpa will be eighty-seven years old if he lives until the 4th day of January next,—a greater age than any of his name ever attained, according to his knowledge."

CHAPTER XXIV.

REST.

T. S. D. TO HIS SON THOMAS.

"BALTIMORE, 8th January, 1885. 98 JOHN STREET.

"MY BELOVED SON,—I find myself overwhelmed by emotions that I am powerless to describe. To-day's mail brought me letters from you and your wife, and from Sue. They are of the same tenor, pretty much, and equally hard to take hold of. I tried just now to

make a start, but had to give it up after spoiling two
sheets of paper. I have known men to live too long,
and have hoped to be spared that humiliation; for a
man may be said to have lived too long when he ceases
to be useful and simply becomes a charge on his friends,
or when he has outlived his reputation, instances of
which I have known, this last being the most deplora-
ble of all. But this last I never feared could befall me.
Money might slip away, health might decay, but I
never could forget that I was born a gentleman, and
incapable, consequently, of a mean action. But it is
one thing to maintain one's self-respect, and another to
take up a too extravagant notion of one's true standing
with his fellow-men. It is not the easiest thing in the
world to see the difference under ordinary circumstances, but next to impossible when the vanity is excited or the judgment muddled by a deluge of assur-
ances from so many partial hearts (not heads) that he
is a marvellous proper man! Such is my present condition, and I have been trying my best to work my
way out of it for about five days, and without success
so far. I have thrown two parts of letters in the fire
through disgust, and I can hardly keep this one out of
it. But I conclude to let it go, as I see no chance of
doing better. You must take the will for the deed,
then, my dear son, as I am absolutely powerless to
thank you as my heart dictates I should for this great
testimony of a son's affection and confidence. I will
write to your dear wife after a while. In the mean
time she may be assured that I will look forward to her
second appearance in this city with more hope than
expectation, I must say. Eighteen months, when piled
on eighty-seven years, amount to something, but for
your sake and hers I will *expect* to see it. Kiss your
sweet wife eighty-seven times for me! Good-by."

T. S. D. TO HIS DAUGHTER EMMY.

"BALTIMORE, 10th January, 1885.

"MY DARLING CHILD,—Your budget reached me on
time. 'Budget' it was, as there are five letters in the
one cover, and all charming letters, too; Ann's equally

prized with the rest, as hers, too, was purely an offering of love. Ann, good girl, regrets that she was not here on my birthday to wash my feet! I call that pure affection, as nothing but affection could have prompted the thought. Tell her that I will write to her soon,—it may be in a week or two, as I have a hatful of such letters to attend to. I think that I received more birthday letters on this last occasion than on all the others combined. I am truly grateful for such evidences of confidence and affection from my dear ones. Those from you and your darling pets are particularly grateful to me, as they always are. Dear little Sophy is sorry that she has no handsome present for grandpapa, but believes he will be satisfied with an evidence of affection. To be sure he is.

"I want only thirteen more years to complete my century. If I live thirteen years more (having been born on the 4th of January, 1798) I will have seen one whole century and parts of two others. Will I see it? Hardly. But many people have exceeded that. How many were glad, and how many sorry, we do not know, but the regrets predominated largely, I am sure.

"You were not well when you wrote, my darling child, but made no complaint. I wish I could get a cheerful letter from you, and will do it when your noble husband straightens out his business affairs; but I cannot hope for it sooner. But this must come sooner or later, and that thought cheers me up. Let it cheer you up also. . . . I have no measure for my admiration of Tom's wife, and I may say the same of Tom. Have I not reason to be proud of my children? Examine them as I may, I can find no trace of meanness in any one. Not a shade of it. And I have ten. The same may be said of my brother's nine."

T. S. D. TO HIS DAUGHTER IDA.

"BALTIMORE, 10th January, 1885.

"MY DARLING CHILD,—I have your birthday letter. Also one from Tom, another from his wife, and still another from Sue. They overpower me. I have not yet been able to make a suitable reply to any of them. I have made three attempts on Tom's, and yet have to write to him. I say I am overpowered. It is by the stream of love and confidence which rushes through these letters that unnerves me. I can hardly see that I can deserve so much affection for doing so little, but my dear children make allowances for my shortcomings. I have omitted to mention Emmy, the dear child who never forgets her old father any more than you do. She not only wrote, but her three children also stuffed in their beautiful offerings to their grandpa. I cannot express myself properly now, nor will I ever be able to do it, as I do not believe the man is alive who has such children as I have. May God bless you, and all of you, my dear, dear children!

"The enclosed letters will answer many of your inquiries, which I send as the best and most convenient method. But I forgot to mention a letter from Heath, from Berlin, which came in on the *very fourth!* Virginius's wife, too, did not forget me. Neither did Ben forget me. He says the cold has been extreme in Bonham, Texas. Every stream frozen solid, so that, although food for ducks abounds in their water-courses, the ducks fly over and seek water elsewhere. Our markets abound in ducks and other game, but they (the ducks) are too high for our purses, and we let them *fly on!*"

T. S. D. TO HIS DAUGHTER SUSAN.

"BALTIMORE, 11th January, 1885.

"MY BELOVED CHILD,—I have received more birthday letters on this last occasion than on all former recurrences of my natal day combined. It appears as if every one with whom I have any correspondence has been wide awake to the fact that I was born on the 4th of January.

"I find myself overwhelmed by the good wishes and loving wishes of so many of my dear children and others, and find myself impotent to make suitable replies, and especially to Tom and his wife. You must all, my dear, take it for granted that your love for me cannot exceed mine for you, and there the matter must rest.... It is difficult to imagine any better people than the James Dabneys, or as good, for that matter. Cousin Em never forgets when giving-time comes, and she accordingly sent us, at Christmas, fully ten pounds of sausage-meat, and a turkey that appeared on our table six times, in spite of its being uncommonly excellent and tender. She availed herself of Evelyn's coming to send up five to six or more gallons of selected oysters, pickled. I have been working on them faithfully from the day of their arrival, and have given my whist club (eleven to twelve persons participated) as many as they could dispose of, and a good many still remain, enough, perhaps, to give my whisters another show at them."

T. S. D. TO MRS. THOMAS S. DABNEY.

"I look forward to your return to Baltimore with more pleasure than I can express, although it may appear absurd for a man to look forward to anything to come off eighteen months hence after he has attained his eighty-seven years. But it costs nothing to hope it, and I therefore indulge in the cheap extravagance."

T. S. D. TO MARTHA C. DABNEY.

"BALTIMORE, 13th January, 1885.

"MY BELOVED NIECE,—Your delightful and cheery letter of the 5th came in this morning, it having missed a coincidence but one day, as the 4th was my natal day,—a thing that you had luckily forgotten, but had been remembered by a sufficient number to keep me writing 'acknowledgments' for a week yet to come. I am very grateful for these evidences of affection from my children and grandchildren, and nieces and nephews, and outside friends; but, to tell the truth, to be congratulated on being eighty-seven years old is rather 'jubus.' However, as you say I am improving on it, I have no right to complain, whether I believe you or not.

... "I hope you may elect to see the Exposition, as in that event you will have placed the Rockies behind you, and will have little bother about coming to Baltimore. Do come, my dear, as it will be the last chance of seeing your old but 'improving' uncle."

On the margin of this letter I find these words:
"As this is the last letter I got from my dearest uncle, I could not bear to send it, and so I copied it for you. Your loving cousin,
"MARTHA."

T. S. D. TO ANN CRAVEN (colored nurse in his daughter Emmy's family).

"BALTIMORE, 14th January, 1885. 98 JOHN STREET.
"DEAR ANN,—Your birthday-letter has been on hand several days, and I now desire to return my sincere thanks for it, and the more because it was unexpected. Why it was unexpected I can't say, as there was nothing unnatural in your wishing to remind as true a friend as I am to you that you thought of me on my birthday. Inclosed with yours were the three letters from my grandchildren, all of whom you nursed from infancy with a care only short of maternal; and their affection for you strictly corresponds to that relation.

"When I reached that part of your letter in which you expressed regret at not being in Baltimore on my birthday *to wash my feet,* I could not suppress a smile, but it was a smile of real pleasure.

"May God bless you, Ann, with many years of good health—an equivalent of happiness, as happiness, after good health, depends exclusively on integrity—is the prayer of Your true friend,
"THOS. S. DABNEY."

The handwriting was as clear as ever, but it was a difficult one to read, and this letter was read to Ann. "If I could get a letter like this once a week, I would be a happier and better woman," she said after hearing it.

George Page's wife wished to send a live, white pig to Baltimore to her master, and was much disappointed on hearing that it was not thought feasible. One day George Page said to Ida,—

"Charlotte say she gwyne to kill an' roas' a tuckey an' sen' him to ole marster. I tell her she fool; Miss Ida ain't gwyne to carry a tuckey to Baltimo'."

"Yes, George, I will. It will please him to see how she loves him."

"Den she ain't sich a fool as I thought. I gwyne tell her to kill an' roas' her tuckey."

A number of the servants sent little baskets of eggs to him.

T. S. D. TO HIS SON BENJAMIN.

"BALTIMORE, 19th January, 1885.

"I am truly sorry that I made the mistake of addressing my letter that was intended for Charley to Ben. Give my love to the dear little fellow, and tell him it was a mistake; that he must not mind, but must write to me again, and I will be sure to send the next to him. As I can never again get to Bonham, you must contrive, by hook or by crook, to visit me occasionally during the remainder of my days. I made it my pious duty to visit my mother every other year during the latter part of her life, taking with me one of her grandchildren on each occasion. I don't mention this for your emulation, as you cannot afford it as well as I could at that time, but you can do the same to some extent."

T. S. D. TO HIS DAUGHTER IDA.

"BALTIMORE, 28th January, 1885.

. . . "The girls, Sophy and Lelia and Evelyn Dabney, and Maria Tabb, daughter of John Henry Tabb, of Gloucester, are off for the theatre to-night, leaving me 'verge and scope' enough to do as I please, and, as I cannot think of anything better, I will dedicate the time to my darling daughter, who has the responsibility of all the affairs of the family on her shoulders, and bravely does she stand under them. May God bless you, my dear child!

. . . "Say how-d'ye to George, Susan, Abby, Louisa,

and any other of my old servants who appear to take an interest in their old master."

T. S. D. TO HIS SON THOMAS.

"BALTIMORE, 12th February, 1885.

... "I have just received a card from Virginius, advising that he will dine with us on Sunday next, and celebrate his semi-centennial with me and his two sisters, who are here. I wish I had some of that fine wine that the army followers of Grant imbibed in the front portico of Burleigh during the war, but, alas and alack! I have it not."

T. S. D. TO HIS DAUGHTER SUSAN.

"BALTIMORE, 15th February, 1885.

"MY BELOVED CHILD,—Virginius dropped in upon us last night, to give us the benefit of his august presence at dinner to-day, this being, as you know, the anniversary of the day on which his first yell saluted the ears of his mother and mine fifty years ago. Many things have happened to him and to us since then. Brothers and sisters have joined him, and some have departed. War, prosperity, adversity, have in their turn crossed the stage of life, leaving each its mark, good, bad, or indifferent. The bad and indifferent perhaps predominate, but still we have cause to thank God for much that remains of the good, among which blessings we rank high on the list the preservation of your life when we thought it was lost; and I think it quite natural that my children should thank God for the preservation of my life for such mysterious purpose as we know not, but will hope not for evil."

T. S. D. TO WILLIAM H. DABNEY.

"BALTIMORE, 17th February, 1885.

"Your late letter (not so late either) has remained unnoticed unreasonably long, as you may think, but the sad event recorded in it was too sad to be either commented on or passed over at the moment. To have a much cherished member of one's family removed forever by death is a calamity to which humanity has fallen heir, and must be met by all; but few, if any, are capable of holding themselves prepared to see them snatched away suddenly when in the full vigor of health, and yet that is one of the conditions under which we ourselves hold to the precarious tenure of life most mysteriously, as a mere 'bodkin' would be sufficient to make us 'shuffle off this mortal coil' in a moment. It is a blessed thing to the departed, but none the less grievous to those who remain."

T. S. D. TO HIS DAUGHTER-IN-LAW, MRS. THOMAS DABNEY.

"BALTIMORE, 22d February, 1885.

"MY BELOVED DAUGHTER,—As Tom tells me in his last that a letter of mine did you *so much good*, I will address this also to you, as not fearing Tom's jealousy, and as helping him in a professional way in the treatment of your ailments. The nostrums of the veriest quacks have been known to work miracles in effecting cures when the remedies known to the regular faculty have utterly failed. But the regular faculty never affected infallibility, although pretenders in medicine, as well as in divinity, do. They both succeed in deluding the credulous, although people die with infallible nostrums in their mouth, and souls go to the wrong place bespattered with holy water!

"And now, at what have I arrived? I believe I started with a proposition of Tom's that my letters did you good. I am glad, indeed, that your ailments, lumbago or what-not, can be assuaged in any degree by such simple remedies as my nonsense. If it is so, I hope this dose, this dash at the Pope and impostors in general, may prove a specific, thorough and complete, and bring you out bright and joyous,—as good as new!"

T. S. D. TO HIS DAUGHTER IDA.

"BALTIMORE, 24th February, 1885.

"MY BELOVED CHILD,—Being square up with my correspondence, I am at liberty, for the nonce, to choose my auditor, and, as I love your prattle hugely, I elect you for my first victim on a new start, under the hope of provoking some of the said prattle. . . . Mr. —— fell on the ice the other day and broke an arm. I boasted immunity from falling, thinking I was too cautious for such a mishap to befall me, and I lost my heels within a few hours after making the boast; but I saved my arms, and was not hurt, as I took care to squat right down when I found I had to go. A good many casualties are reported, as the bad and slippery weather has been long continued. It is ten o'clock, so good-by."

T. S. D. TO HIS DAUGHTER-IN-LAW, MRS. THOMAS DABNEY.

"BALTIMORE, 27th February, 1885. 98 JOHN STREET.

"MY BELOVED DAUGHTER,—My last bulletin from Magazine Street was from Sue, but that has been too long ago, and although it was cheering enough for the time, and as no news is supposed in my family to be good news, I still cannot suppress the fear that the rule may not hold good in this instance. I therefore request that Sue or Tom or your cousin or yourself will break the uncomfortable silence and let me know how matters stand. I request, in addition, that no mail be allowed to leave New Orleans, after receipt of this, without a message to me from one of you. You see, my dear, that I am getting old (getting?), and don't feel that I can spare either of you, as time might not be left me to repair damages.

"Baltimore is undergoing the most rigorous winter of many years. A month ago grave apprehensions were entertained of an ice-famine next summer, but now every ice-house is filled, I suppose, with ice from twelve to eighteen inches thick, and the rivers stacked with ice too formidable for the tugs. The Chesapeake is dangerous for navigation on account of floating ice, too heavy to be encountered at night, and hence travel by the bay has been seriously interrupted. Boats are tied up in all directions. This has only been the case for a day or two, however, but there is no telling how long it may last, as snow resumed falling at 6 P.M. this evening, after a suspension of thirty-six hours, the snow falling piling on one of nine inches, that fell three days ago. So you see we are having a lively time for catching rabbits, sparrows, snowbirds, and the like, to our hearts' content! When a boy, I liked that hugely, but I must confess now that the frost of years, as it fell on my pate, has had the effect of moderating my delight at witnessing the frost of heaven.

"I hope you have seen the orations of Winthrop and Daniels, as delivered on the occasion of the dedication of the Washington Monument at Washington. They are grand specimens of oratory, as the monument is of architecture, and when combined should and will, I hope, go far towards cementing the hearts of our great nation into one loving, irresistible whole, the prating of States-rights people (so called), who have not yet found out that the war is over, to the contrary notwithstanding. Calhoun knew no country but Carolina (he only knew one), and I have lately (and only lately) found that persons actually exist who only know Virginia, for I heard a lady say, after reading those noble orations in honor of Washington, and in which his counsels are commended to his country, that had he not been a Virginian she would have cared nothing for him!

"Why do not the moon and stars fall upon and crush us, I would like to know?

"Having taken breath, I only have to say, with my love to your husband, good-by.

"THOMAS S. DABNEY."

After writing this letter my father posted it himself. It was a cold afternoon, and everything covered with snow. He had paid several calls during the last few days, and was as bright as usual. On this evening his friends came for the semi-weekly game of whist, and he played as well as ever, and enjoyed everything, and went up-stairs to bed in good spirits. As he seldom came down to breakfast before eleven o'clock, and sometimes during this winter as late as twelve or one, no one went to call him until twelve on this day. Only Sophy and Lelia were at home this winter. Sophy had gone off to a sewing-school, in which she was a teacher, at ten o'clock.

As he did not come down at twelve, Lelia, who had

twice during the morning called to know if he was awake, ran up to his room. He appeared to be calmly sleeping, with the dear head resting on the clasped hands, just as he always composed himself for the last refreshing sleep in the morning, that he enjoyed so much. When she found that she could not rouse him, she thought that he had swooned. There was nothing that looked like death in that calm, sleeping figure. The servants helped her to rub him till a physician could be called. He said that the spirit had passed away two hours before. Death had been instantaneous and painless, and had come in his sleep. His prayer had been answered; he had not lived to be helpless, and he had passed away suddenly.

Often in life, when another would have put off a call, he would say, "I will do it at once." It seemed now as if he had answered to those last summons to come, "I will come at once."

Lelia's letters to the absent son and daughters give the last details of the putting away of the honored and precious father.

His children took him to Gloucester, to old Ware Church that his mother and he had loved. Here they laid him under a walnut-tree, within the shadow of the venerable church. On a slab of plain granite, placed there by his four sons and Frederick Dabney, are cut his name and the date of his birth and death. He had said to us that the slabs over his ancestors in the old church-yard on Jamestown Island were the most suitable and enduring that he knew, and he had chosen them as his pattern in the slabs over his dead, and we put the same over him.

As one stands at the head of the green mound one may see beyond the fields and meadows the blue waters that he loved so well.

LELIA TO THE SISTERS AND THOMAS IN NEW ORLEANS.

"BALTIMORE, 4th March, 1885. 98 JOHN STREET.

"MY DEAR SISTER SUE AND THE REST OF MY DEAR SISTERS AND DEAR TOM,—We have just returned from carrying our beloved father to Gloucester. I cannot help hoping his spirit saw the waters of the Chesapeake. If he had been alive he would have loved to stand where he was on the boat. But I must tell you how it was.

"At three o'clock on Monday Mr. Dame read all that part of the service usually read in the house. —— and —— would not allow a notice to be put in the papers, as they said the house was too small. They sent notices or told all our special friends. There were a great many here, but I do not know who they were. I asked —— to give me the list of pall-bearers. They were Mr. Thomas B. Mackall, Mr. Hopkins, Mr. Newton Gray, Mr. Thomas Levering, Dr. E. R. Walker, Dr. Powhatan Clarke, Dr. Marriott, and Mr. William Reynolds.

"Mr. Yeatman, sister Sophy, and I were all who went to the boat with him. Ned had to leave during the service and hurry to a different boat by which he could make better time. Jenkins and his men did everything on the boat. Evelyn could not go with us, but she and Willie met us at Canton that night at eight. We went to the boat immediately after the service. We had the service at three o'clock on brother Virginius's account, so that he could go back to New York.

"Mr. Yeatman did everything for us, and I do not know how we would have done without him. The boat did not leave Baltimore until after eleven o'clock, so he knew we would miss the other boat, but he telegraphed, and the captain promised to wait. He did wait a long time, and then had to start, and came to meet us, I suppose, as we met in the bay. This was a dangerous thing to do. Mr. Yeatman spoke to everybody, and everything was done so respectfully and reverently, you knew that we had to be transferred to the other boat.

"We took this line because it landed us within three miles of the church. When we got to the landing Cousin James and Todd were there waiting for us with everything ready. Ned and Lee had attended to the arrangements in the church-yard. Jimmy had let everybody know. The court was in session. We went directly from the boat to the church, where we did not have to wait long.

"A great many people came and shook hands with us and sympathized with us, and talked so beautifully about him. Our cousins were all they could be. The pall-bearers were Judge Warner Jones, Thomas Taliaferro, General William Taliaferro, Colonel Robbins, Mr. Hairston Sewell, and Major Thompson. More asked to be allowed to be pall-bearers than we wanted. The interment took place on March 3 at 4.30 P.M.

"Every one seemed so much gratified at his love for the place and our taking him there on that account. I think Cousin James's family went as papa's family. I know he did, and Evelyn and Jimmy Duncan. I did not see the others. Evelyn would hold on to me. Cousin James walked with sister Sophy. Lee's voice was so sweet in 'Abide with Me.'

"They begged us to stay, but we heard there was a chance of reaching the boat. Todd said he would try, so we left the church-yard as soon as the services were over, and Todd took us rapidly with his blooded horses, and we were just in time. Cousin Em was not at church. She had no idea we could go home that day, and looked for us at the Exchange.

"When Cousin Parke was here he talked to her as if she were her mother in age, and, as she knew so many of the old stories, with a woman's tact she made him thoroughly enjoy the reminiscences he would run over. Among them he talked a great deal of his mother and her love for Bishop Moore and Ware Church.

"He also told us what I had never heard before, about his beginning a Sunday-school in the Highlands in Gloucester. So like him. He bought a stove and all the books, and made all the preparations that involved money at his own expense and that of a young man who went in with him. But unfortunately they could not get hold of the children. They did all they could to get them, but failed."

LELIA TO HER SISTER SUSAN.

"TOWSON, MD., March 13, 1885.

"I want to write to you about our dear father. I try so hard to bear it right. I want to tell you bright, pleasant things. We have thought, and Mrs. —— agrees with us, that papa slept splendidly this past winter. He not only slept in the morning, but in the night.

"That last night he did not make one sound. E——, who was sitting up-stairs, in the front room, answered my question, 'Have you heard papa stirring?' 'I have not heard one sound from his room.' I ran up-stairs on that, not much frightened, for three times within ten days had I run up to find him sound asleep, and so surprised to hear me tell him how late it was. Once I told him how much frightened I was, and asked him if it was necessary for him to stay in bed until one o'clock, saying, 'Papa, you frighten me so much.' He was greatly amused. It pleased him very much seeing me uneasy about him. But I noticed when I waked him even at half-past eleven he was very drowsy, and I determined not to wake him so early. I thought it only my own nervousness about gas, and would worry myself to death about that, knowing he could not smell it.

"There was some one around his room all the time, and if he had made any sound it would have been heard. But I do not believe that he moved hand or foot after he went to sleep. There was every evidence of this,—the cover tightly tucked around his neck, and smooth all over the bed.

"This is not the letter I meant to write. I tore it, thinking that I would throw it away. But I will send it, and try again to write what I wish to say. . . . Is not that a sweet thought in Cousin Fred, and so far above his means?"

LELIA TO HER SISTER SUSAN.

"BALTIMORE, March 26, 1885. 98 JOHN STREET.

. . . "You could not have felt a farther-off feeling more strongly than we did. It was not as if we had looked for it. But in one sense I had looked for it. That was the third time in that week that he had alarmed me. I had run up to his room to find him asleep, and he was so much amused by my waking him. Once, not long before Evelyn left us for the C——s, I went to the C——s with Evelyn. On my return, I said, 'Has not papa come down yet?' Sister Sophy said, 'No; and it makes me uneasy.' I ran up to his room, and he did not wake until I called once or twice. It was one o'clock. I said to him, 'Do you need to stay in bed this long, for it frightens me nearly to death.' He was so much amused, and said, 'So you keep an eye on me, do you? I like that.'

"I try to think of all the pleasant things. I bring back a great many to my mind. I try not to reproach myself, nor do I do it now as I did. A letter of Ned's gave me so much comfort on that subject."

LELIA TO HER SISTER IDA.

"BALTIMORE, 98 JOHN STREET, March 8, 1885.

... "He had such a sunny disposition; he was so happy over so little, and never stopped to repine over what he might have had. He was as grand in his poverty as a king could be in all his glory. All these friends of his here who knew nothing of him until a year or two ago, look on him just as those do who knew him in his younger and more prosperous days. They love his great heart, his truth, his nobility. How fresh were the wells of love in his ever-youthful heart! He made friends here as if he were a boy. Even the little boys on the street knew and loved him, and would run to meet him, and he would stir them up with his stick, or pretend to try to disperse them in fun. ... I did not know that Mr. —— appreciated him, but he broke completely down when he spoke of him. Mrs. Mackall was so sweet, going close to him, leaning down to his face, as if she were trying to find life where there was none. She would say, 'I love that good man. I love that good man.' ... Mrs. Yeatman sent lovely roses, which we put on his breast at the very first. Mr. Levering sent a large box of cut flowers, not just white flowers, but all-colored roses and other sweet-scented flowers. I laid them on him. Mrs. Gray brought lilies, and they, too, were not made up. He liked them so much better that way. If he was sick I do not think he knew it himself. He did say his legs were stiff, and that was the only reference that he made to his health. He was so busy reading the papers and writing letters, he lost not a moment. And then he went visiting, and enjoyed his friends who called.

"Not many days before (my mind is such a blank I cannot recall the day) Dr. Walker called and saw no one but papa. I asked him if he thought him looking well. He said that he thought him unusually well."

MARTHA DABNEY TO SUSAN.

"SANTA ROSA, CALIFORNIA, April 29.

... "If you could have all the letters that he wrote to my dearest father you would have quite a complete history of his life. Two or three letters every week would pass between them on many subjects,—politics very often, on the occasion of sending a quarter of lamb or a fine piece of beef. These were always occasions for long notes. Of late years I have tried to keep all their letters, but mother has such a passion for sending them away that I have lost some very valuable ones. I *begged* for the last one of my uncle, telling her it might be the last I should ever see from his hand, so I kept it. You will see from reading it what a happy mood was on him. I am sorry not to send you the original, because it won't look so natural to you to have it in another handwriting; but I value it too much to trust it to the mail. I wish you would be so good as to send them all back when you have got what you want from them.

"A school-teacher's lot has little leisure in it, else I would try to write in appropriate terms a tribute to one whom I admired as much as I loved. One who possessed that most excellent of all characters, the rare blending of manly strength with womanly tenderness, a mind of large grasp and delicate discernment, a symmetrical nature, where the intellectual and the moral formed a perfect whole.

"To those who only knew him casually his sagacity in practical affairs must have been very striking. While his neighbors were sending half their cotton North to buy corn, his granaries were overflowing. He had a saying, 'Cattle don't fatten on bought corn.' Don't you remember? It's strange what interest I took as a child in everything he said, and admired his management. 'Plough deep in dry weather' is another of his sayings that I remember. I wondered that all the planters around didn't come to him for instructions.

"His mind was so comprehensive as to embrace everything. He was as much at home in the purely intellectual as the purely practical.

"How I do regret my sweet old uncle! May God bless all his children and grandchildren!"

Of the letters that came to his children a few extracts are here given:

Jennie Eggleston Zimmerman wrote: "I, too, mourn that beautiful life gone from us as a daughter. When I was famishing for home and home-love his father-heart reached out and took me in as heartily and tenderly as if I had been one of his own. I can never forget it. It is one of the sweetest, most cherished memories of my life, and I feel poorer because he has gone out of this life. It seems to me that the most prominent feature of his character was his fatherliness. Even to his grown-up children he seemed to fill the place of both father and mother.

"The manner of his death was especially beautiful. A long, good life, full of tenderness and good deeds, passing away in healthful slumber without a pang of agony. . . . While he discharged all the duties of life with fidelity, while he was an ideal gentleman, he was pre-eminently a father. Thank God for his life!"

Mrs. A. G. Brown wrote: "Many and many a time in our lonely home has he cheered us with his bright, hopeful conversation. We always felt better for his coming."

Mrs. Campbell Smith wrote: "The grand old country gentleman, as I knew him, a very lord in his castle, hospitable and courteous to all. Distant and reticent I've seen him to some few, with good reasons of his own for it, but kindly, familiar, and jovial with those he loved and claimed as friends. . . . I bore him the greatest love and admiration. I love to think of him and contemplate his beautiful life. Such hope and encouragement to those who would follow in his footsteps!"

His son-in-law, Benjamin H. Greene, wrote, after a visit to the home: "Everything about the house looked natural to me except the empty chair and corner which the grand old patriarch occupied upon my former visits. I longed to see him and to hear him talk in his fascinating manner every minute of my stay in his house, more than I had ever before experienced. We know exactly where to find him, and I pray that when the summons comes we may pass away as sweetly and serenely as this grand man did."

His son Edward wrote: "Every letter that I ever received from him was good, eminently good, for he was a hero in the truest and best sense of the word, looking all issues squarely in the face and scorning all subterfuge."

John Dabney wrote: "I wish that the good man's hands had been laid in blessing on the heads of my two children."

The last of his old friends, John Shelton, now himself a man of seventy-one years of age, wrote: "I esteemed him as a most noble man, and one of the very finest specimens of the old Virginia gentleman that it was ever my fortune to know. . . . Leaving behind him a name without fear and above reproach."

A negro woman who had never met him wrote thus of him to her daughter on his death: "he War a very Welthy Man and he all so died very hapy and he did live in the South and all so War good to the Poor and did help Both White and Colard for he war good to all and he War high 'onard By Both White and Colard."

We could not let his old servants hear the tidings of the death of Thomas Dabney from the public journals.

Letters were written to several of them. George Page wrote: "He was a good master to us all. You are all my children, and I love you all alike." He took his letter from the family to two negro churches, where it was read aloud to "our people." George wrote, and we got many affectionate messages from them.

Mammy Maria was in New Orleans, having been taken there by her daughter, with whom she lived. Her mind appeared almost gone; softening of the brain had set in several years before. But her affections were in no way dulled by the disease that had attacked the brain, and she sobbed and wept when any of her white children went to see her. We went ourselves to tell mammy that her master was gone. She asked, quickly, "Was George Page with him?" and then became silent, and looked stolid, as if she had not comprehended the import of the words that she had heard.

But those words had snapped the mainspring of her life. She walked about the house for a week, but she refused to touch food or drink. When urged by her daughter she said, "I got 'nough," and when water was put in her mouth she did not swallow it. At times frightful paroxysms of grief came, but she rarely spoke unless spoken to. At the end of the week she got on her bed and lay there with closed eyes. Her friends prayed and sang around her bed, but she gave no sign except that big tears rolled through the closed lids. From being a stout woman she became emaciated, and on the 24th of March, the twenty-fourth day after hearing of her master's death, she passed away in great agony.

"It 'peared like her heart busted with grief when she heerd of marster's death," her daughter said.

"Oh, Mammy Harriet," one of Thomas Dabney's bereaved children said to her old nurse, "will papa be afraid to meet at God's judgment bar the face of any servant whom he ever owned?"

"Oh, no, no, my good marster, no!" while tears rained down the venerable black face.

ADDENDUM.

The following incidents are related by Edward:

"One night, happening to be a short distance from camp, I heard the beating of the long roll, and, hurrying back, found the men already in line of battle. My duty was to dress the files, and on finding my company I walked down the line, speaking to the men and aligning them properly. Through the gloom I recognized some by voice and some by form. Presently I came to a singularly tall and erect man whom I did not know, and asked his name. 'It is I, marster,' was William's quiet and respectful reply. I ordered him to the rear, telling him to keep out of range of the guns unless Ben or I were wounded and had to be removed from the field.

"At the battle of Baker's Creek my duty was, in case of disaster, to assist in conducting the wagon-trains to a place of safety; on that day, therefore, I was a non-combatant. At an early hour, as the troops were filing past me, I noticed a boy without a haversack, and gave him mine (with two days' cooked rations), knowing that my chances for picking up a dinner that day would be better than his. Afterwards, accompanied by William, I rode to the front to see how the day was going. Our point of observation was none of the safest, and the shriek of a shell or the hiss of a bullet was of frequent occurrence. After a while, William entered a log cabin near by (from which the occupants had fled, leaving everything), and in a short time announced that dinner was served. He had prepared a sumptuous meal—ham and eggs and hot cornbread. During this meal he waited on me with the same quiet and stately deportment as if we had been in a place of perfect safety, and betrayed no anxiety when, owing to a sudden pressure on our lines, the bullets began to rattle briskly on the roof and sides of the cabin."

www.ingramcontent.com/pod-product-compliance
Lightning Source LLC
Chambersburg PA
CBHW030312240426
43673CB00040B/1144